To my family—my brother, Lonny, my sister, Roberta, my brother in-law, Frank, and my sister in-law, Becky, my Aunt Lydia and Uncle Al, and to my loving friend, Richard Kirschenbaum. I thank them for their faith, support, patience, and love.

D. J.

Dedicated to my mother, my husband, Bernard, and my daughter, Shana, for their continued love and support.

G.K.

Teaching Beginning Ballet Technique

Gayle Kassing, PhD
Jacksonville University, Florida

Danielle M. Jay, PhD
Northern Illinois University
DeKalb, Illinois

Human Kinetics

Library of Congress Cataloging-in-Publication Data

Kassing, Gayle.
   Teaching beginning ballet technique / Gayle Kassing and Danielle
Jay.
     p.   cm.
   Includes bibliographical references (p.) and index.
   ISBN 0-87322-997-5
   1. Ballet--Study and teaching.   I. Jay, Danielle, 1947-
II. Title.
   GV1788.5.K37   1988
   792.8'07--dc21   98-23390
                                                       CIP

ISBN: 0-87322-997-5

Acquisitions & Developmental Editor: Judy Patterson Wright, PhD; **Managing Editors:** Joanna Hatzopoulos and Henry Woolsey; **Copyeditor:** Amie Bell; **Proofreader:** Kathy Bennett; **Indexer:** Theresa Schaefer; **Graphic Designer:** Stuart Cartwright; **Graphic Artist:** Angela K. Snyder; **Photo Editor:** Boyd LaFoon; **Cover Designer:** Chuck Nivens; **Photographer:** George Tarbay; **Cover Model:** Heather Kroski; **Illustrators:** Mick Greenberg and Dick Flood; **Printer:** United Graphics

Printed in the United States of America   10 9 8 7

Human Kinetics
Web site: www.HumanKinetics.com

United States: Human Kinetics, P.O. Box 5076, Champaign, IL 61825-5076
800-747-4457
e-mail: humank@hkusa.com

Canada: Human Kinetics, 475 Devonshire Road, Unit 100, Windsor, ON N8Y 2L5
800-465-7301 (in Canada only)
e-mail: orders@hkcanada.com

Europe: Human Kinetics, 107 Bradford Road, Stanningley
Leeds LS28 6AT, United Kingdom
+44 (0) 113 255 5665
e-mail: hk@hkeurope.com

Australia: Human Kinetics, 57A Price Avenue, Lower Mitcham, South Australia 5062
08 8277 1555
e-mail: liaw@hkaustralia.com

New Zealand: Human Kinetics, Division of Sports Distributors NZ Ltd.
P.O. Box 300 226 Albany, North Shore City, Auckland
0064 9 448 1207
e-mail: info@humankinetics.co.nz

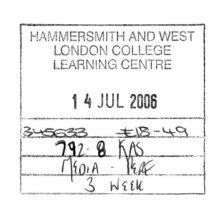

contents

Teaching Beginning Ballet Technique is a guide and reference for teaching students and evaluating beginning ballet technique in an academic setting. This book is for the individual who has not had prior experience in teaching beginning ballet, or for the person who has taught ballet but not in an academic setting. The audience includes dance educators in secondary and higher education. Other audience segments include dance educators who teach pedagogy courses and ballet teachers in private and professional settings.

This book focuses exclusively on the art and science of teaching beginning ballet. It provides a theoretical understanding of classical ballet grounded in educational theory, balanced with the practical progressions of teaching new exercises, steps, principles, and aesthetics to the beginning student. In addition, this book is a text for a dance pedagogy class, a teaching methods course, or for use as a ballet reference book.

The book is divided into two distinct parts: part I, *Preparing to Teach Beginning Ballet Classes*, provides the theoretical knowledge base for teaching the beginning ballet course and part II, *Teaching Progressions for Beginning Ballet Classes*, is a guide to the actual teaching of exercises, steps, principles, and progressions through a series of instructional units.

Chapter 1, *Facilitating the Learning Process*, guides the reader as to what a teacher must know to teach a beginning class, including the format of the ballet class, stages of motor learning, teaching strategies, how to use cues and imagery, and how to build a visual memory. Chapter 2, *Utilizing Teaching Styles Effectively*, discusses the teaching/learning process in ballet, and teaching styles and their vital factors of motivation, discipline, feedback, and management. Chapter 3, *Developing Foundational Principles*, provides explanations of the theoretical framework of ballet technique, including discussion of the basic principles of ballet and rules used at the barre and in the center. Chapter 4, *Constructing the Beginning Ballet Class*, discusses ways to construct beginning barre and center combinations, how to develop combination progressions, and the importance

of music in conjunction with the class. Chapter 5, *Managing the Ballet Class*, covers teacher management of class time for beginning level students, safety, and how to handle short class periods. The final chapter in part I, *Assessing Student Progress*, describes assessment strategies and their implementation as part of the teaching/learning process.

Part II, *Teaching Progressions for Beginning Ballet Classes*, is a series of four units, each approximately three to four weeks, depending on student progress and the length of the term. Each unit builds upon the content from the previous unit and outlines the progression to be followed when building a beginning ballet technique. The units focus on *what* is taught, *when* it is taught, and *how* it is taught. Each unit contains the following features: Principles, Objectives, Teaching Strategies, Assessment Tools, Teacher Responsibilities, and Performance Test Content. A detailed analysis accompanies each exercise, pose, and step in a recommended progression with a definition, verbal depiction, purpose, preparation, music and timing, breathing, and cues and imagery for teaching the exercise or step. The teacher's challenge is to place and progress students along this continuum.

To use the book effectively, read part I first. Then reread chapters 1, 4, and 3, in that order. After you have completed this, read part II. Look at the progressions; these provide pathways for you to explore in relation to your students and your class. Because each class is different, select which approaches you think will work best for your particular class. These units give you alternatives for teaching a beginning ballet class: where to start, what to teach, and where to end the instructional unit.

Reread each unit before teaching it. Then review chapter 2, *Utilizing Teaching Styles Effectively*, and chapter 6, *Assessing Student Progress*, before teaching the unit. Keep a journal to record what choices you have made and their success. Continued analysis of your teaching will help you develop as a teacher.

When you approach the task of teaching ballet, it may feel like you are looking at a thousand-piece puzzle that has to be assembled (see figure 1). Where

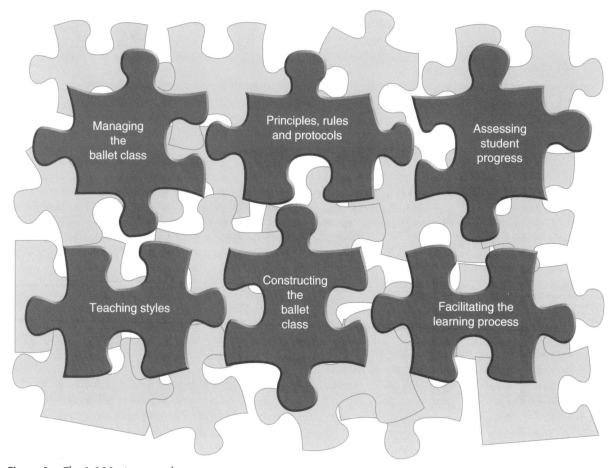

Figure 1. The 1,000-piece puzzle.

do all the pieces fit? So many details have to be considered. What do you teach when? It may seem an overwhelming task! We have tested the methods and teaching progressions and refined them for this book, written especially for beginning teachers in an academic setting. We have prepared a synergetic look at how all the pieces of the puzzle fit together into the larger view of teaching ballet at the beginning level.

As ballet teachers our teaching goal is to instill clear and appropriate movement principles as students acquire a vocabulary of classical ballet that will provide continuous development of ballet technique. Encourage your students to take small risks to accomplish each new challenge in the study of ballet; remember that learning is a joy, and teaching continually a discovery.

Teaching ballet is as much an art as performing it. Classical ballet is performed and taught throughout the world today. Much of the teaching of classical ballet has been an oral tradition, passed down from teacher to student through the centuries. The approach that we should teach our students exactly like our teachers taught us is not possible. We are a product of our environment: the students, the classes we have taken, and the places in which we teach. Like our students, we pass through learning stages as our teaching skills constantly grow. As professional educators, we continually search and strive for new ways to communicate with students. There is a wealth of information in many disciplines from which we as dance educators can gather knowledge that will enhance our teaching. To achieve this, we assimilate the valued traditions from the past with the knowledge of ballet technique and theory. We couple ballet pedagogy with motor learning, teaching styles, assessment, and instructional strategies that provide specific applications to teaching ballet.

Originally this project began when we created an assessment tool for the ballet technique class. We soon realized that a ballet assessment tool was only a part of the teaching/learning process. Classical ballet is a highly codified art form with a complicated internal structure that has developed over three centuries. So, how can the content be assessed without knowing and understanding it? Few ballet technique books are directed to teachers and teaching the ballet class. Most ballet technique books are for students. For many new teachers, learning how to teach ballet is done through trial and error in the classroom. This book has been written specifically for ballet instructors in order to facilitate both the instructor's and the students' learning process.

Most individuals who teach beginning ballet classes have studied ballet or other dance forms for years, but they may be novices at teaching ballet technique. Since your own dance skills are on a much higher level than a beginner's skills, you may have forgotten the components of a beginning ballet class or the stages of learning that beginning dancers go through when learning new exercises and steps. Learning ballet presents many challenges for both teachers and students. The movements require precision in order to perform

exercises and steps that meet an established standard of correctness. The terminology for these exercises and steps are in French, so the written term and spoken term may seem very different. Connecting the ballet term to the step that is performed can also be challenging. To meet these challenges, we hope to stimulate your thinking about instructional strategies to use in the teaching/learning process, and provide criteria and methods for assessing student progress that support ballet education as part of the National Standards in Arts Education.

We acknowledge the work of Joan Lawson in the field of ballet pedagogy. In her writings, she addresses the major principles of ballet and interprets them for twentieth century dancers. Her point of view derives from her English training and focuses upon ballet performance in a setting where children are selected and trained to be professional ballet dancers.

Our approach to teaching ballet comes from an American point of view and with eclectic training from a variety of schools, methods, and techniques. We have taught ballet primarily in academic settings and therefore are accountable for the dancer's knowledge and performance of classical ballet. We have devised a teaching system using 11 interconnecting principles. Students must make both cognitive and physical connections to ballet to build a technique. We have chosen to focus on several of the principles during each unit and integrate them into the class as a foundation for the next set of principles presented in the next unit. Together this compilation identifies, introduces, and applies the principles of classical ballet to the beginning student's work in a manageable way.

Features of the Book

This book focuses on teaching beginning classical ballet. The book is unique; part I presents strategies for teaching, shows application of teaching styles, provides the theoretical foundation of ballet in practical terms, and offers management and assessment plans for the beginning ballet class.

Part II presents the content for beginning ballet students in four units that take the new teacher in a high school or college setting from the first day of class to the end of the term. Each unit contains planning information, including Objectives for the unit, Teaching Strategies, Assessment Tools, Teacher Responsibilities, and Performance Test Content. A detailed explanation accompanies each exercise and step, supplying a definition, explanation of how to perform it, specific cues and images for teaching the step, an assessment checklist, teaching progressions, and suggested combinations.

This book empowers the new ballet teacher with a well-tested plan for teaching beginning ballet that is flexible and can be modified to meet individual teaching situations. The main objectives of this book are to provide the teacher with a foundational knowledge of classical ballet and to present and order the subject matter to meet the expectations and progressions of a beginning ballet class in a number of settings. The book includes practical insights on what to expect and how to handle beginning students in a ballet class.

This book is a labor of love dedicated to ballet as a performance art and, most of all, ballet as arts education. Each of the authors has taught ballet in community, professional, and university setting for over twenty years. Our primary purpose is to share with new teachers the art of introducing students to ballet in a way that gives students a positive learning experience and an appreciation of dance.

CD-ROM Option

At the time of this book's printing, we are in the process of developing an interactive CD-ROM program designed for use hand-in-hand with the units presented in this text. Our CD-ROM is a tool that reinforces what students have learned in the ballet class. For the student, the CD-ROM is like having a personal instructor outside of class; for the teacher, it is like having a teacher's assistant in class. The CD-ROM provides a learning environment that allows the user to

- view a performance of the essential exercises, steps, positions, and poses of beginning ballet;
- see the written French ballet terminology; and
- hear the correct pronunciation of French ballet terminology.

Used in conjunction with the book, the CD-ROM will bring beginning ballet technique to life for both teachers and students. To receive more detailed information, or to find out when the CD-ROM becomes available, you may send e-mail providing your name and address to **cdinfo@hkusa.com**.

Acknowledgments

We would like to thank the following people:

- Dr. Judy Patterson Wright at Human Kinetics for her vision as our Developmental Editor
- George Tarbay, our talented and very patient photographer
- Northern Illinois University Media Service for the support of this book
- Dr. Bischoff, Chairperson of the Department of Physical Education and Dance Education, at Northern Illinois University for use of facilities and support of this project
- Dr. Charles Carter, Department of Physical Education and Dance Education, Northern Illinois University, for sponsoring Isiah Davis as a model
- Northern Illinois University, Department of Physical Education and Dance Education
- Northern Illinois University, Department of Theatre and Dance, for student models
- Judy Chitwood, Associate Professor, Department of Theatre and Dance at Northern Illinois University, for her talent as a model
- Randall Newsom, Coordinator of the Comprehensive Dance Program at Northern Illinois University, for costumes
- Janiese Potempa for her invaluable help with our photo shoot
- Denise Nakaji for her editorial help
- Dancer/Models: Robert Stewart, Denise C. Nakaji, Heather Kroski, Emile Jedlo, Judith Chitwood, Lisette Rodriguez, Kendra Cornett, Isaiah Davis, Sarah Cullen, and Janiese Potempa

Preparing to Teach Beginning Ballet Classes

The seasoned teacher is the one who walks into the classroom with the entire class memorized. This stage of teaching can be reached; but like all of us, you have to first pay your dues. The process begins with doing the necessary preparation before each class meeting. After teaching the course several times, the teacher has acquired enough experience to know what works best in the classroom in order to prepare the class more effectively.

Part I of *Teaching Beginning Ballet Technique* presents the skills you will need to teach beginning ballet. Part I is organized into six chapters that provide you with specific information about teaching the class, understanding the theoretical foundations of ballet, creating the exercise and step progressions, managing the class, and assessing student learning. All of these aspects of teaching a beginning ballet class are utilized during the day-to-day presentation of new positions, exercises, and steps that the students learn while they are in class. Part I gives you the necessary tools as a foundation to teach the content presented in part II of the book.

The first part of this book, chapters 1 and 2, includes a background on ballet and the teaching/learning process. It provides the teacher a variety of teaching tools such as cues, imagery, teaching styles, and teaching strategies. The third chapter covers the content of the ballet class: the basic principles, positions, rules, and protocols that are a part of the ballet barre and center floor components of the class. Chapter 4 describes how to create beginning barre exercises and center combinations, and includes teaching progressions. Chapter 5, *Managing the Ballet Class*, gives practical information about how to organize and conduct the class, safety procedures in the ballet class, teacher-student interaction, and the teacher's expectation of a beginning class. Chapter 6, *Assessing Student Progress*, presents on-going assessment strategies during the teaching/learning process. Different approaches and methods of pre-assessment of body types and knee variances, assessment procedures, and evaluation tools are provided for a variety of testing situations. Detailed explanations offer a step-by-step path through the process of evaluating students' progress.

Even after teaching ballet for many years, we still enjoy teaching beginning ballet. Each new student and every new class is unique. We gain continued satisfaction from learning something new each time we teach the course that helps us refine our teaching. The challenge is to ask oneself: "How can I teach beginning ballet more effectively and efficiently?" and "How can I make it easier for students to gain movement confidence and enjoy the experience so much they want to move to the next level?" We enjoy working to meet these teaching challenges; we hope you will, too.

chapter one

Facilitating the Learning Process

You open the door to the empty studio. Tomorrow it will be filled with 30 students who are enrolled in beginning ballet. You have 10 to 16 weeks of two class meetings a week to teach these students how to perform basic ballet exercises at the barre and beginning center combinations. These students must learn to execute ballet steps and understand the directions given by you in French—a formidable task to accomplish in such a short period of time. Fortunately many teaching strategies are available that can empower you to reach this goal.

The purpose of this chapter is to explore the basics of teaching the beginning ballet class. In a typical ballet class, at the beginning of each barre exercise and center combination, the teacher uses the *part-whole* or *whole-part-whole* methods to present a verbal depiction of the movement sequence using action words and/or ballet terminology in the French language. At the same time, the teacher may model or demonstrate the movements to be learned or performed, keeping in mind the stages of motor learning. During an exercise or combination, the teacher cues the students' execution of the movements or may give an image to help the students achieve a desired placement or movement. While the students dance, the teacher observes their performance.

Within the teaching/learning process, the teacher meets the different levels of learners in the class by giving them feedback via cues, imagery, and demonstration. To make the movement-language connection, the teacher establishes for students an image of correct placement and develops their visual memory of steps and exercises. To achieve these goals the new teacher must plan, prepare, and practice the class before teaching it. These strategies encompass both the art and science of teaching ballet, making the teacher's role important to the study of ballet technique.

rt of Teaching Ballet

Preparation is vital. Although taking ballet classes is important to be able to teach, observing various ballet teachers teaching different levels of classes is essential. Observe the manner in which the teacher explains different steps and exercises, and gives cues for performance or images that communicate movement qualities. By collecting these resources, you build a visual memory of teaching strategies and gain insights into your own teaching. From these collective experiences you can make choices of what and how you will teach in different situations.

Teaching a ballet class requires a different mindset than that of a student taking the class. Students perform the exercises and the combinations that the teacher gives: They solve movement or music problems, and attend to their own personal performance as they acquire skill. As the teacher, you often teach as many as 30 students in a class, with each student having a different background, reason for taking the ballet class, unique body type, and individual learning style. You are accountable for planning the classes, teaching the course, and assessing each student in the class.

In a beginning ballet class the teacher may encounter individuals who have never set foot in a dance studio before as well as students who have studied ballet previously. Keep in mind that many students have probably never experienced these types of movements. Many have never pointed their feet or straightened their knees. Most beginning students have little kinesthetic awareness of their body and its parts and only a basic spatial or directional knowledge about how their bodies move. Some students in the class may have had other dance or sports experiences in the past. Regardless of students' level of previous training and innate abilities, the teacher must be able to communicate the elements of the subject matter to each individual in the class. Regardless of students' movement backgrounds or reasons for taking the class, ensure that they understand the benefits of taking a ballet class to enhance their appreciation of ballet as an art.

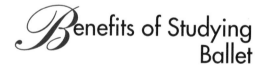

enefits of Studying Ballet

Studying ballet offers many valuable benefits; ballet class

- provides physical conditioning,
- nurtures physical and mental discipline,
- decodes a new nonverbal language,
- develops literacy in the language of ballet,
- teaches the vocabulary of classical ballet,
- improves posture and grace,
- educates individuals so that they can appreciate and support live dance performance, and
- provides connections with a codified dance form based in the Renaissance.

These benefits are consistent with the National Standards for Arts Education: Dance, and with *Goals 2000* (*National Standards for Arts Education* 1994). Performing the ballet class is a ritual for the dancer, regardless of whether the dancer is a novice or a professional. The ballet class has a structure grounded in history and tradition stemming from the Renaissance.

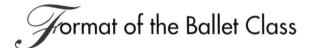ormat of the Ballet Class

The traditional ballet class contains two parts: the barre and the center. Each is addressed in the following sections.

Role of the Barre

The barre is a series of exercises performed at a wooden rail that typically surrounds three sides of the dance studio. At the barre students learn and practice exercises that are the components for steps in the center portion of class. The physical barre provides the support the beginning student needs to acquire basic alignment, balance, and other principles that will be needed for center combinations. Practicing the barre exercises, the dancer integrates mind and body into a working whole. Students explore their attributes, develop their kinesthetic sense, access their mental capabilities, and sculpt the body to make it ready for the work in the center.

Barre exercises warm the muscles and prepare the body for center combinations and moving across the floor. They include bending and rising movements; small to large brushing or gliding movements on and off the floor; rotation of the legs; quick isolated leg and foot movements; striking and beating actions; stretching the legs and torso; transfer of weight; balancing; and slow, controlled movements or poses.

Role of the Center

In the center section of the class, barre exercises connect into steps. The steps combine into everchanging combinations that expand the dancers' skill and memory, not only of executing steps, but also of applying principles, rules, and the aesthetics that make the movement ballet. The center is especially challenging for the teacher and the students. Students perform here without the physical aid of the barre, integrating the principles, rules, and exercises taught at the barre into steps and combinations.

Center floorwork includes exercises to practice classical arm positions and movements; repeating barre exercises in the center; learning spatial directions and classical poses; moving to a slow tempo; executing small and large jump, leap, and hopping steps alone or in combinations; practicing introductory, transitional, and basic turning movements; and learning slow and fast steps and later executing them in short combinations. The beginning level center includes center barre, adagio, petit allégro, and grand allégro.

Relationship Between the Barre and the Center

The traditional ballet class comprises a barre followed by a center. In the beginning ballet class, this traditional division is not so apparent. At the barre the beginning student learns barre exercises. During the center portion of the class, the student returns to the barre to learn and practice steps that will be performed in the center. A binding and cyclic relationship exists between the barre and the center, in which each depends on the development and strength of the other. In the beginning ballet class, the time allocated to the barre and center change during the term as the class gains more ability and stamina to perform center steps and combinations.

The levels of achievement students acquire at the barre support their center work. Teachers should be aware that if barre work appears strong, the center work will not necessarily be of the same strength. The technical performance of the student in the center is likely not to be of the same quality as at the barre. The teacher must

- understand that repetitive practice in the center will make the dancer stronger;
- observe students' work in the center to discover what areas of the barre work need to be reinforced; and
- make the center a smooth and manageable step up from the barre, not a leap across the Grand Canyon!

Beginning students must comprehend the barre exercises, center steps, and combinations to proficiently learn the language of ballet.

Teaching Strategies for the Beginning Ballet Class

Demonstrating movement and having a clear understanding of movement-language connections and the stages of motor learning help the teacher grasp how beginning students learn movement. These teaching strategies are presented next.

Demonstrating the Movement

Demonstrating new exercises and steps to a beginning class is paramount. Strive for demonstrations to be clear, precise, rhythmically accurate, and technically correct. Demonstrations are the source from which students learn the movement by observing and trying to emulate the correct execution of exercises and steps.

One strategy is for the teacher to execute the exercise or step using action words (e.g., "brush out and close"), spoken in rhythm with the sequencing of the movements of the step, first without music and then at a slow tempo. While the teacher repeats these words with each step, the students should repeat these words to themselves when practicing the step so that later they can practice the step on their own.

Making Movement-Language Connections

The connection between movement and language must be developed in the beginning class. Before introducing or practicing an exercise or step, begin by announcing the name of the exercise (e.g., "demi-plié") and then explaining what the name means (e.g., "half-bend"). When demonstrating the teacher should use English action or cue words until the student is able to perform the step without cues. Reaching this level of performance is important. The student must become responsible for performing the exercise or step as soon as possible. Transferring responsibility to the students frees the teacher to teach other aspects of the movement beyond its initial execution.

Although ballet terminology is in French, the movement needs to be introduced using English action words that describe the movement; then the teacher gradually transfers to the French terminology. The correlation between movement and language must also be made between English and French. As you introduce a new exercise or step, write the ballet term on the chalk board so that

students can begin to associate the movements with the terminology. Here are two ways to evaluate whether the vocabulary is being learned:

- Ask students to give the French term for the exercise or step.
- Say the French term and ask students to perform the step.

These devices enable students to remember or associate the step with its name until this connection becomes automatic.

Understanding the Stages of Motor Learning

Parallel to developing the movement-language connection for students is understanding motor learning theory as it applies to ballet. A beginning ballet student goes through the same stages of learning a motor skill as does an athlete: verbal-cognitive, motor, and autonomous. The teacher's role in the beginning ballet class is to shape each student's performance. The movement-language connection establishes a verbal and cognitive basis for learning ballet. This provides a comfort level for students who are used to expressing themselves orally or in written form.

In the initial verbal-cognitive learning stage, it should be expected that students will present a rough execution of the exercises and steps being learned. The teacher imparts feedback to the students with vital knowledge about collective and personal performance with recommendations for improvement. It is important that students understand what is correct technique. This can be learned by

- observing teacher demonstration,
- viewing a videotaped performance,
- listening to a verbal depiction of the exercise or step,
- comparing personal performance through teacher-guided discussion to the image of what is correct or incorrect, and
- creating a mental picture of the correct execution of an exercise or step that the student uses as a guide.

During the motor stage, execution becomes more precise, yet it is also frustrating for students in that the movements may not consistently work the way they intended. Students' movement responses tend to be somewhat inconsistent. Therefore, the teacher's comments need to be clear, concise, and understood in order to motivate students. At this stage, students are able to incorporate the teacher's comments more readily than in the verbal-cognitive stage.

Lastly, in the autonomous stage, the dancer is able to self-correct and has a high degree of consistency in performance. At this stage, the teacher can express the exercises and combinations in French and the dancers can perform the combinations without conscious translation because the terms and exercises and steps have become synonymous. This final stage of motor learning does not always occur during the beginning ballet class.

Two Presentational Methods

Breaking down a movement or a sequence of movements is necessary for students to understand the skills being taught. Two effective ways to teach ballet exercises and steps are the *part-whole* and the *whole-part-whole* methods. Teaching beginners can be complex as you are introducing new vocabulary terms in addition to new movements.

Part-Whole Method

The part-whole method of teaching is used when presenting new material so that students understand the components of any new exercise or step and the sequence in which the movements are performed. The part-whole method combines the parts together to create a whole exercise or step. The teacher uses English action words as the verbal cues while demonstrating each part of the new step or exercise. Present each part of the new material in its sequence twice: first with verbal cues and demonstration, without music, then demonstrating the exercise with counts to the music.

At the beginning of the term, this first presentation is without music so that students can concentrate only on the movement. The "whole" presentation should be a complete verbal depiction of actions along with demonstration of the exercise or step with the music. The teacher does not add comments on how to perform it or pitfalls to avoid.

Whole-Part-Whole Method

In the whole-part-whole method, the teacher presents the entire combination, breaks the combination into

parts, and then repeats the whole combination again. The whole-part-whole method is especially useful later in the term when combining two or three steps. This allows the students to focus on learning the entire exercise or combination. After two presentations of the whole step or combination, you can

- show a particular part to point out specifics that students should incorporate into their performance, and
- review a part that prepares students for a transition in the exercise, a directional or weight change, a tempo change, or added arm or head movement changes within the exercise.

When the presentation is complete, ask if there are any questions. Questions should be answered before students perform the exercise or combination. In subsequent lessons, the presentation of the same material can be shortened to the teacher first demonstrating the movement to music and saying the ballet terminology and then verbally going over the exercise or combination using ballet terminology without music.

The final phase in presenting exercises and steps may occur at the end of the semester. The teacher says the entire exercise or combination in French without demonstrating the movements. This level of understanding requires students to know the movement and the accompanying French terminology to translate the physical and lingual into a performance. A great deal of practice is necessary for students to accomplish this complicated task. The teacher must go step by step in building a movement-language connection for the students to reach this level of translation between words and movement successfully. After the teacher states the entire exercise or step, the students execute the movement with appropriate cues from the teacher.

Using Cues Effectively

Cueing is the verbal and / or rhythmic direction that the teacher gives students during a step or exercise to alert students to what steps are next and how they should be performed. Cueing is an essential skill for the ballet teacher. Choosing the correct method of cueing and the appropriate words or rhythmic direction is important. Cues should be short and memorable. By repeating the same cues over and over, they become slogans for more complex explanations of how a step is performed. Certain classes and individuals respond differently to different cueing methods.

In the early beginning classes, use the English descriptive or kinetic words for the movement instead of French terminology. This makes the movement cues clearer to the student.

What to Cue

Cues must communicate succinctly a concise description of how to perform an exercise, step, combination, or principle. Cueing should be part of the initial verbal presentation of a step or exercise.

Ways to Cue

What are some ways to cue the movement? Some examples follow:

- *Words*: Cue with the names of the movement or steps (eF ., "run, run, leap," or in later units, "run, run, grand jeté").

- *Counting*: Count out the movements (e.g., "& 1" [run], "& 2" [run], "& 3" [leap or grand jeté], "& 4" [hold in fondu]).

- *Nonsense syllables*: Cue the exercise using nonsense syllables instead of words or counts (e.g., "Da, da, yuh, ump, hold").

- *Singing*: Sing the words with the music; rehearse by singing a capella (without music) (e.g., "run, run, l-e-a-p," "run, run, grand j-e-t-é").

- *Part of the phrase*: Cue by calling out only part of the entire phrase; this type of cue is used only when students know all of the combination except a transition or a new step (e.g., [no cue] run, [no cue] run, [cue] "grand j-e-t-é").

- *Clapping*: Clap out the rhythm of the step. Do this both with and without the music so that students can understand the rhythm of the step and how it fits with the music.

- *Vocal emphasis*: Reinforce the words or nonsense syllables with vocal inflection, which may be high or low, soft or loud, slow or fast.

When to Cue

The teacher cues students during a phrase before the movement or change will occur (e.g., cue the downbeat of the next measure on counts 5, 6, 7, 8 of the preceding measure). The teacher must allow students enough time to understand and translate the cue into action. Correct cueing directs effective movement learning.

If cueing in the ballet class is a new skill, the teacher should

- practice giving cues with the music before presenting the phrase in class,

- anticipate cueing before the movement or musical change occurs,

- know the cues listed in the units presented in part II, and

- present the cue at the right time during the learning process.

Cues for the beginning dancer should be specific and visual, for example, "step, hop" for sauté arabesque, or "extend your arms forward in their rounded position, with the hands level with the bottom of the sternum" for First position arms.

In the initial stages of teaching and learning beginning ballet, proper and consistent cueing is crucial. After the students grasp the exercise or step they need time to absorb it into their minds and bodies. Then, students must have quiet time to practice performing the material. This time helps students learn the movement without constant verbal support from the teacher and provides a relaxation time for the teacher's voice. As the term progresses, the teacher

- observes students more,

- cues movement less,

- demonstrates new exercises or steps,

- refines exercises or steps already presented,

- uses different cueing methods,

- repeats the same cues, and

- gives clear cues for refinements in execution.

Cues direct the movement. Images, provided by the teacher, develop and enhance students' understanding of movement and its quality.

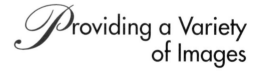

Providing a Variety of Images

Images to help the beginning dancer imagine proper alignment and movement technique should be visual, appropriate, and related to everyday life. The teacher's goal is for students to learn and improve their technique. To achieve this, teachers should develop a repertoire of images from taking ballet class, observing other teachers, and using their own imaginations. Be creative. If the teacher can offer a variety of images, dancers may be able to relate to one of them, sometimes understanding how to execute a step or apply a principle for the first time because they can visualize in their minds and sense internally how their bodies should move. The types of imagery used in teaching dance are visual, kinesthetic, anatomical, and pictorial.

Visual Images

A visual image uses knowledge of a familiar, tangible object or phenomena that can become an analogy of how a step is performed or how a movement principle is applied to an exercise or step. Using external visual images, the dancer develops correct placement and a spatial sense or feeling of a movement. For example, you might explain the demi-plié as follows: "Compare the action of bending the knees to an elevator moving down and up in its shaft. Think of your pelvis and hips as the elevator and your legs as the shaft. The pelvis descends and ascends in the shaft of your legs without tipping forward or tucking under."

Kinesthetic Imagery

Kinesthetic imagery is related to the dancer's sense of what is happening in the body. Using this type of imagery, dancers are able to train or retrain their bodies to perform the movements of ballet. The teacher might direct the students to "Place your weight over your heels; now sense that feeling. Now move your weight forward over your arches; can you sense the difference? That's where your weight should be. Let's do that again so you can feel the difference between when the weight is over your heels and when it is centered correctly over your arches."

Anatomical Imagery

Anatomical imagery is based on understanding and being able to visualize the structure of the body (bones and muscles). For example, to help students stand taller the teacher might give an anatomical image such as "Elongate the spine without losing the three curves (cervical, thoracic, and lumbar)." You may want to take to class a chart of the human skeleton to locate different parts of the body.

Pictorial Imagery

Pictorial imagery is derived from mental pictures that help dancers attain correct body alignment. Dr. Lula Sweigard devised a system called *ideokinesis*, which she presented in her book, *Human Movement Potential: Its Ideokinetic Facilitation* (1974). This method is used to educate the muscles and joints of the body to move in a balanced manner. Muscles relax and tense. The inner structure holds the body in correct alignment through tonic contractions (tonus). Using ideokinesis, internal pictorial images relieve muscle tension and redistribute it so that the body can move in a more effective and efficient manner.

This type of body awareness is important to learning the complex skills required in classical ballet. One of Sweigard's images is

> Imagine your pelvis as a ball of ice cream and your legs are the cone. Tipping the cone down, the ice cream goes forward. The cone needs to be at a level position in order to keep the ice cream in the center of the cone and stable (Sweigard, 1974.).

Franklin has written two books that explore the use of imagery in dance. His first book, *Dynamic Alignment Through Imagery* (1996) generally addresses images in relation to body alignment regardless of dance style. In Franklin's second book, *Dance Imagery for Technique and Performance* (1996), he gives specific examples of imagery as it relates to ballet. These books provide useful supplements to you as a teacher.

Imagery helps students to begin visualizing, thinking about, and sensing parts of the body with which they may never have connected. Body awareness is enhanced through the use of imagery to perform a movement accurately and efficiently so that the movement becomes automatic. It is this combination of imagery the dancer uses to draw with the great toe the same half-circle path on the floor each time for the rond de jambe à terre. An important teaching tool for the ballet teacher, imagery connects students' everyday experiences to the performance of ballet. In this new world of ballet, the students must see and feel the movements of ballet as part of the learning process to build a visual memory.

Building a Visual Memory

A ballet teacher develops a visual memory of combinations and strategies from which to draw upon to support teaching. This visual memory comes from observing and remembering movement, steps, combinations, and even entire dances. The teacher supports and enhances a visual memory by taking classes or recalling personal teaching experiences. A card or computer file of combinations and materials can support and expand memorized resources.

Beginning students learn steps by observing a demonstration. In the ballet class, the teacher shows students how to build a visual memory by directing them to

- observe the entire presentation of an exercise or combination before executing it,

- visualize the exercise or combination before physically performing it,

- rehearse the movements both physically and mentally,

- memorize each action of the step and practice the sequence of movements before performing the step in its entirety, and

- perform the exercise or step to the music.

Accents, directional changes, and the quality of the movement must be pointed out to students, so that in future work students can remember to focus on these aspects as part of an internal checklist. The more advanced dancer memorizes steps in a combination by watching it being performed.

When teaching ballet the teacher demonstrates the same movement many times. The teacher can guide students to build a visual memory using the following techniques. Typically, the students follow the teacher and imitate the movements. If the teacher stops moving, the students stop because they have not yet developed a visual memory on which to rely. The teacher demonstrates the movement repeatedly, enough that the students comprehend the step or exercise. Then the teacher should stop demonstrating and let the students try to perform the movement on their own. Sometimes the teacher should alert the students before stopping, sometimes not.

When beginning students practice movement by themselves they often imitate dancers they see either in front of them or in the mirror. To ascertain if students know the steps or combinations, ask them to perform facing away from the mirror. This strategy helps students determine their knowledge of the step and reminds them of their responsibility to master the step or combination for themselves.

Memorizing the movement and connecting the name of the step to the movement takes commitment and practice, which in turn allows students to develop a visual memory of the step. Using this process the student acquires a vocabulary of ballet movements that are recognizable and repeatable along with a visual memory of basic ballet exercises and steps. Memorizing and picturing the actions of the exercises and steps coupled with imagery helps to develop the beginning dancer's kinesthetic sense, which is further enhanced with mental practice of the movements.

Students should rehearse the movements in their minds by visualizing the sequence of actions with correct timing and accents. Mental rehearsal strengthens the movement and the visual memory of the student and shortens the learning time. Through the development of a visual memory, the student learns ballet exercises and steps that become the basis for gaining competency in using their vocabulary of movements in different combinations.

Teaching/Learning Process

Your major role as the teacher is to instill a love and appreciation of classical ballet and its unique discipline during the learning process. Learning in ballet encompasses the psychomotor or physical, the cognitive or intellectual, and the affective domains. The teaching/learning process is dependent on all of these domains, the experience of the teacher and the student, and the establishment of a learning setting.

Creating a Learning Setting

Teaching a ballet technique class is different from teaching in the academic classroom. The ballet class learns as a group, but also each individual should be guided by the teacher according to his or her learning style. Students hear the French terminology (auditory learning), see the movement demonstrated (visual learning), and experience the movement themselves (kinesthetic learning). Students are also influenced by the attitude of the teacher toward the learner, which may be positive or negative; the physical environment; and the student's prior knowledge of dance in general or ballet in particular.

The openness of the individual, teacher or student, is paramount to the teaching/learning process. The dancer must have faith in and respect for the teacher with regard to the teacher's knowledge, experience, and skill. Likewise, the teacher must show respect for the students and the class. To promote the teaching/learning process, the teacher must create a supportive and safe environment so that all students, regardless of their movement background, will be able to learn and practice new movement skills.

Establishing an Image of Correct Performance

It is imperative that the teacher establish the image of what is correct in the beginning student's mind and body. The teacher must continually review the cues for an exercise or step so the student can understand all the elements that constitute a correct performance. Think of this as bringing a camera lens into focus manually. You have to adjust the lens gently and slowly until you can see a sharp image. As the teacher, over a period of time, you have to continually adjust the students' movements and understanding of the movements to a sharper, clearer performance. A combined effort is required with the teacher and the student both giving and responding. This repeated effort of learning each exercise or step correctly can be expedited as the teacher helps the student build a visual memory of the ballet vocabulary that has been taught in class (see figure 1.1a, b).

Utilizing Levels of Learning

With the introduction and development of each new barre exercise and step in the center, the following process is repeated to progress from one level of learning to the next. When the individual is comfortable performing the exercise or step already learned, he or she is ready to proceed to the next level.

- Level I: Teach the action of the legs.
- Level II: Explain the timing, the accents, and the breath phrasing that are part of the step.
- Level III: Teach simple arm movements. Put the arm and leg movements together.
- Level IV: Incorporate the head movements that accompany the step. Then combine the leg, arm, and head movements together. To perform an exercise or step with coordination of arms, head, accents, and breath phrasing is quite a feat for a beginning dancer!

a

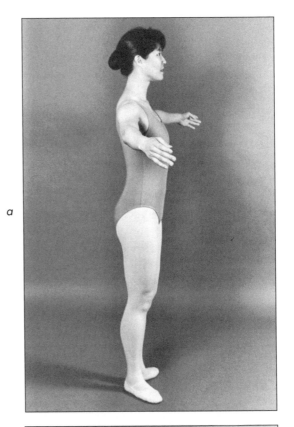

b

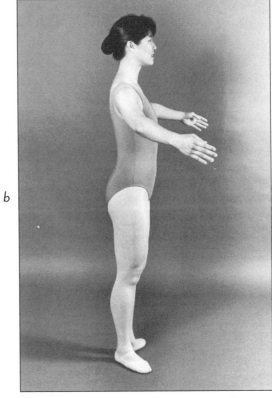

Figure 1.1 Students need to discriminate between a) incorrect arms in Second position, and b) correct arms in Second position (Cecchetti Method).

Learning ballet means gaining a repertory of exercises and steps that increase in difficulty with the addition of one, two, or more variables to the performance. Beginning ballet barre exercises stay the same; once a step is learned it structurally remains the same.

Preparing to Teach

The basic elements of teaching ballet technique have been isolated into parts in this discussion so they could be examined in detail. In the classroom, these elements flow together. If you are new to teaching, the following list provides a guide to creating a class. Remember that the major organizers are *Pre-assess*, *Plan*, and *Practice*.

Pre-assess:

1. Pre-assess each student's physical abilities and skill level the first moving day of class.

2. Continually review the format and purpose of the barre and center parts of the class in relation to your students and where you are in the term.

3. Visualize how your class will move within the studio. Take into consideration the size of the studio and the number of people in the class.

Plan:

1. Prepare and write out on 3 × 5 index cards all of the exercises and steps that you plan to teach before each class.

2. Set time aside to study how each exercise and step will be presented, the English action words, the cues, and the imagery.

3. Select the musical accompaniment from the record or compact disc. If you are fortunate enough to have live accompaniment, set aside sufficient time to go over the music for each exercise and step with the musician for dance.

4. Know the time signature, the length, the tempo, and the quality of the music. Records or compact discs usually list the names of the exercises and their time signatures.

5. Listen to and count to the music.

Practice:

1. Practice each exercise or step, counting out loud to the music to determine how well they work together.

2. Rehearse your class in the studio with the music. Perform the combinations in the center

and across the floor. Adjust any exercises or combinations if necessary. Time the barre and center sections of the class.

3. Memorize the class if at all possible for a professional presentation. If you feel nervous, bring your 3 × 5 written or typed index cards with the exercises and musical information with you to class so that you can refer to them if necessary.

Advance preparation pays off, especially if you are new to teaching. Planning the class, you select the materials that prepare you to teach. Practicing the class, you strengthen your presentation. Presenting the class, you learn to direct the teaching/learning process and adjust it to meet students' needs. Good preparation combined with flexibility helps you address unforeseen developments in the classroom. Being well prepared allows you to orchestrate the teaching/learning process with confidence.

Summary

The role of the teacher is to instill students with a love and appreciation of classical ballet and its unique discipline. The teaching/learning process encompasses the psychomotor, cognitive, and affective domains. Students can benefit greatly from the study of ballet by improved physical conditioning and a disciplined mind and body. The teaching/learning process is enhanced when practiced in an open, positive, and mutually respectful atmosphere.

The ballet class is composed of barre work and center combinations. Teachers should understand the purpose and format of these two major components of the class. Several teaching strategies are recommended, including the part-whole and whole-part-whole methods of presentation. Teachers need to provide movement cues to students throughout the class as well as images from everyday life that students can use to understand alignment and movement principles. Images may be visual, kinesthetic, anatomical, and pictorial. Through providing cues and images, the teacher helps students to make the movement-language connection (connecting the movement to the French vocabulary of classical ballet) and build a visual memory of the steps and exercises presented in class. To do all of this well, preparation is essential to give confidence to the new teacher.

chapter two

*U*tilizing
Teaching Styles
Effectively

Classical ballet is a complicated western theatrical dance form comprising many elements. These elements are combined in creating a hierarchy from the simple to the complex to constitute this highly integrated art form. As an art form, classical ballet provides a clear set of criteria for performance and teaching. Chapter 1 explored the basics of teaching ballet in relationship to presenting content. The purpose of this chapter is to build a new level of understanding about the teaching/learning process utilizing teaching styles. Vital factors of motivation, discipline, feedback, and class management enhance the teaching styles, and therefore the entire teaching process.

eaching Styles

Several teaching styles are available to the teacher for presenting exercises, steps, and principles. The teaching styles applicable to the ballet class are command, practice, reciprocal, self-check, inclusion, and guided discovery. These styles are taken from Mosston and Ashworth's book, *Teaching Physical Education* (1986).

The teaching styles can be placed on a continuum (see figure 2.1). As the continuum moves from left to right, the teaching styles move from teacher-centered to increased student involvement, where the students are making personal choices. At the far left is the command style; in this style, the teacher makes all the decisions on content and how the student will learn. To the right of the command style is the practice style, in which the teacher gives students time to practice. The practice session may be structured as either teacher-directed or student-directed. The next style on the continuum is the reciprocal style. The teacher prepares the exercises, combinations, and performance criteria for the class members. In pairs, one student evaluates another classmate's performance with a subsequent

discussion and change of roles. Next, the self-check style uses teacher- and/or student-created criteria by which the student evaluates personal progress. The inclusive style allows the student to choose several options for performance. This teaching style requires student self-evaluation and a sense of what type of a challenge can be attempted. In the reciprocal, self-check, and inclusive teaching styles, the teacher acts as the facilitator as the student takes on more and more responsibility for learning. On the far right of the continuum is the guided discovery teaching style. The teacher may make statements or ask questions of a student that have only one correct movement answer. The teacher is requesting the student to engage in convergent thinking, thereby using a developed personal mental performance checklist.

Command Style

The command style is the traditional style of learning ballet with the teacher presenting the entire lesson to the students. Demonstration is the primary mode of learning ballet pedagogy. For the beginning student, the teacher simultaneously presents the exercise or combination with a verbal explanation and demonstration. It is important that during the presentation students watch and listen before doing the exercise. This observation helps students build a visual memory of movements and learn the connections between the steps and the terminology. Later, the teacher may use ballet terminology without demonstration to present the exercise.

For example, the teacher demonstrates a petit allégro combination. During the presentation, the teacher says and performs the combinations on both sides without and then with the music. Next, the students perform the combination without and then with the music with the teacher, who says the names of the steps while executing the combination. After you and the students have practiced the combination together, you stop to observe. You may

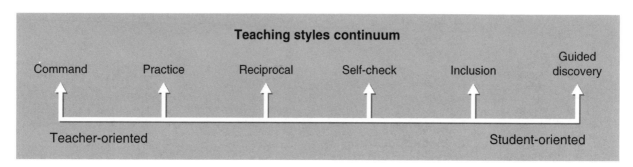

Figure 2.1 Teaching styles continuum.

Teaching Beginning Ballet Technique

continue saying the names of the steps while the students continue to execute the combination. Characteristics of the command teaching style are:

- The students respond to a stimulus (the demonstration) with a performance.
- The students perform the movement together as a group.
- The students strive for accuracy in the movement.

Practice Style

After an exercise or step is introduced to students they need to practice it. The practice style of instruction develops the mind-body connection. Learning to coordinate the body to perform these movements takes time, especially at the beginning level. At this level of training a motor memory is just starting to develop. The teacher encourages mental practice or rehearsal, which in turn helps physical performance.

Students practice the movements mentally by visualizing actively performing a step with the correct rhythm and counts. Scientific evidence supports that mental practice or visualization of an activity enables the individual to learn and remember the exercise or step (Feltz, D.L., and D.M. Landers. 1983). Encourage your students to practice outside of class both with mental and physical practice.

Mental practice or mental rehearsal focuses on thinking of performing the exercise or step from beginning to end in sequence. Research supports that mental practice generates motor learning (Felts and Landers, 1983). To mentally practice the demi-plié in First position, direct the student to focus on the alignment of the body, turn-out from the hips, and placement of the feet. Then ask the dancer to mentally rehearse. The teacher states the cues for executing the exercise, such as "Bend the knees descending as far as possible with the heels remaining on the floor, and direct the knees over the second and third toes." Remind the students that the body counterpulls on the descent of the demi-plié. Guide students on their return from the demi-plié. At the end of the exercise, check alignment and turn-out of the hips. Students can mentally rehearse exercises using the cues that the teacher says in class. This infusion of cues into personal mental rehearsal supports and accelerates the motor learning process.

In the practice style the teacher demonstrates the barre exercise or center combination. Next, the teacher gives students practice time either without or with music. Without the music, students practice at their own pace to sense the actions in a sequence; later, students may practice the exercise or step to music. While the students practice, the teacher goes from student to student giving individual instruction or monitoring the practice and also provides feedback to the entire group. Characteristics of the practice teaching style are:

- The teacher gives students time to rehearse an exercise or step with and/or without music.
- The teacher provides group or individual feedback.

Reciprocal Style

The reciprocal style of teaching gives students chances to apply the principles and correct execution of classical ballet to classroom performance. This teaching style is also known as peer teaching. Using the reciprocal style can be a valuable learning experience for both students and teacher. The teacher learns what principles or parts of the exercise or step have been learned and what areas still need review.

Using reciprocal strategy in the ballet class, each class member finds a partner. One student acts as an observer while the other person performs the exercise or step. The teacher creates a performance criteria checklist for the students to use when looking at the performance of an exercise, step, or combination. With this checklist, the observer can make a judgment as to whether the performer has met the performance criteria. The observer tells the dancer in a constructive manner about his or her performance. This type of teaching/learning gives the students an opportunity to be evaluated by someone other than the teacher. By observing other students, the dancers become more aware of their own performance and more involved in the teaching/learning process.

Using another version of the reciprocal teaching style, the teacher asks students what techniques and principles are part of the performance of a specific exercise or combination. The teacher lists them on the chalkboard. Breaking into pairs, while one partner performs the step or combination the other partner observes, then the couple have a dialogue about the performance. Immediately after they reverse roles, followed by another dialogue. This activity can be repeated so each partner can practice what he or she learned in the dialogue. In a reciprocal learning situation, the teacher can pair the students into couples of equal experience or pair a more experienced dancer with a less experienced dancer.

After the students perform several exercises or combinations, have them change partners. Different people see different things that contribute to improving performance. For example, in peer teaching a jump (sauté) in First position, the checklist of criteria would include:

- The body remains in alignment during the execution of the step.
- The jump begins and ends with a demi-plié.
- The legs fully extend and toes point for the ascent and during the jump.
- The landing is toe, ball, heel, knee in sequence into the demi-plié.

The student reviewing the performance uses the written criteria as a checklist. While observing his or her partner's jumping, the student compares the performance to the checklist. The criteria checklist becomes a springboard for comments about the performance. Characteristics of the reciprocal teaching style are:

- Students work in a partner relationship; one person performs and the other observes.
- The performer, after executing the combination, receives immediate feedback from the partner.
- The observer evaluates according to set criteria (an assessment checklist) developed by the teacher sometimes in conjunction with the students.
- Students learn how to give constructive criticism.

Self-Check Style

With the self-check teaching style, students monitor personal performance with a teacher-developed checklist. Later, the student and the teacher mutually create a specific checklist or set of goals for the student to work on during the course. Using a self-checklist passes more of the responsibility for learning from the teacher to the student. This teaching style works well with students who have had previous ballet experience or later in the term.

In the self-check style, the teacher develops a list of criteria for performing an exercise or step. For example, students should do the following for a

battement tendu:

- Start in Fifth position at the barre.
- Brush strongly from a full foot to pointed foot in each direction (devant, à la seconde, derrière) and return from a pointed foot to a full foot in Fifth position.
- Transfer weight from the evenly balanced starting position to the supporting foot and leg and back again.
- Articulate the working foot completely from a full foot to a pointed foot and back again.
- Lead with the heel out and return to Fifth position leading with the toes.
- The working foot remains in contact with the floor during the exercise.

Characteristics of the self-check style are:

- The student evaluates personal performance in the class.
- The teacher establishes the criteria and the student analyzes personal performance.
- The feedback to the student is immediate.

Inclusive Style

Even in a beginning ballet class, the teacher uses the inclusive style of teaching. This style allows for teaching various skill levels within one class. Most classes have students with different levels of training. At the beginning level, some students may have never set foot in a dance studio before; others may have studied ballet as a child and now want to take a class again. Sometimes students may have had years of training and want to enroll in a beginning ballet class for a variety of reasons: to protect their personal performance, recovery from an injury, and/or for fun.

So that everyone is motivated and not bored or frustrated in the class, the teacher can offer options. These options add performance challenges to both the barre and center at different levels of difficulty. The inclusive style of instruction meets the needs of individual students. This gives a challenge or a choice to test ability.

Individualizing instruction provides levels of difficulty that the teacher can assign to individuals in the class. For the student without previous dance training, it takes an entire semester to achieve the entire exercise and step progression process outlined in part II of this book to some degree of proficiency. For the student with some previous ballet experience, assign a performance option. The teacher must determine if the student is concentrating on achieving what is being taught or if the student is ready to accept a challenge. Here are some examples of options to give students who possess various levels of ability:

- Perform the step or exercise at either a modified or standard tempo.
- Execute the exercise either full foot or on relevé.
- Add arms alone or arms and head movements to exercises and combinations.

Characteristics of the inclusive teaching style are:

- The teacher provides students with options for performance.
- Each student chooses at what level of difficulty a step will be performed.
- The style includes all learners in the class by challenging each student regardless of his or her ability or training.

In using these teaching styles, the teacher engages students in divergent thinking, or thinking from specifics to general. Using divergent thinking, the student learns to apply principles, rules, and protocols to new exercises and steps. The student learns to execute a demi-plié before and after a step and applies this rule to each new step learned. The guided discovery teaching style utilizes convergent thinking. In this mode, the student answers questions or statements that the teacher asks, such as "Is your focus slightly up and forward?"

Guided Discovery Style

The guided discovery teaching style is applicable to teaching classical ballet when the student has a resource of knowledge on which to draw. This style uses a questioning approach directed toward obtaining specific answers. The student must be able to answer the question using previously learned information. In this teaching style the teacher transfers to the student the responsibility for analyzing if the position or movement is correct or how to correct it. For example, the teacher would ask, "Are your shoulders and hips square to the front of the room?" "Are all five toes on the floor?" "Where is your weight on your supporting foot?" This teaching style helps the individual remember and monitor the salient features of executing an exercise or step. Characteristics of the guided discovery teaching style are:

- The teacher poses questions or statements during execution of exercises or steps to refine student movement.
- The student dancer answers self-check questions posed by the teacher by adjusting movement memory. Some of these questions include: Does the dancer perform the exercise or movement correctly? Can the student feel the incorrect and/or correct movement? Is the dancer able to adjust the movement to what is considered correct?

The more ways of presenting the material, the better the chance that the student will respond quicker. Teaching styles provide more avenues through which to reach students in the class, as does presenting material verbally, auditorily, or kinesthetically and/or using cues and images. One student might understand a correction using the command teaching style, whereas another student might respond better to the reciprocal teaching style to learn the same exercise or step. Likewise, the teacher must acquire ways to communicate with each individual and the entire class about all aspects of technical training as well as the intellectual, emotional, and psychological issues related to studying ballet.

Each teaching style is influenced by the vital factors of motivation, discipline, feedback, and management. These vital factors give the teacher conduits that connect the teaching styles to the content (see units I through IV) and the teaching/learning process in the class.

Motivation, Discipline, Feedback, and Management

The vital factors of motivation, discipline, feedback, and management (Mosston and Ashworth, 1986) permeate the teaching styles, cues, and imagery. The vital factors in relation to the teaching styles have changing roles. Each of these vital factors begins as extrinsic or externalized from the point of view of the teacher. As the semester progresses, the vital factors become intrinsic or internalized to students. This transfer occurs as students assume more responsibility for their learning during the semester, which is initiated by the teacher's movement along the teaching styles continuum from teacher-directed to student-directed learning.

The teacher should become aware of how students perceive each of these vital factors. Informally, the teacher learns about students' perceptions through observation and conversation with them. For more definite information, you may wish to pursue active research by asking students to respond in writing regarding these elements in relation to the ballet class.

Motivation

Motivation may be tangible or intangible; it is an incentive, or what moves someone to action. For the student it is that inner drive that propels an individual to continue striving toward a goal or toward reaching a level of self-satisfaction.

Motivation in ballet can be driven by a variety of personal reasons, and it can be a powerful factor in the teaching/learning process. Taking ballet may fulfill the female student wanting to live the childhood fantasy of being a ballerina or the male or female student using ballet as a method through which to refine movement skills to excel in sports. The teacher can use student motivation as a springboard to encouraging the students to become personally responsible for their learning. If a student does not exhibit a strong desire to learn ballet, the teacher plays a pivotal role in fostering the student's motivation. Teachers can motivate students by making positive comments or giving compliments that encourage a student to try harder, attain a new challenge, or work toward the long-term goal of achieving a grade in the course.

Discipline

Discipline means learning, practicing, and demonstrating expected behaviors specifically associated with ballet. From the student viewpoint, discipline comes from the desire to meet and attain the desired results. Taking ballet class develops self-discipline of the body as well as the mind. Practicing ballet physically changes the body, teaching it a way to communicate through movement and respond to music. Executing the ballet barre and center requires the student to focus on the exercises and combinations in logical, sequential phrases that relate to the accompanying music. The student imposes self-discipline to meet the standards of ballet, sometimes calling upon the discipline learned in other arts or academic pursuits. Through committing to the study of ballet, students increase self-discipline

and abilities, which may in turn have a positive effect on learning in other areas of their lives.

The teacher views discipline as a commitment to practicing the structure, rules, and etiquette of the ballet class. Applying each of these components contributes to developing a foundation for understanding the aesthetics of ballet as an art. Discipline in the classroom connects dancers to the rich history of ballet, which dates to the courts of the Renaissance and the formalistic traditions that have become classroom heritage. This connection to tradition results in infusing students' performance with an appreciation for the beauty of this dance form that has existed for over three hundred years. Aesthetic awareness for beginning students allows them to sense the spirit of the art, or what it is like to be a ballet dancer. Becoming a dancer requires accepting feedback from the teacher.

Feedback

Feedback is information that enables the individual to improve his or her performance. In a beginning ballet class the teacher must create an atmosphere that is positive and encouraging. Teacher feedback is directly linked to teacher observation.

Beginning ballet students are very fragile and self-conscious as they learn new movements. Early in the term the teacher should concentrate on helping students develop their self-perception as dancers. Comments should be made to the class as a whole to improve collectively their performance. Very few comments should be made to individuals; there is safety in being part of the group. After the teacher has developed a comfortable relationship with each student, the teacher begins to make constructive comments to individuals while continuing to give feedback to the class as a whole. Try to phrase all comments as positive reinforcement, with a suggestion for improvement. The teacher must make the class safe so that beginning students will risk making mistakes so that they can learn from them.

Feedback in each of the teaching styles may be verbal or non-verbal. As the students move along the continuum of the teaching styles, feedback, like the other vital factors, moves from external to internal. Throughout this process the teacher remains as an "outside eye," monitoring student application of self-check, choosing options, and evaluating the degree of student success. The teacher provides feedback to the students as a teachable moment. For this moment with a student, the teacher may plan or through spontaneous dialogue provide insight into the execution of a movement or understanding of a principle. If the teacher sees that the student is steadily working toward accomplishing a goal, letting the student achieve on his or her own is the best feedback the teacher can give. The teacher praises the student's efforts during the process and once the goal has been accomplished.

Management

Management of the class is teacher-directed. The teacher decides content, organization of the barre and center, level of instruction, pace of the class, and the options offered to students to challenge them in an orderly teaching/learning atmosphere. The teacher manages students' work by observing, listening, and demonstrating the exercises and steps. The teacher is the role model for the expected behavior in class. Through the eyes of the students, management requires that the teacher is the constant guide who supports and provides challenges for each student throughout the course.

Management is how the teacher implements the teaching styles and guides the students through the process of learning ballet. The teacher is a firm but friendly guide. The learning experience for students should be positive while they experience each of the teaching styles. This type of management requires that the teacher gently guide the students into new areas of learning using the teaching styles discussed earlier, while supporting their development with a strong but unobtrusive leadership role in the class.

Summary

Chapters 1 and 2 described the external and internal layers or tracks of teaching a beginning ballet class. In the studio classroom, the teacher must operate with such a two-track mind in order to include both layers of the teaching/learning process. On the external track, the teacher presents the exercises and steps to the class using movement, language, cueing, and imagery. On the internal track, the teacher infuses the lesson with the teaching styles: command, practice, reciprocal, self-check, inclusion, and guided discovery (see figure 2.2). The vital factors of motivation, discipline, feedback, and management, in conjunction with the teaching styles, guide students through the teaching/learning process. It takes students time to put the pieces of the beginning ballet puzzle together. Likewise, it takes teachers time to understand how the elements presented in these first two chapters work together in the teaching/learning process to achieve the goal of teaching ballet technique.

Figure 2.2 Two-track teaching.

*D*eveloping Foundational Principles

Classical ballet is a very logical art form. The core of classical ballet comprises a vocabulary of exercises, steps, positions, and poses for which the terminology is in French. Principles, rules, and protocols govern how to perform exercises and steps. Rules and protocols distinguish ballet from other dance forms. The theoretical structure provides a framework that, applied correctly, meets the classical standards demanded by the art. Aesthetic concepts encapsulate the core and theoretical structure. All these components make ballet unique for its clarity of expressive movement and pureness which renders it a classical art form. It is imperative that the ballet teacher understands these principles, rules, positions, and protocols and how they apply in order to communicate them to students.

The purpose of this chapter is to introduce the principles, rules, poses, and protocols that form the basis for the barre and center. Ballet uses classical positions of the feet, arms, hands, head, and body. The foundation of the barre incorporates the center line; the working and supporting leg; positions at the barre; and the protocols practiced at the barre during the preparation, execution, and ending of exercises. The center utilizes protocols for preparation, endings, and during the execution of steps and combinations. Within the center structure are the center barre, adagio, and allégro combinations. The class closes with a bow or curtsy known as the révérence.

Principles of Classical Ballet

The general principles of classical ballet encompass alignment, turn-out, weight distribution, stance, transfer of weight, squareness, pull-up or lift, counterpull, counterbalance, aplomb, and balance. Although the principles are examined individually in this chapter, in the ballet class they are interrelated. It is difficult to study one principle without looking at its relationship to others. But for the beginning student, introduce each principle separately and in a progression, which is explained in the units in part II. This strategy allows the beginning student to concentrate on applying one principle before adding the next principle. Learning and applying the principles of classical ballet is a layering process. The teacher gauges this process so that students continue to integrate these principles intellectually and kinesthetically. New principles blend with learned principles into the students' movement experiences, thereby creating a solid basic ballet technique (see figure 3.1). The pyramid helps to understand how the principles build upon each other and integrate into the units.

Alignment

Body alignment is good posture in its most classic sense. Proper alignment is the foundation for all ballet technique. For the ballet dancer, body alignment constantly integrates the head, torso, arms, and legs into a cohesive whole while moving through space or holding a pose. Alignment is a primary and dynamic ballet principle to which all ballet principles depend upon or relate. Figure 3.2 shows a dancer in proper alignment viewed from both the front and side of the body. The components of alignment are examined in detail and context in part II, unit 1.

Turn-Out

Turn-out, the outward rotation of the legs and feet, is the most distinctive characteristic of classical ballet. Turn-out emanates from the hip joint. The femur rotates in the hip joint from the six deep rotators of the hip: piriformis, abductor internus, quadraters femoris, gemelli interior, gemelli superior, and obdurator externus. Muscular control of the pelvis, legs, and abdominal muscles is essential to maintain correct alignment of the body and to facilitate turn-out.

Turn-out extends from the hip joints through the upper and lower legs and feet. Align knees with the pelvis and the foot. The kneecap (patella) falls directly between the second and third toes. The ankle is perpendicular to the floor so that the foot does not roll either inward or outward. The vertical alignment of the hips, legs, knees, ankles, and feet is maintained regardless of whether the joints are straight or flexed. Give the following teaching cue for turn-out in executing the demi-plié: "Direct your knees over the second and third toes of each foot."

Ideal turn-out is 180 degrees. For the beginning dancer, turn-out is the dancer's natural rotation from the hip joints, approximately 90 to 100 degrees. To maintain equal turn-out on both legs requires proper alignment, squareness of the torso, and centering of weight (see figure 3.3). Natural turn-out increases as the dancer

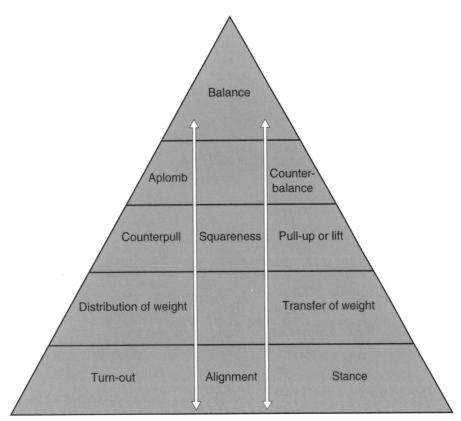

Balance

Aplomb

Counter-
balance

Counterpull

Squareness

Pull-up or lift

Distribution of weight

Transfer of weight

Turn-out

Alignment

Stance

Figure 3.1 Pyramid of principles of classical ballet.

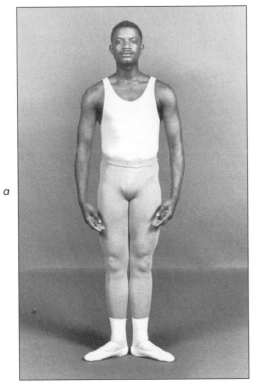

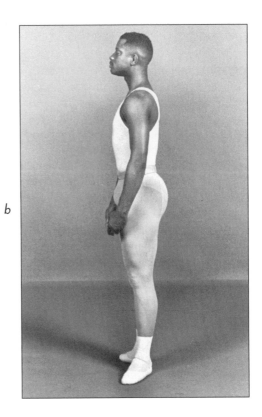

a

b

Figure 3.2 Alignment: a) Front view b) Side view.

applies these principles and gains muscular control.

Turn-out is a primary principle that applies to all of ballet technique. During the Renaissance ballet was performed first in the ballroom and then moved to the stage. The clothing that the dancers wore made turn-out the most efficient and aesthetic way of moving in all directions and assuming any of the classical positions while facing the audience. Turn-out is the hallmark of classical ballet.

An image that helps dancers understand the principle of turn-out is the "magic spiral" (see figure 3.4). Imagine a spiral that initiates from the hip bone, goes in back of the buttock, and passes over the inner thigh rotating it outward. Then the spiral passes behind the knee and wraps around the middle of the calf turning the calf forward. The spiral wraps around the shin and pushes the heel forward. The spiral continues wrapping around the top part of the foot and around the toes pushing the toes to the outward and back. The opposite direction can be retraced with the spiral wrapping around the leg from the toes to the hip bone.

Weight Distribution

Distribution of weight is crucial to how well the dancer balances and moves efficiently. Body alignment is central to proper weight distribution. Turn-out interrelates to the distribution of weight on one or two feet. As the dancer moves, body weight continually recenters over one or both feet.

In the full-foot position all five toes and the sole of the foot contact the floor to support the weight of the body. The body weight centers vertically over an area of the foot that is triangular in shape (see figure 3.5a). The foot triangle connects the metatarsal of the great toe, the fifth metatarsal, and the heel. The dancer places the weight over the center of this triangle to connect the vertical alignment of the body. By centering the weight over the foot in this manner, the dancer is able to move in any direction instantaneously.

In the three-quarter relevé position, distribute the body weight over the metatarsals and all five toes. The weight vertically centers between the second and third metatarsals to prevent the foot from rolling in or out. In the relevé position, with the weight centered on this small base, the foot flexes at the base of the metatarsals and the heel lifts so that the

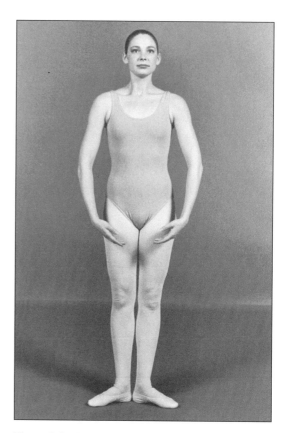

Figure 3.3 Turn-out in First position.

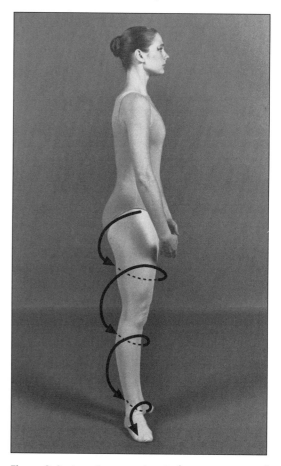

Figure 3.4 Imagine a magic spiral wrapping around the legs to understand turn-out.

Teaching Beginning Ballet Technique

longitudinal arch is perpendicular to the floor (see figure 3.5b).

Stance

In exercises and combinations the dancer momentarily assumes a stance with weight on both feet when passing through the classical foot positions. To assume proper stance, the body weight should be centered equally over the arches (see figure 3.6). Learning to assume a proper stance with weight equally centered on both feet is especially important for the beginning dancer. The beginning dancer assumes the classical foot positions to learn the position kinesthetically, to rest, and to regain balance before shifting weight to one foot or in a different direction.

Transfer of Weight

The action of shifting weight from two feet to one or the reverse is part of achieving stance in ballet. The dancer makes the transfer of weight appear effortless. Breathing with the movement, using turnout, and stretching the body upward disguises the actual shift of weight. Being able to execute the weight shift is crucial to achieving the smooth changes of the feet and directions that are salient features of ballet.

Before the body weight transfers from two feet to one foot, the body stretches slightly upward and sideways on a diagonal through the legs and pelvis. Completely shift the weight to one leg, then center the body weight forward and over the arch of the supporting foot. The shift from two legs to one leg is barely noticeable. Figure 3.7 shows the shift of weight from First position to one foot and then to Second position front. Use the following teaching cue: "Stretch upward and forward to center your weight over the supporting foot."

As the weight transfers from one to two feet, the body stretches upward through the legs and pelvis. Complete the shift of weight, then center the body weight over each foot distributing the weight equally between both feet. You can cue students by reminding them to "Stretch upward as you place the weight onto two feet."

Squareness

Squareness refers to keeping the shoulders and the hips on the same plane and parallel to each other and the floor. This principle enables the dancer to increase directional acuity as the working leg moves in different directions. The torso

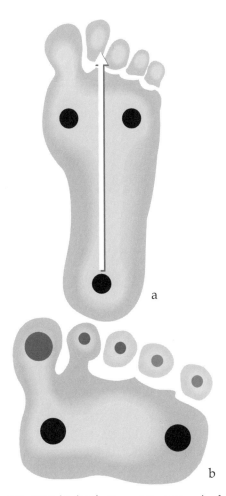

Figure 3.5 Weight distribution: a) Foot triangle, full-foot position, b) Three-quarter relevé.

in classical ballet works as a unit and has often been perceived as immobile, which is untrue. In reality, the torso moves subtly in relation to the breath phrasing of movement and combinations. Squareness of the torso provides stability in opposition to the stretching of the working leg in various directions, while the supporting leg lifts upward. The dancer's kinesthetic sense of torso and squareness becomes more important with the integration of directional changes at the barre and in the center. With these ideas in mind, establish the principle of squareness in the beginning student first at the barre (see figure 3.8a), then in the center when facing the front of the studio (see figure 3.8b), and later when facing the corners of the room (see figure 3.8c).

When the leg lifts off the floor in various directions, this usually involves an adjustment of the pelvis and the spine. When the working leg extends forward, the pelvis and the spine begin to move after 60 degrees. Movement of the leg to the side is limited to about 45 degrees without spine or hip

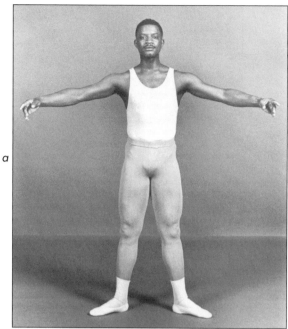

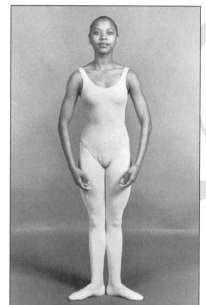

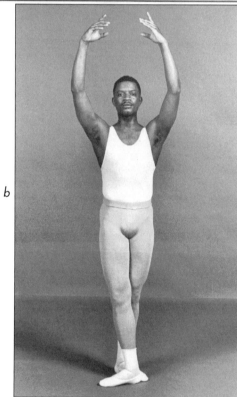

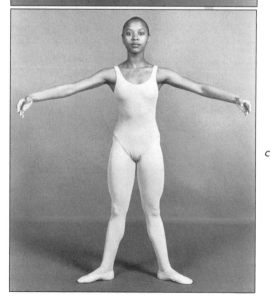

Figure 3.6 Stance: a) Second position. b) Fifth position; weight is equally centered on both feet.

Figure 3.7 Transfer of weight from a) First position, to b) One foot, to c) Second position.

Teaching Beginning Ballet Technique

movement. The spine and pelvis stabilize up to 15 degrees in the back.

The idea of squareness of the hips is misleading because of the anatomical structure of the body. The dancer strives to keep the hip line (iliac crests) level. The dancer always keeps in mind the image of the hips facing forward on the horizontal plane. For stability, weight distribution and counterpull work in conjunction with squareness.

If the hips tilt upward, squareness alters and weight distribution shifts to the heels (see figure 3.9a). To regain squareness, the spine lengthens, the hips move under the shoulders, and body weight centers over the triangle of each foot (see figure 3.9b). In arabesque, squareness is essential for balance and the correct aesthetic line. If the hip opens on the side of the working leg, the dancer leans or spirals toward the supporting leg rendering the dancer off balance, which in turn may cause the shoulders to twist open toward the raised leg.

Pull-Up or Lift

Pulling up through the legs by stretching upward from the floor, engaging the abdominals and lifting the torso off the legs is an important part of ballet technique and contributes to its aesthetic (see figure 3.10). Pull-up or lift is three-dimensional. When the supporting leg (or legs if standing on both feet as in figure 3.10) pulls up, it stretches upward into the pelvis to maintain maximum length. This keeps the dancer from sinking into the supporting leg and hip. Likewise, the pelvis and torso lift off the legs for ease of movement. The dancer engages the

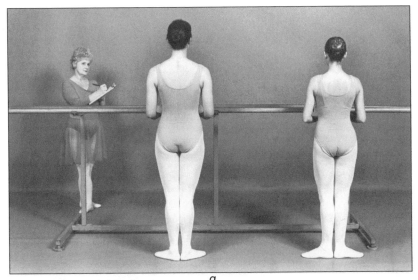

a

b

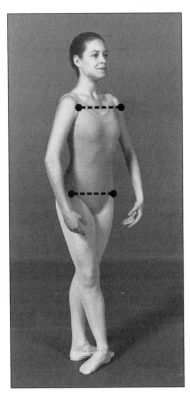

c

Figure 3.8 Squareness: a) At the barre. b) in the center. c) Facing the corner.

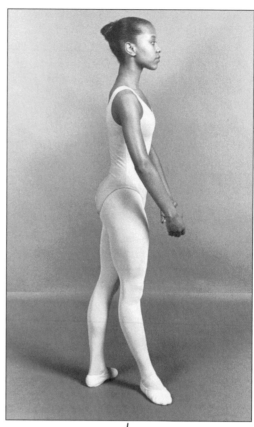

a b

Figure 3.9 Squareness in Fourth position: a) Incorrect. b) Correct.

abdominals, lifting them upward from the pubic bone to the sternum, and lengthening the distance between the ribs and the hips while compressing to make a waistline. This action simultaneously accompanies the back elongating downward toward the floor, but maintaining its three curves: cervical, thoracic, and lumbar. These counteractions give lift and vertical centering to the torso and consequently free the legs to move easily while the body seems to float above them. To be effective the principle of pull-up or lift integrates good alignment, breath phrasing, and aplomb. Using pull-up and lift, the dancer appears light and able to defy gravity.

Counterpull

Counterpull deals with the opposing forces that are at work in the body. Gravity and the weight of the body exert a downward force; the muscles supply the upward force. When the tension in the muscles lessens, with proper body alignment, the dancer performs movement with ease (see figure 3.11). Breathing becomes unhampered and the dancer performs as a well-tuned and efficient instrument.

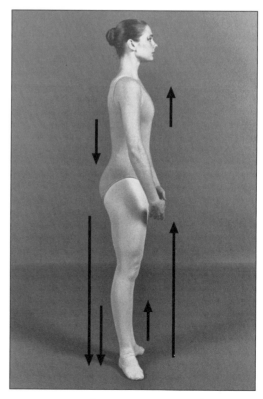

Figure 3.10 Pulling up through the legs and lifting the torso allows for freedom of movement.

Teaching Beginning Ballet Technique

For every action there is an opposite and equal reaction. When executing a downward motion, the body lifts before it descends. In classical ballet technique, the dancer attempts never to sink in the body or give in to gravity. If the working leg moves, the working side of the body tends to move either forward or backward. These actions usually occur in the shoulders, the hips, or both. Counterpull prevents the loss of squareness and pull-up.

Counterbalance

Counterbalance is the upward and slightly forward tilt of the torso when the leg lifts beyond 20 degrees back, or derrière (développé derrière and arabesque). Because of the structure of the back of the hip joint, counterbalance or tilt allows the working leg to extend upward without straining the back (see figure 3.12a). The body continues to maintain squareness during counterbalance. The front of the body stretches upward on a forward tilted angle while the leg stretches backward. The body returns to its aligned position on the completion of the movement or movements back-

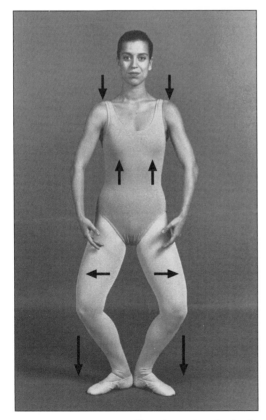

Figure 3.11 Counterpull in demi-plié; the body lifts before it descends.

ward (see figure 3.12b). The elongation of the cervical, thoracic, and lumbar spine is essential to this process.

Aplomb

Aplomb is an imaginary vertical line the teacher uses to assess alignment and vertical centering in the dancer. View aplomb from two directions. From the front, view the dancer standing in classical First position. The aplomb line (also called the center line) runs from the top of the head, through the middle of the nose, mouth, chin, sternum, navel, middle of the pelvis, and between the heels (see figure 3.13a). From the side, the aplomb line runs from the top of the head, in front of the ear, through the middle of the shoulder, hip, and knee, and falling in front of the ankle bone (see figures 3.13b).

By centering the body weight before rising from demi-plié to relevé, the dancer appears to move vertically without a visible forward shift of the body (see figure 3.14a, b).

On the return from relevé to a full-foot position, the dancer inhales and counterpulls. If the dancer centers the body weight properly on relevé for the return to full foot, the dancer appears to descend vertically and exhales on the way down. These upward and downward actions are central to the idea of aplomb. The dancer's goal is to execute these actions with an effortless quality.

The principle of aplomb also applies to the moving dancer. In that context, aplomb is the dancer's ability to change levels from demi-plié to relevé and the reverse while controlling and centering the body weight along its vertical axis. As the dancer executes movements from two feet or one foot, balance, stance, weight transfer, and aplomb integrate. When the dancer moves all the body parts constantly readjust to realign. Aplomb allows the dancer to move vertically up and down or through space with confidence and grace.

Balance

Classical ballet views balance both anatomically and aesthetically. To achieve balance anatomically, the three planes of the body intersect. The three planes are the frontal plane, the front half and back half; the sagittal plane, the right side and left side; and the transverse plane, the top half and bottom half (see figure 3.15).

Figure 3.12 Counterbalance allows the working leg to extend in arabesque beyond 20 degrees: a) First arabesque en l'air, b) First arabesque à terre.

Balance is a dynamic principle that the dancer tries to maintain throughout the body while stationary or moving. To be in balance, the dancer continually readjusts the internal relationship of one or more body parts while in a pose, moving in various directions, or turning. To achieve balance, center the body's weight on one or two feet; balance incorporates turn-out, pull-up, and alignment into an integrated whole.

Balance has an internal as well as an external dynamic. To find balance the dancer learns to sense it internally as well as see it externally by focusing on it in the mirror. Viewed as an aesthetic principle of ballet, balance refers to choosing the correct proportions for parts of a combination, showing the harmony of all the parts in their everchanging relationships.

To gain balance the dancer assimilates the internal structure of exercises and steps through the classical ballet positions. These positions are the framework through which movement in ballet flows and what make ballet a plastique, three-dimensional art form.

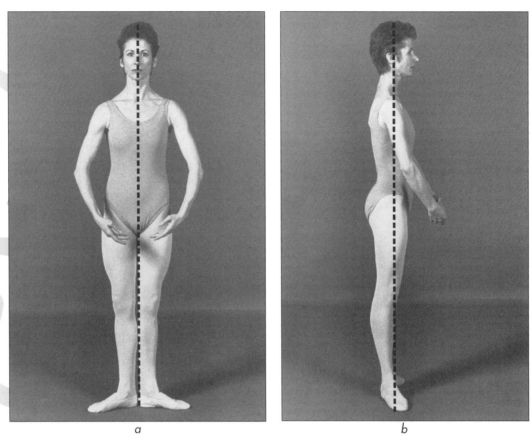

Figure 3.13 Aplomb. First position: a) Front view. b) Side view.

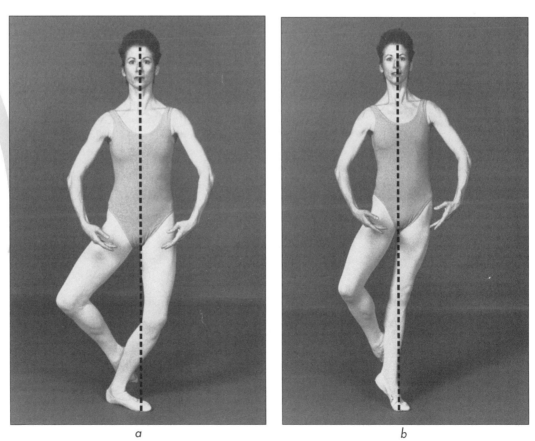

Figure 3.14 Aplomb: Coupé derrière. a) Front view: Coupé derrière fordu. b) Front view, three-quarter relevé.

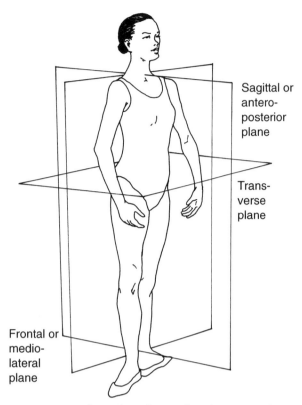

Sagittal or antero-posterior plane

Transverse plane

Frontal or medio-lateral plane

Figure 3.15 Balance: frontal, sagittal, and transverse planes intersect.

lassical Ballet Positions

Classical ballet uses positions of the feet and active foot positions on the leg. Classical arm positions extend to the hands and incorporate head positions. Dancers pass through or hold for a short duration classical foot and arm positions while executing movements or positions. The classical ballet positions and movements distinguish ballet from other dance forms.

As ballet developed and spread throughout western Europe and Russia, several schools and methods emerged. The Cecchetti Method and elements of the Russian School and the Royal Academy of Dance are most appropriate for training the beginning student. There are many interpretations or variations of how exercises and steps are executed, even within a single school. For the purposes of this book we are focusing on teaching basic ballet technique; more advanced nuances of the movements are not covered here.

Positions of the Feet

The placement of the feet is in relationship to the turn-out from the hip socket. In classical ballet, all movements of the legs and feet begin and end in a turned-out position. The five basic positions of the feet are First, Second, Third, Fourth, and Fifth positions. These five positions are described in greater detail in part II, unit I.

In the basic feet positions, the entire foot rests on the floor in the full-foot position. This position provides the foundation for supporting the body weight. The body weight centers vertically on top of the arch, distributing the weight over a triangular area that connects the first and fifth metatarsals to the heel. A line extending from the heel, or the apex of the foot triangle, bisects the base of the triangle between the metatarsals. This imaginary line provides a guide to discerning if the weight centers over the arch. If the weight falls on the inside of the foot, the arch drops and the foot pronates, or rolls inward. If the weight falls on the outside of the foot the ankle weakens and the foot, it supinates, or rolls outward. Both of these foot conditions are the consequence of poor alignment and incorrect or too much turn-out.

Active Foot Positions

Active foot positions refers to the category of relevés, or rises, where the body raises from full foot to balance on all five toes and the metatarsals. The standard relevé is a three-quarter relevé on the longitudinal arch. To execute a relevé there are several different ways to ascend to three-quarter relevé position and descend to the full-foot position (see unit II, barre).

Positions of the Foot on the Leg

The foot of the working leg (leg doing the action) is placed on the supporting leg in several positions. Positions of the working foot on the supporting leg include

- at the ankle,
- between the ankle and the knee, and
- at the knee.

These foot positions provide approaches from which to begin steps and transitions between movements. In all of these positions,

- align and square the body;
- keep hip crests level;

- center weight vertically over the supporting leg and foot, which are well turned-out;

- turn out the working leg; and

- flex the hip and knee of the working leg (in the sur le cou-de-pied position, the ankle flexes).

Pointing the Foot

In classical ballet the pointed or plantar flexed foot is an important technical and aesthetic consideration. The foot points when it is in the air (*en l'air*). How the dancer points the foot is very important to the dancer's technique and development of line (see figure 3.16).

When the foot does not point along the line bisecting the foot triangle the result is called *sickling*, whether pointing the foot on the floor, in the air, in active foot positions, or resting the pointed foot on the supporting leg. In active foot positions, if the foot sickles in (inversion), the body weight moves toward the outside of the foot. Or, if the foot sickles out (eversion), the body weight moves toward the inside of the foot. Either of these problems weakens the ankles and contributes to poor alignment, weight placement, and balance.

Pointing the feet in the air or resting the foot on the leg requires correct foot placement. Connecting kinesthetically with pointing along the center line

Rules:

When the foot touches the supporting leg, the side of the little toe touches the front of the leg, such as the retiré devant position; the heel touches the back of the leg, such as in the retiré derrière position.

of the foot is essential for correct physical placement and meeting the aesthetics of classical ballet.

The importance of pointing the foot correctly is especially critical when jumping. The sequential action of the foot (heel, metarsal, toe) releasing into the air along its center line gives power to the jump. A proper landing demands that the toes, metatarsals, and heels return on this center line bisecting the foot to avoid injury and to maintain alignment.

Classical Arm Positions

Classical ballet arm positions originate from the anatomical position; the arms extending down from the shoulder held near the body with the elbows and palms facing in toward the dancer. To achieve classical ballet arm positions, the elbows and wrists flex slightly to create a subtle and graceful curve throughout the arms and hands. For most classical arm positions, the arms curve with the palms facing the dancer. The classical arm positions include the Preparatory position (or Fifth en bas), First, Second, Third, Fourth, Fifth positions, and variations (see unit I, center).

The arms move with the participation and support of the torso. Arm movements coordinate with leg gestures and focus of the head. Among the major ballet schools and methods, there are many arm positions; some positions are repetitive or variations of others. For the beginning student it is best to keep the arm positions simple.

Positions of the Hands

The hand in classical ballet is an extension of the dancer's arm positions. Stretch the hand and extend the fingers; there is space between the fingers, with the second and fourth fingers lifted slightly above the third and fifth. The thumb extends parallel to the index finger on the side of the palm. In most classical hand positions, the palm faces the dancer. In the Cecchetti Method, the wrist is slightly flexed, and the thumb and third finger are close together. In Second position, the palm is on a slight downward angle to the

Figure 3.16 Pointing the foot.

floor. An exception to the classical hand is the arabesque poses. In an arabesques, the palms face down to the floor.

The classical ballet hand position differs slightly for the man and the woman. For men, the hand position stretches almost flat, with the second, third, and fourth fingers slightly curved, rather than the delicate curve that the fingers add to the woman's classical hand position (see figure 3.17, a-c).

Positions of the Head

The head is the focal point of the body in classical ballet. To achieve classical alignment, the head balances on the top of the spine. The head changes position throughout the exercises and combinations to compliment classical poses and positions, and to direct the audience's eye toward the direction in which the step moves.

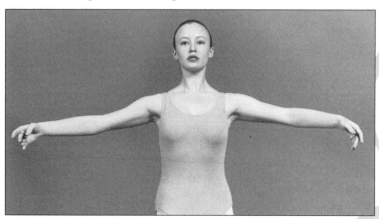

a

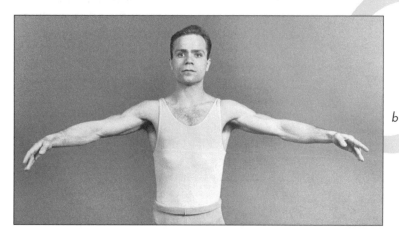

b

c

Figure 3.17 Position of the hand: a) Woman's hand. b) Man's hand. c) Arabesque hand.

Teaching Beginning Ballet Technique

An important part of head positions is the dancer's eye focus. The eyes are part of the head positions and relate to the stage space and the audience. For the beginning dancer, positions of the head are simple and integrate into the work with arm movements (see figure 3.18, a-c).

Learning the classical positions of the feet, arms, head, and torso is like learning the alphabet. Once learned, these classical positions combine with movement to create exercises that in turn become the basis for center steps and combinations. At the barre, students learn the foundations, specific rules,

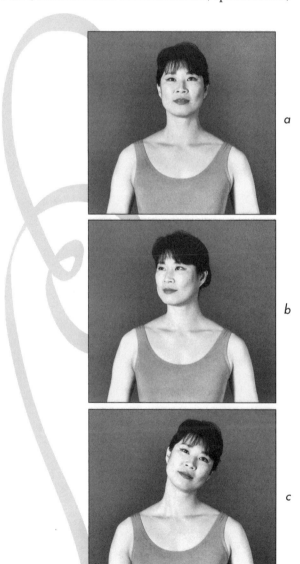

Figure 3.18 Position of the head: a) Centered. b) Turned. c) Inclined.

protocols, and ways of working that give them a beginning level fluency in using the classical positions and the different movements that connect them.

Foundations of the Barre

The foundation of the barre is all important to the beginning student for the successful acquisition of technique and principles. At the barre, the student learns exercises that integrate positions and applies the rules and protocols that stem from tradition. The student learns preparations, patterns for exercises, and breathing techniques that form a basis for the work to come later in the center. The purpose of the barre differs according to the level of the dancer. The beginning dancer relies on the barre a great deal. It helps the student learn how to control his or her body weight before, during, and after an exercise. Often in the beginning class, the student returns to the barre to learn and practice steps facing the barre before performing them in the center.

Barre Exercises

The word *barre* has two meanings: 1) the wooden or metal railing along the wall that the dancer uses and 2) the series of exercises performed during the first part of a ballet class. The standard height of the barre ranges from 42 to 47 inches. Two barres attach to the wall, one low and the other high. The physical barre acts as a stabilizer to the supporting side of the body, so that the working side learns the movements. The support of the barre frees the beginning dancer to concentrate on performing the movement.

The beginning barre exercises include demi-plié, grand plié, battement tendu, battement tendu relevé, battement dégagé, battement dégagé en cloche, rond de jambe à terre, port de corp, battement frappé, petit battement sur le cou-de-pied, battement développé, and grand battement. This series of exercises warms up the body parts, develops strength, and increases flexibility. Performing the barre exercises

- warms up the core temperature of the muscles,
- develops technique,
- prepares the dancer for the center or choreography,
- allows the student to apply principles at the barre for later use in the center, and

- provides a structure enabling the student to expand focus from executing the exercise to include patterns, arm and head coordination, and breath phrasing.

The repetitious practice of the basic ballet movements at the barre builds the foundation for the dancer's technique. Performing the barre exercises precisely and concisely are important factors for executing steps and combinations in the center. This is part of building and developing a strong technique.

Positions at the Barre

The two fundamental positions for the beginning dancer at the barre are 1) the student places two hands on the barre, facing it or 2) the student uses only one hand on the barre and is facing the side of the room.

Two Hands on the Barre

When learning and practicing new exercises, the beginning student faces the barre and places both hands on it. This position helps the student sense

- squareness of the body,
- directions of the working leg, and
- principles of turn-out and weight distribution.

When beginning dancers face the barre, there are two ways to place their hands on the barre:

1. The arms relax down from the shoulder girdle. The upper arms are near the sides of the body. The forearm extends directly forward, and the hands are placed on the barre in line with the forearms (see figure 3.19a).
2. Or, the dancer crosses the hands at the wrist, centering them in front of the body (see figure 3.19b).

For some barre exercises, students face the center of the room with both arms extended along the barre. In this position it is crucial to prevent pelvis, back, and shoulder misalignment.

One Hand on the Barre

After learning an exercise facing the barre, the beginning student then performs the exercise with only one hand on the barre. Traditionally, the student places the left hand on the barre and begins the exercise on the right side and with the right working leg (see figure 3.20).

The dancer stands near the barre to place the hand on it at the appropriate distance. The dancer

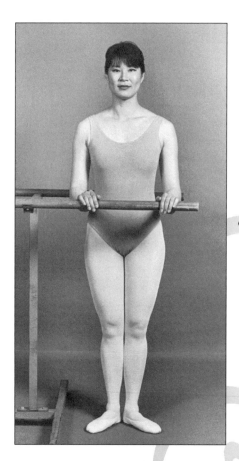

a

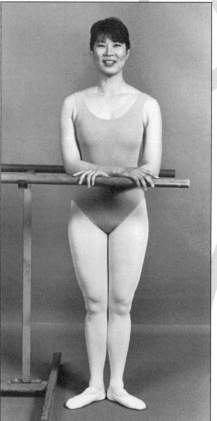

b

Figure 3.19 Two hands on the barre: a) Hands in line with the forearms. b) Hands cross at the wrists.

Teaching Beginning Ballet Technique

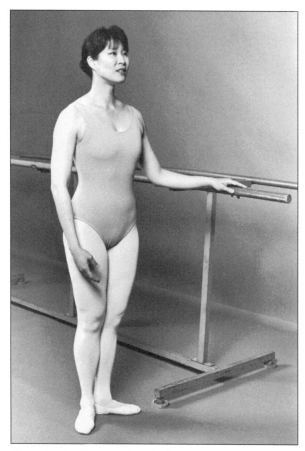

Figure 3.20 One hand on the barre.

places the hand on top of the barre and forward so that the elbow remains bent and near the side of the body in a neutral position. To accommodate a transfer of weight forward or backward during an exercise, the dancer slides the hand forward and back along the barre (see figure 3.21).

Traditionally, fingers curve easily around the barre with the thumb near the fingers. The hand should not grip the barre, nor should the forearm be tense.

Rules:

- Grabbing the barre too tightly causes the "white knuckle syndrome."

- The distance the student stands from the barre is very important to relaxation, control, and balance, especially on the side of the body nearest the barre. If the dancer stands too close to the barre, the body loses alignment and squareness. Likewise, if the dancer stands too far from the barre, the body becomes misaligned, uncentered, and off balance.

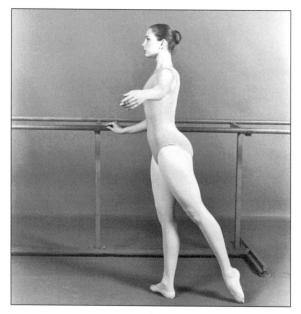

a

b

Figure 3.21 Sliding hand position on the barre: a) A la quatrième derrière à terre, b) A la quatrième derrière en l'air.

Center Line

Classical ballet uses symmetry as a design and aesthetic concept. The dancer trains both sides of the body to achieve this aesthetic ideal. The center line vertically bisects the sagittal plane of the dancer into two halves through the nose, sternum, navel, and on down. Positions and movements seldom cross this imaginary vertical line that extends beyond the body into the dancer's personal space.

Supporting Leg and Working Leg

The leg that supports the weight of the body during the execution of a barre exercise is the supporting leg. For the beginning dancer, this leg is typically the one closest to the barre. The working leg executes the leg actions of the step. The relationship between the supporting and working legs is symbiotic. Before, during, and after an exercise, the weight of the body transfers from two legs to one and from one to two. Both the supporting leg and the working leg are equally important to the development of technique and ease of movement. Each leg requires strength, which develops through executing the barre exercises on both sides; this strength then transfers to the center work.

Breath and Breath Phrasing

Learning and applying correct, consistent breathing and breath phrasing is an important basic element of executing every exercise and combination. The beginning student should practice breathing during each exercise and combination. As a natural accompaniment to the movement, breath phrasing provides the dancer with adequate breath support and gives a movement sequence phrasing and dynamics. See Breath Phrasing for Barre Exercises later in this chapter.

Protocols at the Barre

Good form in ballet requires performing certain protocols with exercises at the barre. Protocols include applying certain rules of performance to an exercise, such as

- standing in position with the arms in the Preparatory position (Fifth position en bas) before beginning an exercise;
- moving the arms from Fifth en haut through Second position to Fifth position en bas using an outside path as a transition during the exercise; and
- pausing momentarily in the ending position of an exercise with the arms in Fifth position en bas.

These protocols give the barre exercises consistency to meet classical standards. Protocols are important guidelines for beginning dancers so that they may begin to understand how every piece of the seemingly giant puzzle of ballet preparations, steps, arms, and head movements fit together into a seamless, logical, balanced, aesthetic form.

Standard Introductory Movements or Preparation

The standard introductory movements to an exercise or step are called a *preparation* in ballet. A preparation is like a preface that the dancer performs before beginning an exercise or combination. During this time, the dancer mentally and physically prepares to execute the exercise or combination. The preparation sets the mood and tempo for the exercise or combination that follows. The preparation always includes arm movements (*port de bras*) and head movements; it may include foot position changes. Timing for preparations is either "5, 6, 7, 8" or "7, 8" of the measure preceding the beginning of the exercise or combination. Timing choices are a matter of preference that varies with the level of study, the school, and the stylistic preference of the teacher.

Arm Movements for Preparation

Before executing a preparation at the barre, the dancer begins with both arms in the Preparatory position (Fifth position en bas). Both arms or the arm nearest the center of the studio execute the port de bras. For students to concentrate on stance and other principles before the preparation, begin with both arms in the Preparatory position. From this position, the arms raise to First position and open to Second position. The arm preparation may end in Second position or return to the Preparatory position before starting the exercise (if facing sideways, the preparation ends with one hand resting gently on the barre). This preparation derives from the First position port de bras (see unit 1).

Head Movements for Preparation

The head coordination begins with the standard tilt toward the foot nearest the barre; as the arms move toward First position, the head straightens to a neutral, or centered, position, poised easily on top of the spine. The head leads the port de bras toward the center of the room as the arms extend to Second position. The head follows the working arm on its transitional pattern to the starting position for the exercise.

Breathing on the Preparation

It is important to maintain a natural breathing pattern. Holding the breath deters efficiency of movement. The port de bras utilizes breath phrasing as a preparation for the exercise. As the arms lift in front of the body to First position, the dancer inhales. As the arms extend to Second position, the dancer exhales. For positions of the arms, see unit I, center.

Executing Exercises

For the beginning dancer, the pattern of the barre exercise is very important. The dancer needs to gain strength in the legs without becoming overly tired while performing the exercise. Adequate time after a movement allows the student to assume stance on both feet before executing a new movement, direction, or transfer of weight. The dancer needs enough time to complete this transition successfully to train the body for faster and more intricate transitions in the future.

Beginning students repeat basic exercises to experience how it feels to perform them correctly. The patterns for the exercises are

- simple patterns to remember so that students can concentrate on executing the exercise;
- performed a consistent number of times in each direction; and
- first directional changes, then weight changes, before combining these two components together.

Creating barre exercises in a variety of patterns develops

- directional acuity, or finding the correct direction;
- change of directions during movement sequences;
- strength in the supporting leg;
- learning stance and transfer of weight as the working leg moves in different directions; and
- transfer of weight from one leg to another.

Patterns and their progressions are discussed in depth in chapter 4.

Arm Movements During Barre Exercises

While performing an exercise the novice dancer holds the arm away from the barre in several positions:

- The arm rests across the body with the hand placed on the shoulder of the arm next to the barre.
- The arm extends in a relaxed position down along the working side of the body.
- The arm extends in Second position (see unit I, center).

When the arm moves to the Second position and remains there during an exercise, it requires the students to gain strength as well as to retain proper placement of the arm in its relationship to the entire body. This is the first level of arm movement (port de bras) for the dancer.

Beginning port de bras is simple, thus allowing students to concentrate on body placement and leg and foot movements during execution of an exercise or combination. Generally, in beginning ballet class, the arm away from the barre is held in Second position. As the dancer gains control and coordination in executing exercises and combinations, the port de bras likewise becomes more demanding. Introducing standard arm positions depends on how fast the class learns.

It is important that students use arm movements with exercises and steps. To present a coordinated picture of the dancer moving through space, the port de bras accompanies the movement with correct timing and breath phrasing.

Breath Phrasing for Barre Exercises

Breath phrasing is used in executing a single step, three to four repetitions of a step, a phrase of the movement sequence, or one set of the exercise in one direction that is no longer than eight counts. This extension of the breath develops breath control and phrasing.

When performing an upward and outward movement (e.g., port de bras from First to Second position), inhale at the beginning of the movement and exhale as the movement or movement phrase ends. When performing a relevé or balancing on relevé, the dancer inhales on the ascent and exhales on the descent. Executing the demi-plié, inhale on the descent and exhale on the ascent. Natural breath phrasing coincides with the dynamics of the exercise.

Turning at the Barre

Between sides of barre exercises, the dancer turns toward the barre and ends facing the other direction. Turning to the opposite side is performed in two ways. One is casual, in which the dancer simply turns to the other side. In the more formal way, the dancer performs a sustained (soutenu) turn toward the barre. To begin the turn, the supporting leg demi-pliés (bends) while the working leg extends off the floor in dégagé à la seconde. The working leg closes in either First or Fifth position relevé, and the dancer turns toward the barre to end facing the opposite direction, then lowers to both feet with either First or Fifth position outside foot in front.

Ending the Exercise

To formally end an exercise, hold the final position and place the arms in Fifth position en bas. The head turns toward the center of the room and tilts toward the outside shoulder. The students remain in this position until the teacher indicates by words or gesture that they may relax. Finishing the exercise completely is an important protocol that gives a formal ending to every exercise. Practicing this protocol is essential to learning the discipline and traditions of classical ballet.

Seven Movements of Dance

Ballet exercises and steps build upon the seven movements of dance. Most of these movements are part of the barre exercises, but they are more apparent in the center and in specific steps. These movements are sometimes performed by themselves but most often combine in many ways to create a ballet vocabulary. The seven movements of ballet are listed next and described in the following sections:

- To bend—plier
- To stretch—étendre
- To raise—relever
- To glide—glisser
- To jump—sauter
- To dart— élancer
- To turn— tourner

To Bend (Plier)

Most steps begin and end in a demi-plié. This action is a bridge between every step to provide the necessary relaxation and preparation for the dancer. Even more important is the demi-plié to jumping, allégro combinations. The demi-plié is the crucial ingredient to keeping the light, bouncing quality or "ballon" in the combination. The press downward of the demi-plié acts as a shock absorber to support repeated maximum extension of the body and legs extending into the air.

To Stretch (Etendre)

The stretch, or étendre, movement is basic to all of ballet vocabulary. The stretch is the opposite to the relax of the demi-plié. The stretch is slow or fast depending on the step or movement. The stretch includes not only the legs, but also the arms and the entire body moves upward away from the floor. This stretch gives the dancer the necessary lightness or lift and gravity-defying aesthetic of classical ballet.

To Raise (Relever)

To raise, or relever, is also opposite to the demi-plié. In the center, relevé is part of the change of levels

that begins with studies at the barre. The relevé is essential and fundamental to performance of much of classical ballet vocabulary.

To Glide (Glisser)

The ballet dancer glides in many center steps. This gliding quality is not only essential to adagio work but also to preparation steps and parts of allégro steps both in combination or contrast with other qualities.

To Jump (Sauter)

To jump, or sauter, is the heart of allégro in all of its many forms. Jumping steps are performed with a variety of beginnings and endings. All jumping steps by themselves or in combination provide the great diversity of allégro steps in ballet, which are both small and large, for men as well as for women. Sauté is a general term that covers movements that defy gravity and pretend to stop in mid-air before the dancer descends like a feather.

To Dart (Elancer)

In many steps the dancer darts in a direction while jumping. To dart is a challenge to the dancer to propel the body in a new direction or change direction with a jump while in the air. Elancer requires dancers to use and refine their body line in space and through space while darting and changing direction.

To Turn (Tourner)

Turning either partially or completely is an important component of the center. Turning takes place in a fixed position, across the floor, or in the air. Teaching beginners the preparation and elements for turning is crucial, especially because pirouettes are a large component of the center in more advanced work. The principles and elements include transfer of weight, balance, and relevé.

Foundations in the Center

The second part of the ballet class is the center. Dancing in the center of the studio, the dancer performs without the support and / or benefit of the physical barre but with the freedom to move through the space. In the center, the dancer concentrates on

- learning a vocabulary of basic steps,
- performing them correctly, and
- incorporating and transferring the principles of classical ballet.

The center part of the beginning class structure includes performing a variety of combinations:

1. Repeating barre exercises in the center (center barre)
2. Slow movements (adagio)
3. Jumping movements (sautés)
4. Small, brisk jumping movements (petit allégro)
5. Introductory and transitional steps that may be performed either slowly in an adagio style, or briskly in an allégro style
6. Introductory turning steps
7. Large, jumping movements in the air (grand allégro)

Beginning level ballet combinations are simple and generally contain only one to three steps. By performing these brief dance combinations, the student develops technical accuracy and competency.

Purpose of the Center

Learning to dance takes place in the center. Beginning students gain movement confidence performing steps and simple combinations striving to create a performance level that includes the aesthetics of ballet, such as balance, harmony, and dynamics. The work in the center is a many-layered process pursued one step at a time to create a technical foundation. The beginning dancer performs many intricate physical and mental tasks even to do one movement, or an overlapping sequencing of movements, in which the student applies principles, musicality, and aesthetics.

The challenge in structuring the center for any teacher of beginning students is to

- develop a working vocabulary of steps and principles,
- build a strong technical and theoretical foundation,
- guide students through work in the center that is appropriate to the beginning level,
- support new work in the center by previous work at the barre, and
- give students the ability to perform steps with confidence before performing in the center.

Barre and Center Connections

There are no barres in the center of the studio; dancers must rely upon their own technique. Technique begins at the barre. For beginning dancers, the transition between executing steps at the barre, with the security it

provides, and in the center, on their own two feet, is very difficult. Teachers make the transition from barre work to center work easier by having students

1. learn and practice a step at the barre before they attempt to perform the step in the center,
2. understand and work on any technical corrections given at the barre in order to perform the step correctly in the center, and
3. return to the barre during the center for additional practice.

The direct connection between the barre and the center must be clearly understood by the teacher in order to communicate it to students.

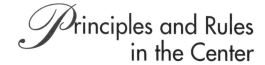

Principles and Rules in the Center

The principles of classical ballet in the center build upon those taught at the barre. The principles of the barre transfer to the center and become its foundation. The principles applied in the center work involve making the dancer self-sufficient and in control of many variables to create a complete performance of a combination of steps. In the center, principles, rules, and protocols define the structure of this part of the class.

Protocols in the Center

Ballet protocols dictate how the student approaches the components of the center. These protocols of performance give ballet its unique blend of formality, tradition, and hence its classical quality. Some ballet center protocols parallel those at the barre. Others are a result of traditions from centuries past or are an outgrowth of classroom procedure. Ballet protocols in the center are based on presenting the dancer to the audience.

Preparations and Endings

In the center, or Au milieu, the dancer faces the appropriate stage direction and steps into Fifth or another position. The dancer stands with arms in the Preparatory position with the head tilted toward the downstage shoulder before executing the First port de bras preparation for the combination.

When beginning a combination facing a corner, both shoulders and hips face the corner, enabling the audience to see the entire front of the body. Continuing to refine this position, the dancer gains a strong sense of how to maximize body lines in relation to the audience and the stage space.

Most of the time, the dancer steps into Fifth position before preparing for the combination. Some petit allégro and grand allégro combinations begin in the "B+" position or attitude derrière pointe tendu à terre. In this position, both legs turn out. If standing on the left foot, the right leg bends with the right knee directly beside the back of the left knee. The right foot points with only the tip of the great toe touching the floor. In the B+ position for female dancers, the legs are together. For male dancers, there is a space between the knees.

At the end of a center combination, the dancer finishes the movement and holds the Fifth position for a brief moment. This pause is like putting a period at the end of a sentence.

Head Movements for Center Preparation

A preparation for a center combination presents the dancer to the audience. Accompanying the port de bras, the head tilts upstage and then faces out into the audience. This head movement comes from the tradition of the dancer first looking at the teacher, who also played the violin for class, before looking at the audience to begin performing.

Components of the Center

In a beginning level class, the center takes the components of classical ballet practiced at the barre as exercises and puts them into a vocabulary of steps that, in turn, become part of combinations. First, basic rules for head movements and breath phrasing are presented, which apply to all portions of work in the center. Next introductory and transitional steps are discussed. Last, the three basic categories of center combinations are examined: center barre, adagio, and allégro.

Rules:

When the working leg extends in a specific direction or when traveling, the head moves according to the following rules.

- When the working the leg extends front, the head tilts over the supporting leg.

- When the working leg extends to the side, the head remains centered.

- When the working leg extends back, the head tilts over it.

- When traveling forward the head turns to the direction of the working leg or the foot closing in front.

- When traveling backward the head tilts over the supporting leg.

Basic Rules for Head Movements

The head positions are centered, turned or tilted, or both turned and tilted.

Breath and Breath Phrasing for the Center

The dancer learns breath and breath phrasing at the barre and further develops it in the center. Breath and breath phrasing for performing steps parallels performing exercises at the barre. In the center, breath phrasing permeates all combinations, giving the dancer the freedom to dance the combinations with the proper dynamics.

Center Barre

The center barre exercises enable students to gain strength by performing barre exercises without the barre. The teacher selects barre exercises and repeats them in the center. Performing the center barre provides a reality check of how much strength and control the students have and what they need to gain to perform in the center successfully.

Battement tendus (see unit I, barre) are exercises that begin center barre work. Other exercises that use the working leg in the air, require constructing short exercises that progress in difficulty. These exercises include battement tendu relevé, dégagé, and grand battement (see unit I and II, barre). Perform short barre exercises on each side individually and then with a transition so that the combination includes both sides. Continuing to perform the center barre exercises refines basic exercises and the student's balance. The center barre is a prelude to the more intensive parts of the center.

Adagio

Adagio comprises slow, sustained movements that continuously unfold and flow through poses, extensions, and circular movements. These movements connect with smooth transfers of weight, transitions, and balances on one foot in various positions. Performing adagio requires immense control of many elements happening consecutively or simultaneously using different facings and changes of level.

Adagio demands a great deal of technique from the dancer. In adagio, time is stretched to make the movements fluid. The dancer mirrors the music with the movement. Often the dancer strives to create the longest possible body lines in space, the longest and fullest movement within a given time frame. Performing adagio presents a personal challenge and competition for the beginning dancer.

Set adagios such as learning the classical body positions, arabesque poses, and développés are very appropriate for the beginning student. Set adagios give students time to learn, memorize, and refine important poses that are used throughout their ballet studies. These adagios teach the contrast of the body facing croisé, effacé, and en face (see unit II), provide a structure for learning to connect movement, and use breath and body control. Later, when the dancer is ready to memorize more complicated movement sequences, the teacher may lengthen the adagio combination and add variations. Adagio construction is discussed in chapter 4.

Classical Positions of the Body

One of the major attributes of classical ballet is the body positions in various directions that

- show the lines of the body,
- add versatility, and
- give three-dimensionality to a dancer's performance.

Classical positions of the body include specific poses with variations facing different directions (see unit II, center). These body positions are performed together in a sequence or individually integrated into various steps. The beginning dancer learns the positions of the body as a series.

Classical Ballet Poses: Arabesques and Attitudes

Arabesque and attitude are the two beautiful distinctive and dramatic poses that are the hallmark of classical ballet. Although the dancer must be capable of performing both poses in beginning training, the teacher presents the basic arabesques (see unit III, center). The arabesque is a pose that extends the dancer's line to its maximum through arms, legs, and torso.

Turns

Performing turns and turning movements is complex, since they include coordination of the body, leg gestures, arm movements, and spotting technique. The beginning student studies the elements of turns: balance on one leg, relevé and the accompanying principles of alignment, transfer of weight, squareness, pull-up and counterpull. Near the end of the term, the student may try the three-step turn, which is an introduction to chaînés, or tours chaînés deboulés (see unit IV).

Introduction and Transitional Steps

When creating a center combination of one or more steps, introduction and transitional steps contrib-

ute to dynamics and flow of the combination. Steps that introduce and link the combination are adaptable to both adagio and allégro. These steps are important parts of the ballet vocabulary that deserve individual study at the beginning level, such as glissade, chassé, and temps levé (see units I–III). In later study they become infused into more complicated combinations.

Allégro

In allégro, clarity of movement, precise technique, musicality, and breathing are all important. Some authors have called allégro the "heart of ballet." Good jumping technique is the basis of allégro performance. Jumping technique becomes increasingly demanding and intricate as allégro combinations progress in difficulty. Musicality and breath phrasing are important to perform allégro efficiently and effectively.

Jumps (Sautés)

Jumps, or sautés, are the basis for allégro steps. Perform jumps, or sautés in the center before petit allégro combinations or before the end of class. When simple jumping combinations precede the petit allégro, they warm up the legs and feet for the following allégro combinations. As the last center combination, jumps such as sautés, changements, and échappé sautés decrease energy from previous allégro combinations and center the dancer for the end of class (see units III and IV).

Jumping Technique

To execute any jump or movement in the air, the legs press downward in a demi-plié. The legs and feet push the body into the air. The feet release from the floor sequencing through the heel, the metatarsals, and then the toes as the body stretches upward away from the floor. On the descent from the jump, the feet extend until they land. The landing sequence starts first with the toes, then metatarsals, then heels, flexing as each part of the foot reaches the floor. Then the ankle and knee flex into a demi-plié. This action provides a shock absorber for the body that prevents injury to the back, hip, knee, and ankle joints.

Types of Jumps

Allégro steps use several types of weight changes in the air:

- Jumps from two feet to two feet
- Jumps from two feet to one foot
- Jumps from one foot to two feet

- Hops on one foot
- Leaps from one foot to the other

For the beginning dancer, the most basic type of jump is from two feet to two feet such as sautés in First and Second position, changements, and échappé sauté (see units III and IV). However, most allégro steps require more complicated weight changes in the air, the dancer begins learning steps that contain them, such as glissade, pas de chat, assemblé, jeté, and temps levé. Introduction and transitional steps in allégro include pas de bourree, chasse, glissade, temps levé, and coupé (see units I, II, and III). These steps cement allégro combinations together and provide breathing time for the dancer.

Within allégro, there are several types ranging from small (or petit) to large (or grand). Petit allégro combinations are usually short and intense. They encompass

- fast footwork,
- quick changes of direction,
- transfer of weight from one foot to another, and
- jumping or steps that rebound.

Allégro demands quick thinking about many small changes in the combination.

The culminating event in class is the grand allégro combinations that travel through space with long air movements. Many grand allégro steps are jumps or leaps in the air (see unit IV). In performing grand allégro the dancer strives to give the illusion of being suspended in the air for long periods of time. Consequently, the approaches to many grand allégro steps are swift and powerful runs and chassés. The dancer uses most of the music for the grand allégro step, such as a leap, by shortening the approach and expanding the time spent in the air.

Ending the Ballet Class

One of the most enduring ballet center protocols is ending the class. Traditionally, students perform a reverence at the end of class; this is a curtsy for women and a bow for men directed toward the teacher to thank her for teaching the class. Follow-ing this formal combination, the students applaud the teacher and the musician for dance, if there is one.

Historically, each student shook hands while bowing or curtsying to the teacher or male students kissed the female teacher's hand before leaving the studio. During this brief individual encounter, the teacher imparted a comment to the student regarding personal performance. In most ballet classes today, very little time is allocated for the reverence or the individual moment with the teacher. But, students applaud the teacher and the musician for dance at the end of class.

Summary

There is more to teaching ballet than just the steps. This chapter is your reference for the principles, rules, positions, and protocols of beginning classical ballet. In this chapter the pyramid of principles includes alignment, turn-out, weight distribution, stance, transfer of weight, squareness, pull-up, counterpull and counterbalance, aplomb, and balance. Classical ballet uses a devised system of positions of the feet and active foot positions on the leg through which all steps begin, move through, and end. Classical positions of the arm, hand, and head always accompany exercises and steps. Classical body positions and poses give ballet its three-dimensionality.

The seven movements of dance (to bend [plier], to stretch [étendre], to raise [relever], to glide [glisser], to jump [sauter], to dart [élancer], and to turn [tourner]) permeate the barre and center. These movements connect into various types of exercises and steps, which are the foundation of the barre and center. The components of the center include center barre, adagio, turns, and petit and grand allégro. Preparations, endings, and breathing during exercises at the barre and in the center correlate to rules and protocols. The principles, rules, poses, and protocols are important foundational building blocks that embody the barre and center of the ballet class, giving the class its formal discipline and tying the class to the long tradition of classical ballet.

chapter four

Constructing the Beginning Ballet Class

The teacher is responsible for constructing the barre exercises and center, which includes center barre, adagio, introductory or transitional steps and petit and grand allégro. The barre and center for beginners are not as complex as in a more advanced class. Regardless, the teacher must view each of the exercises at the barre and combinations in the center as little dances.

The purpose of this chapter is to explain how to construct the barre exercises and center combinations for the beginning ballet class. This chapter explores direction, patterns, and number of repetitions within the exercises or combinations and the use of set exercises and combinations. The number of steps and exercise progressions increase as the dancer gains knowledge and experience. Musical considerations in the ballet class encompass timing, accents, choosing the music, musicality, and working with live or recorded music.

Concepts of Class Construction

Two overall concepts are basic to the construction of beginning ballet classes: simplicity and repetition. The beginning class employs extremely simple exercises and combinations. Repetition is a guiding concept for constructing the beginning class. Repetition, however, does not always equate with quality. Emphasize quality versus quantity. Striving for quality of movement must be ingrained in the minds and bodies of beginners. This mind-set is all-important to reaching for perfection in one's performance. The intertwining of repetition with emphasis on quality of movement supports the foundation for future study.

Use of Repetition

In beginning ballet classes, the barre work and center combinations must be simple and repetitious. The major focus of the class is acquiring a strong, clear performance of exercises and the application of principles. It is better for the beginning student to execute a few steps well, as a foundation for further study, than to execute a great number of steps in a slovenly manner.

Repetition is important to learning ballet. In order to remember the movement kinesthetically, practicing the movement is essential so that it becomes automatic and appears natural. The repetitive practice of the same steps allows the beginning dancer to develop a motor memory of the movement. This ability to remember motor patterns is essential to learning classical ballet. When motor memory takes over, exercises and steps are performed without having to stop to consciously think of each element that makes up an exercise or step.

Repeating simple barre and center combinations gives beginning students the opportunity to focus on the execution of each exercise and step before they combine into combinations. When creating the mind-body connection for each step, students completely synthesize the movements for a step on both sides of the body. This must occur before linking to other exercises or steps.

For students to develop a sound ballet technique, the teacher continually monitors adequate and correct practice of beginning exercises, steps, and application of ballet principles. Apply these critical elements of repetitious practice in your beginning level class:

- Use cue words that are simple, accurate, and consistent.

- Stress the quality of practice as paramount to the quantity.

- Emphasize concentration on performing an exercise completely and accurately.

- Select elements from the center and repeat them several times in barre exercises.

Quality Versus Quantity

The old adage applied to practice, "more is better," has been replaced by the idea that "less is better when performed with quality." The idea that the more a student performs a movement the better is a misconception. A delicate balance must be achieved between the quality and quantity of practice in the beginning level ballet class.

Do it right, or don't do it at all. This standard supports the principles and expectations of classical ballet. In some schools of thought, quantity is encouraged, but overtraining or overworking the dancer can lead to injury and/or enlarged muscles. For example, doing a grand battement 16 times en croix is excessive. By the time the exercise finishes, the dancer performs this exercise incorrectly only to accomplish the task. Quality versus quantity is the standard for practice and performance in all ballet, especially in the beginning class.

$\mathcal{R}$elationship Between Center and the Barre

In the beginning class, a strong link exists between what the student performs in the center and at the barre. The elements and steps of center combinations are first learned as barre exercises. Students must execute barre exercises with some competency before attempting them as part of center work. For the beginning dancer there is a big difference between work at the barre and work in the center. The center barre becomes a bridge between the barre and center steps and combinations. The goal for the dancer is to close the gap between them so that the barre becomes a means of testing balance and strength.

To create tomorrow's ballet class, the teacher analyzes today's class. Analyzing the class just taught identifies components that need to be reviewed in the next or subsequent classes. When constructing the combinations and exercises, begin with the center. Create center combinations with the objective of student success, tempered with a bit of challenge. Music plays an indispensable role to making exercises and combinations become dance. Musical considerations are addressed later in this chapter. The process of constructing the class is the first consideration for the teacher, and it begins with the barre.

$\mathcal{C}$onstructing the Beginning Barre

When constructing barre exercises, the teacher considers the repetitions, directional changes, and transfer of weight studied at the barre and applied in the center. These variables intertwine, but consider each separately when teaching the beginning dancer.

Learning to execute barre exercises is basic, but executing them with alignment, balance, transitions, weight transfers, and directional changes is the foundation of technique. The teacher constructs barre exercises to teach all these important components. It is like performing a balancing act; the teacher continually strives for proportion by weighing one factor against another as to its importance. The goals of the barre are to strengthen the supporting leg, the working leg, and to attain accurate execution of the exercises. When students achieve

these goals, their emphasis shifts to change of weight, directional changes, and other principles. Through practice the dancer gains movement proficiency. Once students have learned the exercises, the teacher creates more varied combinations; but be careful not to clutter the exercises so that the important basics are lost.

For the beginning dancer, the barre exercise patterns are very important. The dancer must gain strength but not become overly tired while performing the exercise. Adequate time after a movement allows the student to assume stance on both feet before executing a new movement, direction, or transfer of weight. Give the student enough time to complete this transition successfully in order to train the body for faster and more intricate transitions in the future.

Basic Exercise Patterns at the Barre

Barre exercises can be created in a variety of patterns. These patterns

- develop directional acuity,
- facilitate change of directions during movement sequences,
- promote strength in the supporting leg, and
- contribute to learning stance and change of weight as the working leg moves in different directions and the weight is transferred from one leg to the other.

Beginning students repeat basic exercises to experience how it feels to perform them correctly. The pattern of the exercise must be simple to remember. The number of times an exercise is executed in each direction must be consistent. The pattern for the exercise should concentrate first on either a directional change or a weight change, before combining these two components together. Each exercise must be performed on both sides of the body.

Directional Changes

When creating exercises at the barre with a focus on directional changes, consider the number of repetitions in each direction. The dancer must learn to change the direction of the working leg while maintaining a strong supporting leg. When creating such an exercise, the teacher considers the amount of time allocated to the working leg and the supporting leg before their roles change in the exercise.

First the student learns directions—front (or *devant*), side (or *à la seconde*), and back (or *derrière*)—and understands the directions both visually and kinesthetically (see figure 4.1 a-c). Devant from First position is directly under the shoulder of the working side with the great toe of the working foot in line with the ear. When devant is from Fifth position, the great toe of the working foot should be directly in line with the heel of the supporting foot or under the center of the head. The derrière, or back, direction is comparable to devant. To find à la seconde, ask students to stand in classical First position. Then brush the foot out to the Second position under the shoulder with the great toes of both the working and the supporting foot in a straight line parallel to the direction the dancers are facing. This à la seconde position allows the beginning student to use natural turn-out in relation to squareness.

En Croix Patterns

One of the most basic patterns for a barre exercise is an exercise performed in the shape of a cross (or *en croix*). The supporting foot makes one line of the cross; the working foot draws the other three lines. Performing an exercise en croix means the dancer executes an exercise to the front (*devant*), to the Second position (*à la seconde*), to the back (*derrière*), and again to the Second position (see figure 4.2). The en croix pattern can be executed starting from either front or back, or combined into a longer pattern where the en croix is performed first starting front and then repeated starting back. This pattern can be used for many exercises at the barre.

To perform four battement tendus en croix, or four brushes on the floor in the shape of a cross, the dancer executes this sequence, returning after each brush to First position:

1. four battement tendus devant,
2. four battement tendus à la seconde,
3. four battement tendus derrière, and
4. four battement tendus à la seconde.

The beginning dancer acquires skill in changing directions using the en croix pattern. If the actions of the working leg are repeated too many times, however, the supporting leg overtires and both the leg and body lose their pulled-up, lifted quality.

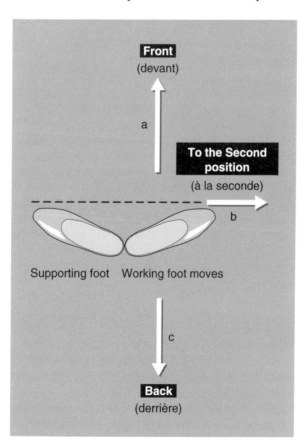

Figure 4.1 Directions: a) Front (devant), b) to the Second position (à la seconde), c) Back (derrière).

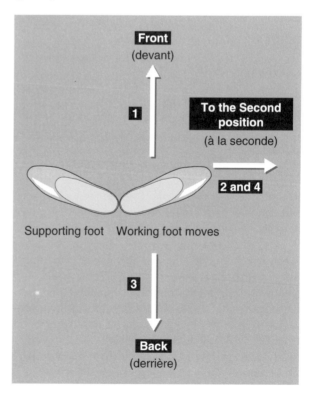

Figure 4.2 En croix pattern.

Teaching Beginning Ballet Technique

Performing eight repetitions of a step in an en croix pattern (e.g., eight battement tendus to the front, à la seconde, back, and à la seconde) is too taxing for the beginning dancer. Four repetitions en croix provides a good starting point from which, over a period of time, the number increases to eight repetitions or may gradually decrease from four to two times. Finally, the beginning dancer learns to perform a step once en croix.

To perform one battement tendu en croix four times, the dancer executes one battement tendu devant, à la seconde, derrière, and à la seconde and repeats this sequence for a total of four times. Performing either of these en croix patterns (four battement tendus in each direction once, or one battement tendu in each direction four times) requires that the dancer has sufficient strength on the supporting leg for the length of the exercise. This training is important for the kinesthetic understanding of spatial patterns.

Other Barre Exercise Patterns

At the barre some beginning exercises repeat the step eight times before changing direction or working foot, decreasing gradually to one repetition over the course. This pattern, the 8, 4, 2, 1 pattern system, gives students adequate time to repeat the movement and prepare for the transition to the next part of the exercise. To use this pattern in class,

- decrease the number of repetitions of the step from eight to four, to two, then to one;
- increase the number of repetitions of the entire exercise to two, then four times;
- decrease the number of steps performed to twice in one direction with successful transitions to the next direction; and
- create exercises using the step once with a directional transition.

Some alternative patterns include performing a number of repetitions of the step in different directions. In a 4, 4, 8 pattern the dancer

- performs a step 4 times front or devant,
- repeats the step 4 times back or derrière, and
- performs eight repetitions à la seconde.

The 4, 4, 8 pattern gives the dancer time to think about the execution of the step and prepare for transfer of weight before executing the step in a new direction. The eight repetitions à la seconde

are long enough to build strength, but not too long to overtire the supporting leg. This pattern also can be taught at the beginning of the next level of study.

When repeating a short combination of alternating or sequential exercises or steps for two or more times, use the term *sets*, which refers to the number of repetitions. For example, you might instruct students to execute "two sets of two battement tendus en croix, then two sets battement tendus with demi-plié en croix.

Even and Odd Numbers of Steps

After performing an exercise set à la seconde, the dancer closes either in Fifth position front or back to continue the next section of the exercise. The number of repetitions of the step and the new direction determines where the dancer closes in Fifth position.

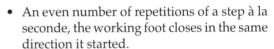

> **Rules:**
> - An even number of repetitions of a step à la seconde, the working foot closes in the same direction it started.
> - An uneven number of repetitions of a step à la seconde, the working foot closes in the new direction.

Adding Steps to Simple Barre Exercises

At first, the beginning dancer concentrates on performing only one exercise or step. The student must perform it well before combining it with others. Create combinations that are easy to remember and no longer than four measures.

Start with variations of an exercise that easily blend into a more advanced exercise, such as battement tendus and battement tendus with demi-plié. The dancer learns first to change from sets of one variation to the other; later, the teacher should construct the exercise to alternate sets between two variations. Combining two steps in a barre exercise

- gives variety to the exercise,
- creates new types of transitions for the dancer to experience, and
- builds sequencing skills.

Combine three steps into a short movement sequence for no longer than four measures performed in a variety of directions (e.g., battement tendu, battement tendu with demi-plié, and battement tendu relevé with demi-plié), or add an ending to the exercise (e.g., balance in relevé for 4 counts). The key to constructing a movement sequence with three different steps is to make it short, simple, and memorable. In this process, the dancer sharpens mental skills by remembering the pattern of the exercise, the sequence, and concentrating on how it is executed.

Exercise Endings

At the end of barre exercises, the beginning dancer holds in Fifth position with arms in Fifth position en bas (low), and the head tilts, focusing over the shoulder away from the barre. This puts a period to the movement sentence.

An eight-measure musical tag gives students time to gain, hold, and then close from a balance

- on full-foot on both feet;
- on relevé in a closed Fifth position with the feet tightly crossed under-over (sous-sus), arms in Fifth position en haut (high);
- on full-foot on one leg;
- in retiré devant (with the working leg extending devant, à la seconde, or derriére under 45 degrees) full foot;
- in Second arabesque on full foot facing the barre, using the natural opposition of the body; and
- in Second arabesque fondu (knee of the supporting leg is bent) facing the barre.

Full foot, relevé, and fondu balances are appropriate endings for many barre exercises.

The dancer practices these balances first facing the barre and then with one hand on the barre. Before ending an exercise with a balance, the teacher may instruct students to practice the balance informally without music. Letting students practice balancing on one leg informally allows them to learn about their personal balance. When the teacher observes students performing full-foot balances competently on one leg, they are ready to explore a one-foot balance on a bent leg (en fondu).

Objectives of Barre Exercise Construction

Another tier of constructing basic barre exercises requires the teacher to address motor abilities and application of principles. This section discusses how to construct exercises to reach the objectives of developing directional acuity, transfer of weight, sequencing, and strength. Next, teaching strategies are suggested for teaching students to apply the principles of ballet, such as turn-out, alignment, and weight distribution to their work at the barre.

Directional Acuity and Transfer of Weight

For the beginning dancer, solid directional acuity and well-executed transfer of weight from two legs to one leg and from one leg to two are formidable goals that should be developed as part of fundamental ballet technique.

Transfer of weight from two feet to one foot presents a major challenge for the beginning student. The teacher creates exercises that

- bridge the number of repetitions of the exercise with this principle,
- change the supporting leg to give each leg time to develop stability without tiring,
- require pull-up in the supporting leg as the working and supporting legs switch roles during a combination, and
- change the working leg and the directions it moves as a basis for later work.

By the end of the course, the student should successfully execute a basic ballet barre in a variety of directional and transfer of weight patterns.

Sequencing and Strength

Beginning exercises at the barre consist of one movement or step repeatedly before doing the other side. When students learn to perform an exercise, the teacher monitors the strength of both the working and the supporting leg during the execution of the exercise. The supporting leg tires easily in the beginning. Therefore, the teacher constructs the exercise so that the beginning dancer learns the exercise and gains supporting leg strength without overtiring. The teacher limits the number of repetitions of an exercise. Executing the barre exercises correctly develops basic principles of weight distribution, balance, and transfer of weight from one leg to the other as efficiently and smoothly as possible.

Teaching Strategy for Ballet Principles

When teaching an exercise or step to beginning students, the teacher must continually check and remind students before they move to integrate ballet principles into their work.

- Remind students to distribute their weight over the center of the foot before, during, and after the step.

- Review the weight transfers that will take place during the exercise or step.

- Communicate to students to self-check alignment and turn-out on both the working and the supporting leg while executing exercises and steps.

- Guide students to think about the ballet principles by asking them questions that encourage them to analyze their own work.

By repeatedly reminding students to remember the ballet principles and using guided questions, the teacher enlarges the students' focus in the class. After students have heard these comments repeated over and over, they become more and more responsible for implementing the principles of turn-out, weight distribution, alignment, and so on, into their own work.

Constructing the Beginning Center

Creating center combinations for beginning dancers is a challenge for the teacher. Students have a small but growing vocabulary of steps. Learning and practicing steps is the primary focus of developing the beginning center. The teacher must construct simple combinations, and the student must learn to transpose to the other side and apply principles and rules. For the beginning dancer, even simple combinations are challenging to visualize and to perform, as demonstrated in the following examples.

The first barre exercise performed in the center is battement tendu. First, teach four battement tendu en croix, then stop and repeat on the other side. This reinforces the directions taught at the barre, but in the center the focal point is on direction 5, the audience. Later, perform this combination on both sides without stopping. The next phase of this exercise includes transfer of weight using eight battement tendu as the dancer walks (*promenades*) forward (*en avant*) and back (*en arrière*). In this combination the weight shifts to the alternate leg between each of the battement tendu.

1. The battement tendu alternates from one foot to the other as the dancer moves en avant.

2. The dancer stops and rests.

3. The dancer performs eight battement tendu walking backward, or en promenade en arrière, moving away from the audience.

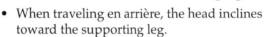

Rules:

- When traveling en avant, the head inclines to the same direction as the working leg.

- When traveling en arrière, the head inclines toward the supporting leg.

The difference between leg gestures in specific directions—devant, à la seconde, and derrière—and the body moving forward and back—en avant and en arrière—must be explained to the students. While moving en avant and en arrière, the body moves forward or back, but the leg gesture may be in a different direction, such as à la seconde.

These patterns alternate from one side to the other. For example, execute seven glissades devant or derrière and one glissade changée to the right; repeat the pattern to the left. The pattern may decrease to one glissade devant or derrière and one glissade changee right and left for a total of four times.

These are the steps through which the teacher takes the beginning student in the center:

1. Alternate the same step to each side decreasing the number of repetitions from eight to four then two.

2. Perform one step in different directions. Generally the dancer moves either side to side or forward and back.

3. As the dancers gain a spatial sense of moving front, side, and back, have them execute two different steps together, moving in several directions.

Not all beginning dancers can acquire spatial or kinesthetic sense of their legs, arms, and bodies, either remaining stationary in space, moving in one direction, or moving in several different directions all at the same time.

Objectives for Center Construction

In center combinations, several patterns aid in developing balance, transfer of weight, and sequencing. Center combinations are constructed in this order:

1. Transfer barre exercises, such as battement tendu, with directional and repetition changes to the center barre.

2. Perform the same step on alternate sides to develop transfer of weight and transposing skills.

3. Develop combinations of one, then two steps.

4. Perform combinations with a rest before proceeding to the other side; then connect both sides.

5. Continue to progress to three- and possibly four-step combinations by the end of the term.

This chain of events begins with taking exercises learned at the barre and practicing them in the center as a center barre. The components of the center are presented in their traditional order; however, in the beginning ballet class they are not taught in that order. The sequence in which these individual steps and components are taught to beginners is outlined in units I through IV.

Components of the Center

The traditional center portion of class includes the center barre, the adagio, pirouettes, and the petit and grand allégro. The beginning student studies the components of pirouettes and may execute a simple three-step turn (see unit IV). Throughout the center portion of the class, the teacher must remind students to apply the principles learned at the barre.

Center Barre

Center combinations of barre exercises repeat patterns used at the barre. This gives the dancer practice performing exercises without the barre to test balance. Performing the same exercise in these two settings gives the dancer a frame of reference of how much the dancer relies on the barre for support and the personal strength and control needed to perform the exercises without the barre.

Adagio Combinations

Adagio comprises slow, flowing, sustained movements that require immense control. Adagio is difficult for the beginning student. Adagio steps are practiced as barre exercises to gain strength and balance before being performed in the center.

A beginning adagio in the center is very short. Later the adagio becomes longer with more difficult movements. The beginning adagio has a balance between movements that are on the ground (à terre) and in the air (en l'air). In addition, the adagio alternates supporting legs at least every eight counts.

These two variables change as the dancer acquires more skill and strength to perform poses and steps, such as *battement développé* (unfolding leg movement). Beginning students should not raise the working leg above 45 degrees. At this point in their training, body alignment, balance, weight transfer, centering over the supporting leg, turn-out, and many other factors are more important than the height of the leg. Adagio for the beginning dancer includes these steps:

- Battement tendu
- Eight positions of the body
- Low développé
- Arabesque

Introduction and transition steps in adagio combinations include

- demi-plié,
- balancé,
- relevé,
- ballet walks,
- sous-sus,
- pas de bourrée,
- chassé, and
- glissade.

In creating adagios, the teacher begins with all movements à terre, or on the floor. Introductory adagios focus on finding directions and working with weight changes. The progressions for teaching the eight classical positions of the body, as outlined in part II, provide an excellent study for learning directions. The arabesque pose is initially taught à terre, then held en l'air for a brief moment. The time en l'air as well as the number of arabesques executed can be extended as appropriate for your students. When teaching adagio, you must proceed slowly and evaluate student progress carefully to provide smooth progressions to more difficult work.

Until the later half of the term, adagios will be short and à terre. The adagio exercises at the barre have to be developed before transferring them to the center. Learning to perform adagio in the center progresses as follows:

- Start with very short movement sequences, no more than eight measures, and then build to 16 measures.

- Perform each side of the combination separately. Incorporate short rest periods before executing the second side.

- Combine both sides for a total of no more than 32 measures.
- Control breath phrasing throughout the adagio movements.

The teacher facilitates learning and refining movements during adagio and other center combinations. These are the types of teaching roles:

- Cueing the upcoming step or pose. For example, on counts 7 and 8 of the preceding measure, prepare the students by saying the name of the next step or pose. Cueing helps students to think ahead during performance to handle transfers of weight and directional changes.
- Observing students performing the first side of the combination.
- Utilizing the rest period between sides of the combination to talk about what the students should focus on when dancing the second side.
- Giving students a moment to review the movement sequence on the other side and ask questions before they perform it.
- Preparing students by discussing problems that occurred on the first side before they execute the second side of the combination, rather than just letting them repeat the same mistakes.

Performing the adagio on both sides allows students to remember cues and comments to integrate into their dancing. Repeat the combination beginning on the other side, this time letting students execute the adagio without your cues. This forces them to think on their feet and accept responsibility for their own work. Students repeat the adagio in a subsequent class. You can facilitate this process by asking students about specific cues and comments that were given at the last class. Encourage students to review and analyze previous work so that they can apply technical corrections to the same combination or to new combinations as the course progresses.

In adagio or other center combinations, the teacher selects transition steps so that students gain a variety of experiences in introducing steps and in phrasing movement sequences. To lengthen center combinations both sides combine into a whole that repeats, beginning on the other side. Often combinations repeat several times as in petit allégro. In ballet, the dancer performs steps beginning with either the right or left foot. Learning to transpose movement is an important skill the beginning student acquires through practice. When teaching center combinations and adagio, the teacher gives stu-

dents time to practice transposing simple, short combinations and adagio, the teacher and the class review their choices by marking the combination together to both sides before the students perform the combination in small groups. Remind students that if they encounter a problem in transposing, they should review the step or transition from the first side of the combination to study its components in order to transpose it to the other side.

Adagio combinations are performed in a slow tempo, which allows students time to think about the next movement. The measures allotted to movements give the time to execute it and time to completely close in Fifth position before going on or ending the combination.

The music for a beginning level adagio should be in a moderate to slow tempo in either 4/4 or 3/4 time signature with a strong primary beat. The student should

- recognize the time signature,
- hear the primary beat (first beat) of the measure, and
- count the music to themselves while performing the combination.

Introductory and Transitional Steps

Steps that introduce a combination or serve as a transition are presented as single-step or two-step combinations (e.g., walking, chassé, glissade, pas de bourrée, pas de basque). Teach each of these steps separately for their own value before inserting them into combinations. Transitional steps introduce and connect movement together in both adagio and allégro combinations. It is important to emphasize clarity in performance of these steps so that when they become part of combinations, they retain their identity. Choose music that gives the beginning dancer time to complete the movement and establish the mind-body connection for all the actions of the step.

Sauté (Jumping) Combinations

Beginning level jumping combinations are simple repetitions of one or two steps no longer than an eight-count phrase, with a rest between each set. These are the progressions for jumping combinations:

1. Execute eight repetitions of sautés, changements, or échappé sautés.
2. Combine two jumps; alternate four of one followed by four of the other.
3. Decrease the number of alternating repetitions to two of each of the two jumps repeated for a total of eight jumps.

The music for jumps must keep the "ballon," or light, bouncing quality of a jump, but be slow enough for students to land from the jump completely with the heel(s) in contact with the floor and execute a demi-plié. For beginning students, the music selection should allow a pause in the demi-plié between each jump to ensure that correct landing and take-off for the next jump is achieved. Jumping combinations precede the petit allégro combinations in the class or are used as the last combination of the class.

Petit Allégro (Small, Quick) Combinations

A petit allégro combination has an introductory step; one or more small, quick jumps; and/or a closing step that will allow the combination to alternate to the other side. Petit allégro differs from the grand allégro in that the movements are small, vertical, darting, or contained steps, whereas grand allégro movements use large vertical and horizontal travelling steps. At the start of the semester, the beginning student moves along the progression from transferring barre exercises to the center to performing basic allégro steps (e.g., pas de chat, jeté, assemblé) into short combinations. By the end of the term, the petit allégro combination

- is a short combination,
- has no more than three or four different steps, and
- progresses gradually to no more than an eight-measure sequence.

Teaching students to coordinate their feet in a step with a jump, hop, or leap is essential. Sometimes performing the movement à terre without the jump, hop, or leap helps the motor process to assimilate where the weight is and where it will go. Teach the components of the step in their sequence à terre. Once the student understands the sequence of movements the feet and legs make, add the jump, hop, or leap into the sequence.

The teacher cues the students to the actions of the jumping step. Cue a sauté in First position by telling students: "Stand in First position, demi-plié, straighten the knees, rise to three-quarter relevé. Now demi-plié in First position, jump vertically into the air, keep your legs straight and your feet pointed. Land toe, ball, heel and bend your knees." After the students understand the actions and their sequence, cue the jump with key words: "and jump [sauté]" or "bend [demi-plié] and up." At this time in the motor learning process, focus on the movement sequencing, later, on timing and other variables.

The beginning dancer learns sequencing skills starting with short, repeated movement combina-

tions. The dancer concentrates on performing each step, and the transition between each step, correctly, changing the weight and coordinating the rhythm of the step in time to the music. Later, the dancer adds arm movements, breath phrasing, and basic head movements to the combination.

Petit allégro combinations include directional changes. The beginning dancer must learn to control the transfer of weight between and during steps coupled with the change of direction. At the beginning of the term, teach single-step combinations, progress to two-step combinations and by the end of the term simple three- or four-step combinations.

1. Expand a single-step combination by adding a transition step: pas de chat, pas de chat, pas de chat, battement tendu à la seconde; close front; repeat other side.

2. Substitute a changement for the battement tendu, making it a two-step combination. Another example of a two-step combination is glissade derrière, assemblé dessus (over, or in front of the supporting foot); glissade derrière, assemblé dessus; alternating a total of four times for eight counts or one set.

3. Combine three, or at the most, four different steps. An example of a three-step combination is glissade, jeté, jeté, assemblé. The phrase for the three- or four-step combination should be no more than four measures in length.

4. Create a four-step combination: glissade, jeté, temps levé, assemblé (see unit III).

The beginning dancer must first process the information for each element of the combination with a conscious effort. Only later, when the mind-body connection has been made, can the dancer think the name of the step and perform it. Then the emphasis shifts to include the transitions between steps.

Music for the beginning student performing petit allégro combinations is usually counted with two measures for each step. As the term progresses,

- increase the tempo of the music gradually, and
- perform each step to one measure, as an option.

The goal for the end of the term is for students to execute a petit allégro combination with one measure for each step in a slower, or perhaps at even standard tempo.

For example, glissade (measures 1 and 2), assemblé (measures 3 and 4); repeat other side. As the term progresses, the tempo of the music is gradually increased. The option may be presented for some students to use one measure for each step. By the end of the term, the beginning dancer may be able to execute a petit allégro combination with one measure for each step but at a tempo slower than the standard.

Grand Allégro (Large, Brisk) Combinations

Grand allégro combinations are large, brisk jumping, hopping, or leaping steps that move across the studio from side to side or along a diagonal (*en diagonale*) and fill the space. The teacher constructs these combinations so that the student either performs one combination that moves to the other side of the studio, stops, and returns or a combination that connects both sides without stopping. These two types of combinations make the student practice sequencing and alternating skills.

When practicing grand allégro combinations, teaching of beginning students follows this progression:

1. Execute a new step in a series across the floor, first in a straight line to the other side of the room and later perhaps on a diagonal line from a back corner to a front corner.

2. Repeat the series of steps starting from the other side or corner of the room.

3. Combine two grand allégro steps with introductory and transitional steps.

4. Expand this short sequence as the students progress to a movement sequence of eight measures across the floor. These sequences should contain no more than three elements.

Building grand allégro combinations in this progression helps students develop their motor memory not only of steps, but also of transitions and arm and head movements that are all part of dancing the combination.

Single steps such as ballet walks, runs, and chassés across the floor prepare students for grand allégro. First arabesque provides a good starting place. Students know First arabesque from practice in adagio at the barre.

1. Perform across the floor: walk, walk, step, First arabesque; the combination then alternates to the other side.

2. Augment the First arabesque by adding a hop (sauté) and stretching the landing into a demi-plié on one leg (fondu).

3. Replace the walks with runs, and increase the tempo.

4. Alternate the combination from one side to another. Transposing to the other side requires a great deal of thought on the part of the student.

5. Replace the runs with a chassé before the arabesque sauté.

Next, the student learns leaps (or *grand jetés*). A basic grand jeté combination consists of two runs between each grand jeté; have the students hold the landing pose of the grand jeté, which is an arabesque on a bent knee (fondu). If the students are capable, begin alternating movement sequences, for example, run, run, First arabesque sauté; run, run, grand jeté. This should take the students completely across the floor, teaching them how to expand some movements and shorten others. Students need to grasp the concept of "proportion" in grand allégro, in that some steps need to be very large; others medium sized; and yet others very, very small.

By the end of the term, grand allégro combinations, like petit allégro combinations, contain three or four steps. Follow the same progression as for the petit allégro combinations:

1. Alternate steps or repeat them to extend the combination.

2. Increase the combination from four to eight counts, increasing the number of counts gradually; this amount doubles to 16 counts when both sides are performed together.

Grand allégro requires a great deal of strength, energy, and breath control to perform to ballet standards. Remember when constructing grand allégros to consider energy and memory demands, vocabulary, and length of the combination.

Utilizing Set Exercises and Combinations

As the teacher, you must weigh the benefits for students between presenting new combinations and repeating learned, or set, exercises and combinations.

- Find a balance for each class between new and set exercises and combinations.

- Give students an opportunity to perfect an exercise or transition.

- Repeat a familiar exercise to promote performance confidence.

- Focus attention on details that might have been missed before when the students were concentrating on remembering the exercise.

Some teachers present set barres. The dancers know all the exercises and work at refining their performance. At times a set barre is appropriate for beginning students since it allows them to focus on the simplest form of the exercise to which the teacher adds elements as the students progress. Set classes are constructed and practiced for testing purposes.

*M*aximizing Student Energy

Marking is a method by which the student concentrates on the foot positions, leg gestures, and arm positions while moving through the actions of a step. In marking a step, the student

- does not fully execute the step;
- eliminates jump, hops, and leaps in the step; and
- reviews the sequence and timing of foot, leg, and arm actions.
- remembers the motor pattern of the steps.

The advantages of marking the step is that it conserves energy so that the step can be repeated many times without fatigue and helps the student learn and remember the basic motor pattern slowly, completely, and correctly.

*M*usical Considerations

The dancer and the dance are married to the music. How the dancer uses music is extremely important to creating a symbiotic relationship that in turn conveys the dynamics and aesthetics of the dance. The dancer internalizes technical and kinesthetic components and translates them into outward movement with musical relationships. This highly integrated and challenging inner dance begins with a clear understanding in the body of musical components.

Timing

Every movement has a tempo that is fast or slow and a rhythm that is either even or uneven. Basic 4/4, 3/4, 2/4, and 6/8 time signatures support beginning exercises and combinations. Follow this progression:

1. Teach a new exercise or step in a slower time frame, such as double time (twice as long), so that students can execute all parts of the exercise successfully.
2. Emphasize simple timing so that students concentrate primarily upon executing the exercise.
3. Provide time to rest between each step and repetition of an exercise.
4. Execute the step in standard time.
5. Add accents. Some steps become more rhythmically complicated with the addition of "&, a, one," or "Ee, &, a, one."

Counting music as a ballet teacher or dancer is different from counting music as a musician. The beats of the music serve as signposts for actions in a step or port de bras. The dancer has to be at a certain place on a certain beat of the music.

Music is counted in several ways. Adagio movements and grand allégro steps are counted by measures. It takes four measures of 3/4 time to execute a battement développé devant. The time frame for adagio and grand allégro is longer because the movement is larger or slower. These types of combinations are choreographed in phrases of 8 measures, or sometimes 12 measures, leaving four measures for one group of dancers to exit the center and the next group to enter the space and run to their respective places. The quick, precise movements of petit and grand allégro demand the dancer use each beat of the music.

> **Rule:**
> Remember ballet movements have an inherent rhythm in themselves, but they must interweave and be one with the music.

Accents

In many exercises at the barre, there is an accent, or stress, on certain parts of a movement. Different steps require different accents.

- Accents often fall before the primary beat (i.e., the downbeat), which requires quick action from the student such as on the battement frappé and the petit battement sur le cou-de-pied.
- Directional accents focus on the the outward action of the step, as in battement tendu, or the

inward (or closing) action, as in battement dégagé.

- Transfer of weight accents concentrate on the "& 1" beat of the music (e.g., in the glissade).

- Level change accents highlight the relevé, or rising action, or the descending action to full foot.

- Petit and grand allégro accents occur on the upward action, the "&" before the primary beat of the measure, or the anacrusis (downbeat).

Choosing Music for Your Class

Choosing the music for class is a vital part of the teaching process. For the beginning dancer, the music mirrors the movement and the quality of the exercise or step.

1. Select music with simple rhythms and phrasing so that the students can hear the primary beat of the measure. Students can most successfully count the music when they hear a stress on the first beat in the measure.

2. Count the measures of the exercise or combination.

3. Count the music so that it has an equal number of measures as the number of measures in the movement.

4. Construct short exercises and combinations. Usually standard barre exercises for beginners build to equal 32 measures. By then the working and the supporting leg are strong enough to support this length of work. The goal is for students to perform the steps and exercises in time with the music correctly.

In class, the teacher counts the music for students when presenting the exercise or step. Each movement coincides with a specific count. When students become comfortable with counting for themselves, they begin to feel and express the music in their dancing. Then you can stop counting for them, which makes students more responsible for their performance and allows you to focus in on giving feedback on students' work. Change the music frequently to broaden students' music and movement experience.

Musicality

In classical ballet, musicality, the ability to be one with the music, is vital. Movements usually blend with the music. Musicality is about learning how to phrase steps within the phrases of the music. From the beginning of the course, students should aim to perform the exercise with the correct tempo and rhythm. A teacher can sing to impart accent, phrasing, and musical qualities to the dancers. Each exercise and step must be danced with the music because ballet is a performing art whether it is done at the barre, in class, or on stage. This must be stressed throughout a dancer's studies. Beyond timing, the dancer must exhibit a flow of movement that meshes with the music. Being one with the music is essential to performing classical ballet.

Live or Recorded Music

Live accompaniment can be a wonderful experience if the musician for dance understands the relationship to music in the ballet class. Live music helps to maintain the energy of the dance class. It makes the students feel like dancing. For a beginning teacher with little experience, working with live music or a musician for dance can be a challenge. The teacher and the musician must communicate constantly before, during, and after the exercise or combination. The items about which you communicate to the musician in class include the following:

1. Setting the tempo, meter, and quality of the music. For example, a rond de jambe à terre exercise is performed in a moderate waltz (3/4 time signature). The teacher will say, "1 - 2 - 3, 2 - 2- 3, 3 - 2 - 3" in the tempo of the exercise.

2. Knowing when to start and when to stop playing.

3. Changing the tempo to either slower or faster.

4. Playing the selection of music before the exercise to check tempo, meter, and quality. To save time, meet with the musician before the class and review the selections for the exercises and combinations of the class. Many of these musical selections become standards, but be sure to vary them so that students can gain experience working with new music.

Teachers and musicians communicate both verbally and nonverbally. For instance, eye contact with the musician for dance is important in this dialogue, and hand gestures may be used during the exercise so that the dancers can continue without stopping for a change in tempo.

Recorded music for ballet class includes compact discs, records, or cassettes. Many good recordings are available. If possible, read the descriptions of the music to determine if it is for a beginning class. Select music that possesses the correct time signature, tempo, and quality for the exercise or combination. A speed control on a record player or cassette is an excellent investment. The speed control is extremely useful in teaching the beginning class, when the music must be slow enough for the dancers to execute the movement. The disadvantages of using records are that more than one record will be used during class, and starting and stopping to change records can be very time-consuming. To mitigate this, designate the record selections before class so that a minimum amount of time is spent changing records between each exercise and combination. Records get scratched and skip. Cross out selections on the record if they have a defect so you do not use them again in class.

A cassette player is another musical option for class. Recording your records gives you a copy while preserving the original record. The disadvantage of recording an entire record on one cassette is finding the next piece of music. One way to save time is to create a tape of all plié music, a tape of all battement tendu music, a tape of all petit allégro 4/4 music, and so on, for each type of exercise. Before class, select the music and cue the tape to the selection. Cueing the music is extremely important, especially if your cassette player does not have a counter. If possible, try to purchase a high-quality cassette recorder/player with a counter and a speed control; these are more expensive but very practical. Counter numbers enable you to quickly find your selections. The speed control provides you with the same advantages as the record player.

Compact disc players are simple to use because you select and press a button. The disadvantage is that most compact discs do not have speed controls. The selection of ballet music on compact disc is constantly growing, and the cost for a compact disc is often comparable to a record. If properly cared for, the compact disc will last longer than a record.

Many times the choice of musical accompaniment depends on the financial and scheduling resources of the setting in which a teacher is working. Although live music is exciting, recorded music, if chosen with care, is an excellent alternative. Choose records specifically designed for ballet and especially for beginning ballet students.

Planning for the Entire Term

Begin planning with a clear picture of what you want to teach during the term. Before starting the course, create a scope and sequence plan (what is learned and in what order) as an overall guide. The teacher develops objectives for each lesson before creating the class (see units I, II, III, IV). Allow for flexibility in your class plan because each group of students and the individuals in every class are different.

Summary

Learning to construct exercises and combinations effectively is an integral part of the learning progressions for beginning students. The continued relationship of dance and music must be supported and nurtured by the teacher so that the dancers gain movement confidence in performing with the music. For the beginning teacher it is often a challenge to keep these two strands of the class working synergistically, but the movement and the music that accompanies it are the heart of ballet.

chapter five

Managing the Ballet Class

The ballet class is highly organized. Students must learn certain rules of decorum as part of participating in the class. Many of these management procedures emanate from the internal structure of the ballet class. The teacher uses them to move students through the barre and center of each class.

The purpose of this chapter is to describe how to manage the class from different perspectives. The teacher or the program for which the teacher works defines the expectations for students' behavior, class attire, and attendance. Safety in the classroom is also the teacher's responsibility. Rules at the barre and in the center provide a predetermined system for students moving in an orderly manner using correct protocols throughout the class. Time management consists of pacing and adapting the class. The teacher creates the class atmosphere, in which teacher-student interaction occurs with observation and through verbal and nonverbal feedback.

Some management procedures practiced in the ballet class are traditions. Others are decisions the teacher contemplates before the first day of class and throughout the rest of the course. The teacher acts as a guide, communicating to students with understanding and insight how to navigate through the world of ballet.

Teacher Expectations

The ballet class requires an expected decorum that is a part of its tradition. An air of formality and discipline in the class reflects the aesthetic quality of ballet as an art. Order and concentration are important components of a ballet class environment. The teacher gives the students exercises and combinations; the students perform them, and the teacher responds to their performance with constructive feedback. Students strive to correct or improve their performance which is motivated by the teacher's comments and their own desire to improve.

During the class, students are quiet while the teacher gives the instructions for combinations or offers a correction. Talking in class to your neighbor is prohibited. If the student has a question, the student raises a hand and is acknowledged by the teacher to speak. Obviously, gum chewing is unsafe and unsightly in the ballet class, distracting students' concentration.

Class Attire

The dancers' and teacher's attire for class contribute to professionalism and class atmosphere. The teacher decides how stringent a dress code to establish for the class, or the class attire is sometimes predetermined by the department or school. Many first-time dancers feel uncomfortable and extremely self-conscious in the body-revealing dance attire they wear to class. This is a risk that must be taken. Those students who have never danced before may not understand the purpose of proper dance attire. At the first class meeting, the teacher explains to the students that dance attire serves several purposes. For students, dance attire allows them to move freely and without constraint. Dance attire enables students and the teacher to see the lines the body creates in space. To provide appropriate feedback the teacher must clearly see each student's body alignment and movement at a glance. Students should meet the dress standards required of a ballet dancer in the beginning class.

The teacher decides what color leotards and tights students wear in class, or if they may choose color and type of dancewear. Traditional dance attire helps students acquire the dancer's image. Female students typically wear the traditional black leotard and pink tights. The teacher may also require that female students wear a belt or elastic band at the waist. This simple device creates a waistline for the dancer and provides a means for the teacher to evaluate the relationship of the hips, waist, and shoulders at a glance. The female dancer should wear a bra that provides proper support for the vigorous activity of class.

For men, the traditional dance attire has been a white T-shirt, black tights, a dance belt, and white socks. You may choose to suggest alternative attire for men. Some teachers allow men to wear biker shorts or even sweat pants in class. Many teachers choose to modify traditional dance attire rather than have the dress code dissuade anyone from taking the class.

Some teachers prohibit students from wearing leg warmers, skirts, shorts, sweaters, sweat pants, and all other baggy clothing in class. If the climate is cold, some warm-up clothing items are acceptable, providing they are close-fitting to the body. Quite often beginning dancers copy the "baggy" look that more seasoned dancers choose.

There are other personal items the teacher must address the first day of class. Long hair should be pulled away from the face and can be worn in a bun at the back of the head. Hair that is loose could potentially hit the dancer in the eye when the head turns quickly. Keeping the hair off the neck allows the teacher to visually assess alignment and how the dancer holds the neck in relation to the head and torso. Some types of jewelry should not be worn in class such as long, hanging earrings, noisy bracelets, and heavy necklaces that bounce when the dancer jumps. These items cause safety concerns, not only for the dancer wearing them but also if they come into contact with other dancers.

Classical ballet is performed in ballet slippers. The expense of purchasing the slippers is justified by the safety slippers provide in performing the movements. The teacher should decide if the standard colors of pink for women and black or white for men will be worn. If students own ballet slippers, the teacher checks if they fit correctly. At the first meeting of the class, the teacher instructs students on purchasing ballet slippers, how to tie them, and how to sew on the elastic straps. These few minutes devoted to preparing shoes for class work save time later.

New ballet slippers must fit like a glove because the leather stretches to conform to the foot. Before buying the slippers, make sure all five toes reach the end of the shoe, without the toes curling under. Men wear socks with their ballet slippers. When purchasing slippers men should wear the socks they plan to wear with their slippers to ensure proper fit.

Ballet slippers are usually one to two sizes smaller than regular shoes. At first, the shoes may be a little uncomfortable. If shoes are too big, however, it is difficult to see the shape of the foot. Likewise, shoes that are too large also present a safety concern because the dancer can trip over the tip of the shoe while dancing. Before the term begins, ascertain where dance attire and shoes can be purchased, such as men's dance belts and shoes in hard-to-find sizes. Post a list of local stores where dancewear is available, and refer students to the list. If these supplies are unavailable locally or in stores in nearby cities, use mail-order firms that provide quick service. The students need their dance attire and shoes as soon as possible.

Personal hygiene is important in the ballet class, which requires intense physical activity. The dancer should wear deodorant and shower frequently, before and especially after class. Dance attire for each class should be clean, otherwise it will be offensive to the teacher and other members of the class.

Attendance

For some courses, students could read a book and learn how to do some things on their own, without attending the class. This is not true for ballet. The students cannot learn ballet without attending class regularly and practicing the exercises and steps over and over again.

The teacher should take attendance promptly at the same time before each class begins. The teacher chooses what portion of the grade relates to attendance. Before the term begins, the teacher establishes for use in the attendance record symbols for presence, absence, illness, and observing the class instead of dancing. The record includes a list of the dates for performance tests, written examination, and a place for grades unless using an electronic grade book.

Performance Attitude

Dressing like a dancer contributes to the performance attitude. This attitude emanates from within the dancer. Acting like a dancer can be achieved initially by meeting class expectations for attire and behavior.

Beginning students can start to feel like performers by holding their head so that the eyes are focused slightly higher than eye level, as if they are looking out at the audience. Achieving a performance attitude in class is clearly an outcome of the dancer gaining movement confidence. With this confidence, the student's performance attitude begins to grow. Often for adult students performing ballet is realizing a childhood dream, and these students bring the performance attitude naturally to the class. From the first day, students should be taught that ballet is a performance art and that, at least for the time they are in class, they are dancers.

Practicing Protocols

Teaching and practicing protocols in relation to steps and combinations is the entry into the cultural and aesthetic aspects of ballet. Knowing the protocols speaks volumes about the individual participating in an art form that is more than three centuries old. No matter where you are teaching, be it a state-of-the-art dance studio, a gymnasium, or a cafetorium, the protocols remain the same. Using protocols establishes the sophistication, the grace, the formal traditions that communicate that this person is performing classical ballet. Teaching students protocols is like teaching them how to use a new language in an eloquent manner.

Safety in the Studio

Before each class, the teacher ensures that the studio is safe and ready for dancing. It is the teacher's responsibility to inspect the studio. Either the janitorial staff or the teacher is responsible for the following safety precautions:

- Clear away any extraneous equipment.

- Sweep or clean the vinyl or wood floor on a regular basis.

- Check vinyl floor seams to ensure that they are not loose.

- Examine the entire floor regularly for slick spots that should have immediate attention as they are potentially hazardous.

- Clean the mirrors.

- Dust the studio frequently.

The temperature in the studio should be comfortable, and the room should be well ventilated. If the temperature is too warm, the dancers get a false sense that their bodies are warmed-up. Even in a warm studio, muscles must be adequately warmed up to avoid injury. If the studio is cold or drafty, plan a longer barre because it takes longer to warm-up under these conditions. Allow students to wear a sweater and leg warmers at the beginning of class, but later they should remove them. If the room is extremely warm and humid, a student may become light-headed. If this occurs, make the student sit down, between his or her knees, or lie down in the fetal position. An air-conditioned studio dispels humidity and keeps the studio cool, but not cold. In warm and humid conditions, encourage students to drink water throughout the day to avoid dehydration during class time.

Rules at the Barre

In the beginning of class, students stand at the barre with enough distance between them that they do not kick each other when they extend their legs. Each student requires a personal space large enough in which to move comfortably without fear of encountering others. This puts students at ease so that they can concentrate on the movement.

Rules in the Center

In the center part of the class, there is a certain decorum that studnets must learn as part of partici-

pating in class. In the center, students stand in lines from the front to the back of the studio. Each student must have a personal space in which to move. If someone stands directly behind another person, the teacher is unable to see that student's performance. Likewise the student is unable to see the mirror to monitor his or her own performance.

In some traditional classes, the teacher selects the dancers who stand in the front line. Generally, women stand in the front and the men in the back of the studio. In some classes students choose where they want to stand. Dancers in the front line must be ready to perform the combination first. Usually the more seasoned dancers gravitate to the front of the class. Those students who want to observe the combination performed before executing it themselves usually stand in the middle of the class.

Changing Lines

Traditionally, changing lines between center combinations requires that the students in the front move to the back of the studio, and the students in the back move to the front efficiently and quickly. To manage this effectively and professionally:

1. The class divides into two groups: one in the front and one at the back.

2. The front group splits down the middle and exits by moving forward and then to the closest side of the room, stage right or left (see figure 5.1a).

3. The front group continues walking along the side of the room, and repositions in lines in the back half of the room.

4. At the same time, the back group moves forward to become the new front group (see figure 5.1b).

Group Work

If the class is large, the teacher divides it into two or more groups so that the dancers have more room to perform. This allows the teacher to see the individuals in each group. While one group performs, the other group or groups wait at the back or side of the studio so that they can take their places in the center as quickly as possible when it is their turn. During the performance of the combination, the waiting dancers should stand quietly and attentively.

When performing in groups, the teacher should indicate first, second, third group, and so on. The

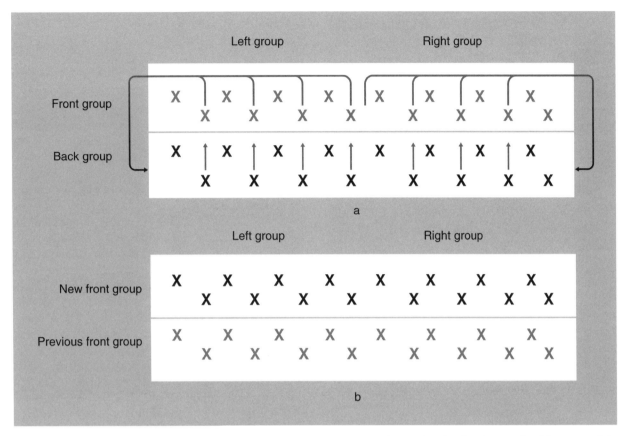

Figure 5.1 Changing lines in the center: a) The front group splits and moves forward and to the closest side of the room while the back group moves forward to take their places. b) The previous front group repositions in back half of the room.

first group begins in the center or enters on the introductory music to begin the combination. After performing the combination, the first group separates to each side of the room and the second group enters from the back of the studio. Another option is that the first group leaves together to the side opposite from the next group's entrance.

Grand allégro combinations generally move from the upstage (rear) corners of the studio on a diagonal to the downstage (front) corners. For this section of the class, beginning students often perform the steps or simple combinations in lines across the studio. Depending on the width of the studio, dancers perform the grand allégro in lines or groups of twos, threes, or fours. Traveling in small numbers gives everyone space to perform the combination. The next line or group usually starts the combination every four or eight counts after the previous line.

Before performing combinations in the center or going across the floor, the teacher specifies how many counts of music will be between each group's performance. Beginning students require more music in which to make this transition. The teacher needs to consider

- the tempo of the music,
- how far the group will travel, and
- what is sufficient time for dancers to run to their places and execute the preparation.

Generally men in the class are the last group to perform the grand allégro combination. The accompaniment is often slowed down to allow the male dancers to use their full range of air movements during the combination. The slower tempo encourages men to jump higher and execute larger movements.

Révérence

At the end of the class, the teacher directs the dancers to form lines in the center to perform a révérence or bow. The teacher performs the bow facing the students. The class claps for the teacher and the musician for dance, and the teacher bows to the class and then turns and gestures by extending the arm with palm up toward the musician.

ime Management

Time management of the class includes the duties before class, the barre, the center, and class closure duties. The teacher is in the studio before students arrive for class. Begin the class on time, immediately after taking the roll and making announcements. Before beginning every exercise, the teacher quickly observes that all students

- are facing the same direction,
- have the correct foot position,
- have the correct foot in front, and
- are ready to start the exercise.

Present the exercise efficiently and effectively and answer questions before the students execute the exercise. Be sure to ask again if students have any questions before starting the second side.

Pacing the Class

In every class, the teacher is responsible for how fast or how slow the class proceeds. The teacher has to decide how much time to spend on certain parts of the class. Learning to pace a beginning ballet class requires the teacher to plan each class and monitor its execution one class at a time but with a view of the entire term.

In structuring any class, allow for flexibility and include adequate time for teaching and practice. For students to learn a new step without feeling rushed, they need enough time to grasp the movements. It is important that students feel that they complete an exercise or combination before moving on to the next part of the class. Once they learn the step, they should be able to perform it as part of an exercise with a quick review and a minimum amount of practice.

Focus on accomplishing the objectives for each class meeting. The teacher controls and directs the class; students should not be allowed to change the teacher's direction. It is equally prudent for the new teacher to prepare more exercises and combinations than is anticipated for each class. Overplanning for a class serves as a precaution or provides alternatives to teach, if an exercise or combination is inappropriate for most of the class. Some students require more individual attention than time permits in the class. Confer with these students outside the class to work on aspects with which they are having particular difficulty.

In a beginning class, the teacher emphasizes the barre more than on the center. After the barre and center develop, the two parts combine gradually into a balanced ballet class that develops technique symbiotically.

Teaching the Shorter Class

Depending on the setting, the beginning ballet class ranges from less than 50 minutes to as long as one hour and 30 minutes. If your class period is only 50 minutes, the ballet class format changes to make the most effective use of the class time.

During the first few weeks of classes, teaching the barre and its exercises takes most of the class period. It is during this time that students learn the barre exercises and basic steps used in center combinations. The students acquire strength and control in order to perform basic steps in the center. During this early part of the term, the center part of the class includes practicing barre exercises and learning steps. Near the completion of teaching the barre exercises, the center portion of the class expands beyond performing single steps to performing short combinations in petit allégro, adagio, sautés, and grand allégro.

In the next part of the term, solidify the basic barre exercises and condense the amount of time it takes to execute them. Meanwhile, expand the number and types of center combinations. By three quarters through the term, the beginning ballet class reaches its standard format. The barre contains all the elements that make up the basic ballet center at a beginning level of movement competency. The students know the exercises and perform them to the best of their ability. Refine the barre exercises and add options. The center combinations incorporate two or three different steps. Now you and the students can concentrate on dancing. In every class it is important for students to gain a sense of accomplishment about their work and to feel like they are dancing. Sometimes, you sacrifice perfection of execution, to let the spirit soar and dance.

eacher-Student Interaction

The teaching/learning atmosphere strongly supports student learning and the interaction between the teacher and the students. This interaction develops through observation and feedback.

Class Atmosphere

The dancer learns in an open atmosphere in which there is mutual respect between the teacher and the students. Within this atmosphere of mutual respect, a student gains movement confidence and tenacity. In an open atmosphere, a student does not fear making mistakes, is open to the teacher's corrections, and strives for perfection without getting discouraged. The teacher is responsible for creating this type of atmosphere from the very first day of class. Often students are self-conscious about their appearance and their movement. Help students gain confidence by expressing patience, compassion, and encouragement, and by persevering firmly in a positive manner.

Teacher Observation

The teacher develops and hones observation skills to teach ballet. To manage the class, the teacher constantly observes and monitors performance. These observations become movement memories. From these memories, the teacher can provide feedback to the whole class or to individuals and gather information for developing future lessons. A series of movement memories about a specific student provides the teacher with a movement profile of the student that changes throughout the term. Movement memories provide a resource from which the teacher draws in the future to foresee alternative ways of handling a classroom situation, or adapt a movement cue.

Teaching Locations

During the barre exercises, the teacher selects a place in the class where all individuals can see and hear the demonstration easily. While the students perform barre exercises, the teacher walks the length of the barre observing student performance. To gather information and provide feedback to students, the teacher

- circulates throughout the room, collecting information with which to provide feedback to the whole class and to individuals about performance;

- makes eye contact with each student during the barre;

- acknowledges each student in the class at least once; and

- utilizes facial expression, tone of voice, and body language during observation and feedback.

In the center portion of class, the teacher presents the combinations at the front of the classroom or the longest mirrored wall. Face the class while describing combinations verbally. The direction the teacher faces when demonstrating movement is important so that students do not have to transfer the movement to the other foot. Either face students and mirror the movement for them (i.e., begin the combination on the foot opposite from the one on which they begin) or you and the students face the mirror to learn the combination. For example, when facing students if you say "Fifth position, right foot front" then you do a Fifth position, left foot in front. Facing the students and mirroring their movements takes practice, but you will find that it becomes much easier as you gain experience.

Mirror all of the directions of the combination while facing the students and telling them what steps to execute. Presenting combinations facing the students builds a strong rapport with them. Performing while facing the students during a demonstration requires three-track teaching:

1. Say the actions or names of the step or combination.

2. Perform the combination with the opposite foot in the opposite direction.

3. Observe the students face to face while gathering information for feedback on their performance.

Yes, three-track teaching is possible, and a presentation strategy you should learn and use!

Sometimes, however, mirroring students on the opposite foot is not always the easiest way for the students to follow the combination. The other way of presenting center combinations is facing the mirror with the students performing behind the teacher, so that they see the movement as they perform it. Facing the mirror, the teacher observes most of the class performing and give cues and feedback. Use this facing to teach complicated steps. Since both teacher and students use the same foot while learning the step, it avoids confusion.

When students perform combinations across the floor the teacher stands at the front of the class to observe the groups as they dance. You may choose to stand behind the students or move around the classroom to observe. At the end of the class, the teacher faces the students, and both perform the révérence.

Types of Feedback

Feedback may be either verbal or nonverbal, depending on the situation. Another valuable form of feedback is guided manipulation, in which the teacher physically manipulates a body part to make a technical correction more clear. Regardless of the type of feedback being used, comments from the teacher should be constructive and focused on the student's technique, not the student.

Verbal Feedback

Verbal feedback from the teacher gives specific information such as a technical correction, a recognition of good work, a challenge to improve performance, or a compliment on execution. Verbal feedback to students is of four general types: prescriptive, acknowledgment, corrective, and negative.

- *Prescriptive* is a positive comment that provides the student with information on how to improve performance (e.g., "Your working leg in the battement tendu devant is well turned-out; if you lead with the heel even more forward and lifted that will reveal your pointed foot").

- *Acknowledgment* is a comment to recognize proper execution or improved performance (e.g., "That was a beautiful rond de jambe à terre en dehors; it demonstrates how well you can rotate your working leg while keeping the hip stable").

- *Corrective* feedback states the solution to the problem the student encounters (e.g., "When you perform a jump from two feet, the demi-plié before and after each jump must be performed with both heels pressing into the floor and the body weight equally centered over your feet").

- *Negative* feedback should be used sparingly and as a last resort. Negative feedback comprises a look, a comment, or sometimes peer pressure that influences the student's behavior before the teacher intervenes. When the teacher uses this form of feedback it communicates the solution to the movement or behavioral problem and is not directed toward the person. For example, if one student is repeatedly not ready to execute the preparation for a barre exercise, the teacher might say, "We will begin the exercise when everyone is ready." The teacher does not begin the exercise until everyone is quiet and ready.

Nonverbal Feedback

Nonverbal feedback from the teacher can be used by itself or to reinforce verbal feedback. Nonverbal communication is an important way to interact with students and entails

- smiling;
- making eye contact with a student or with the class;
- nodding to indicate correct execution; and
- looking quizzical, mildly teasing, or surprised.

The teacher has to have a sense of humor in the ballet class. Use humor in such a way that students are able to laugh at themselves and not feel that their efforts are being ridiculed. For instance, when a student performs a combination but changes the steps, the teacher may respond with a comment such as: "Oh, that was very creative."

Another way to give non verbal feedback is when the teacher performs the exercise either for the class or with the class. Sometimes the teacher demonstrates the exercise to teach correct timing, sequencing, and accents or to refine performance. Ask students to simply observe the performance. The teacher may accompany the performance with verbal cues to reinforce correct execution of the step.

Since ballet is a visual, nonverbal art form, much of the communication in the classroom employs movement. Many beginning students have limited observation skills and get lost in the complexity of the entire step. Avoid this by asking students to concentrate only on the leg gestures or the arm movements performed. This directive focuses the attention of the students to the appropriate moving body part. Later in a beginning class, the teacher asks students to look at the entire body while demonstrating a step or combination. This shift of focus is important for the student to understand the coordination of body parts in performing the step.

Guided Manipulation

Since ballet is a very physically demanding art, the teacher may elect to move or manipulate a student's body part to clarify a movement or principle. At the first class meeting, tell the students that to teach ballet, you sometimes have to physically move their bodies so that they kinesthetically feel the correct position. For example, in a pose, the teacher stretches the student's arm to extend her line, or in an exercise the teacher lifts a student's heel forward as his foot brushes along the floor.

At the first class, the teacher asks if any students prefer not to be touched or manipulated. The teacher explains the purpose of guided manipulation used in the ballet class. Request that students who choose not to be manipulated tell you before the next class. Because of legal implications, the teacher must have permission to manipulate a student.

During class, the teacher senses whether or not a student wants to be manipulated. It may be better to wait until after the class to ask the student, or let the student ask for your help. Before touching the student, specifically describe what body part will be moved and why. Gently move the body part. Ask the student if he feels the difference from his original position. He may or may not feel the correct position or movement.

Sometimes a one-on-one conversation with a student takes the place of guided manipulation. Describe and/or demonstrate how to perform the pose or movement correctly. Ask the student to perform the pose or movement and observe if the correction is made and understood. If the student accomplishes the change on her own, the teaching point becomes a part of her performance.

Training Students to Provide Their Own Feedback

The teacher constantly "looks and listens" to obtain feedback about student performance. The teacher trains students to actively monitor and analyze personal performance. Then, the student begins to apply what is learned from one performance to the next. Applying personal feedback to performance is an important attribute of understanding and gaining technique. Train students to listen to and apply all group corrections, as well as comments to individuals in the class, as a self-check. The more responsibility the student accepts for personal performance, the more the student monitors internal feedback. Learning to apply personal feedback enhances

- body image,
- concentration,
- movement confidence,
- self-confidence, and
- self-esteem.

Teacher observation and feedback directly links to the management of the ballet class.

Teacher Management Expectations

As the manager of the ballet class, the teacher is a facilitator. You are the person on whom students depend to steer them through the process of learning beginning ballet. You guide them through the frustrating realization that ballet is not an "instant" art form but one that requires patience and practice. Achieving immediate perfection is not the rule in learning ballet. Experiencing the joy of movement and self-expression, however, can be a part of learning ballet from the very start.

It is helpful to keep in mind that few if any of the students in the beginning ballet class want dance as a career goal. Many students come to the ballet class frightened that they will not succeed. They often compare their work to someone better in the class. As the teacher puts them at ease, and show them that each individual has a personal challenge they can achieve by learning ballet. You instill in them that learning ballet is more than just the physical aspects of the art. The elements of ballet—grace, posture, self-expression, discipline, commitment—transfer to their lives, giving them new inner resources. Ballet is a logical art that has a prescribed discipline. Through teacher management, the discipline of taking ballet class becomes a self-discipline that students apply while in class and perhaps in their lives.

Learning to teach ballet is a journey for you and for your students. Like the students, as a new teacher, you too are learning to steer through the process of teaching beginning ballet. Teaching requires practice and patience to master the skills presented in this chapter. Your management skills will grow with your experience. You should not expect instant perfection, any more than should your students. Often, new teachers feel they must tell students everything they need to know about performing a step or exercise at one time. Instead, offer knowledge in small digestible portions. The adage "less is more" also applies to teaching. If you hold their hands, continually demonstrating the movement and saying the names of the steps, your students cannot learn to do it for themselves. The teacher learns when to let students try dancing on their own. If they fail, that is all right. You are there to help them try again.

Summary

Managing the beginning ballet class is both challenging and rewarding. Begin by having clear expectations of your students concerning class attire, attendance, and performance attitude. Safety in the studio is a paramount concern; make sure that temperature and conditions of the floor and studio are suitable.

Managing the class is made easier by the formalized rules at the barre and in the center. Organize students' movement by making sure they have enough space in which to move. The systematic changing of lines and entering and exiting for group work are important for safety and learning efficiency and reduce the amount of time that might be wasted when transitioning between groups.

Time management, pace, and adapting content to the length of the class are also vital aspects of teacher management. The pace of the class depends on how fast the students learn.

Class atmosphere reflects the discipline of the art practiced in an open environment that allows students to take risks in the class. Where the teacher stands in relationship to the students throughout the class is important to demonstration, observation, and correction. Provide positive, constructive feedback to your students both verbally and nonverbally, and encourage students to monitor their own work. Guided manipulation is a form of nonverbal feedback that helps the student to feel correct movement or positions kinesthetically. Have realistic expectations of your beginning students, but continue to nurture them to explore their full potential as dancers.

chapter six

*Assessing
Student
Progress*

Accountability and assessment are important aspects of education for students, teachers, and administrators. In academic settings, student performance is reflected in grades and grade point averages. In the academic ballet class, the ballet teacher is responsible for teaching students ballet technique to achieve established performance levels. As a professional educator the ballet teacher evaluates student performance. To make accurate and consistent judgments, the instructor uses criteria upon which to base judgements to determine what grade the student earns for the course. Assessment is a global term; it refers to gathering evidence and then reporting it. Evaluation requires quantitative or qualitative judgments. The purpose of this chapter is to identify different kinds of evaluation tools and their use in ballet class for assessing student progress.

At the beginning of the term, the teacher conducts a physical pre-assessment profile of the students in the class. This profile determines each student's body types and any variances in the structure of the knees. These knee types influence how individuals move, and some types may indicate retraining. In any class, evaluation is either formative (short term) or summative (long term).

Teaching classical ballet involves the three domains of learning: psychomotor, cognitive, and affective. The psychomotor domain relates to acquiring skills. In this domain, performance examinations derive from criterion-referenced evaluation. This type of evaluation uses a checklist or rating scale. The cognitive domain refers to the acquisition of the knowledge of ballet. Written tests and reports are a part of this domain. In most ballet classes, the affective domain is not tested. Rather, the teacher notices changes in self-confidence, body image, and poise. Performance exams, attendance, written examinations, and reports on dance concerts comprise the total grade in the academic ballet class.

$\mathscr{A}$ssessment in the Ballet Class

Assessment appraises student performance over a period of time. In the ballet class, assessment begins with

1. developing the objectives for the unit,
2. selecting the exercises and steps taught in the unit,
3. pre-assessing students,
4. choosing the teaching styles that accomplish the objectives, and
5. assessing the psychomotor and cognitive domains of learning.

Assessment in the ballet class is a cyclic model in which all of the steps are connected and are interdependent. Assessment is not limited to testing situations but is continuous throughout the course.

$\mathscr{P}$hysical Pre-Assessment

The teacher begins the assessment process at the beginning of the course. For the first assessment the teacher conducts a physical pre-assessment of each student in the class. This information is vital; since it predicts how students with various body and knee types will move in relation to the content of the class.

At the first moving ballet class, the teacher conducts an informal assessment of students' body types and knee structures. The pre-assessment becomes the basis for the teacher's mental profile of each student in the class. This profile identifies the student's body type; any physical problems; skill level; and, later, includes a performance profile. To teach effectively, keep a clear picture in mind of each student's body type and work as they progress through the class and acquire technique.

Body Types

Body types vary from individual to individual. W. H. Sheldon investigated and compiled his findings about body types in the *Atlas of Man* (1954). Through his research, he concluded that there were three body types (somatotyping): mesomorph, ectomorph, and endomorph. Tissue types are the foundation of his theory. His findings state that the mesomorph body tissue has a predominance of connective and muscular tissue, ectomorph tissue consists mostly of nerve tissue, and the endomorph has a large amount of endocrine tissue. No one individual adheres completely to these types, but these categories give useful insights into certain bodily tendencies.

Hereditary and genetic predispositions affect the psychology and physical structure of the student.

• The mesomorph is an individual with a solid, square musculature, almost athletic in appearance. This individual usually excels in muscular strength and endurance activities. A mesomorph can perform large vigorous movements over a long period of time. Jumps and grand allégro are typically strong points. The major attributes for this individual body type are strength, endurance, and power. Flexibility and mobility present a constant struggle that the individual strives to maintain through daily workout.

• The ectomorph has a long, narrow, lean, and slender figure with an almost fragile structure. This individual is usually very flexible and possesses great mobility. Arabesques, high grand battements, and flexibility are the hallmark of this body type. However, if the ectomorph overstretches, loss of control ensues. The ectomorph performs quick movements well because of the well-developed nervous system and its relationship to the skeletal system. This body type limits the efficiency of the cardiovascular system. Strength and muscular endurance activities are difficult for the ectomorph; but strength, endurance, and relaxation exercises can improve the ectomorph's performance.

• The endomorph has a rounded body contour with an excessive amount of fatty tissue (Sheldon, 1954). This individual performs petit allégro combinations well because of the body type's predisposition to move quickly. An endomorph possesses strength, flexibility, and endurance and maintains these capacities. Weight control is often a problem for an individual with this body type, so endurance exercises are part of the daily workout.

From the 1930s through the 1960s the mesomorph body type predominated ballet. From the 1970s to the present, the ectomorph has been the popular choice of ballet choreographers.

Regardless of the student's body type, teachers take into consideration other physical attributes such as the proportions of the body and leg length. If the dancer has a long back and short legs, he or she will have difficulty acquiring extension. Although classical proportions are most desirable for performing classical ballet, students with all different body types will be enroll in the beginning ballet class.

Knee Variances

Individual differences in bone structure of the knee affect the performance of the dancer and the aesthetic line that the dancer's body creates. The shape of the pelvis and position of the thigh determines the straightness of the legs. There are several variances in the shape of the knees: knock-knees, bowlegs, tibial torsion, and hyperextension. Dancers with knee variances adjust body alignment to move

quickly and with control. Adjustments focus on straightening and aligning the body and legs to create a line perpendicular from the hip through the leg and the foot. The entire body alignment compensates to become balanced, to create the classic line that enables the dancer to move efficiently. Knee variances require retraining through a conscious effort that adjusts with every exercise and movement. To get this result, the teacher makes students aware of correct body and knee placement throughout the class.

Knock-Knees (Jarreté)

The term *jarreté*, characterized by Jean Georges Noverre, an eighteenth-century theoretician of ballet technique, translates as "closed legged," or "knock-kneed." In this type of knee, the medial condyle of the femur is taller than the lateral condyle. When a jarreté dancer stands in First position turned-out with the calves touching or nearly touching, the heels separate.

The knock-kneed dancer is typically loose-limbed and supple, with the weight of the body resting on the heels. Usually, the knee joint is slack. A dancer with this type of legs usually has high insteps that are often weak. For the knock-kneed dancer acquiring speed and good elevation may be a problem.

> **Simple Test:**
>
> To decide if a dancer is knock-kneed, view the dancer from the back in First position (approximately 90 degrees turn-out). There should be no more than one to two inches between the heels. If more than two inches is between the heels, the dancer may encounter problems typical of a knock-kneed dancer.

Bowlegs (Arqué)

The term *arqué*, identified by Noverre, translates as "arched," or "bowlegged." With bowlegs the lateral condyle of the femur is taller than the medial condyle. Usually occurring in men, the femur is normal, but the tibia has an outward curve. With this condition the tendency is to supinate, or roll outward, on the feet. Because of this misalignment, the dancer is more prone to injury on the medial side of the knee. When a dancer with bowlegs stands in First position, the knees have space between them.

The hip joint turns inward as a result of the bowlegged condition. This knee variance interferes with the technical ability of the dancer. Dancers with bowlegs are typically strong and stiff; extensions are never high, but the dancer has power and ballon. This knee variance in females is not aesthetically pleasing.

> ### *Simple Test:*
> To decide if a dancer is bowlegged, view the dancer from the back in parallel First position and then in a natural turned-out First position (approximately 90 degrees turn-out). If the dancer is bowlegged, the knees have a space between them and hyperextend.

Tibial Torsion ("Cross-Eyed")

Tibial torsion is a variant of bowlegs, in which the patella shifts toward the medial side of the knee. This condition causes incorrect alignment of the foot and alters the angle at which the legs propel from the foot. Tibial torsion impairs dancer's balance and elevation.

> ### *Simple Test:*
> To determine if a dancer has tibial torsion, ask the dancer to stand in parallel First position. View the dancer's knees from the front and notice if the knee caps are off center. This indicates tibial torsion.

Hyperextension

Hyperextension occurs when the knees press too far back and the ligaments behind the knee permanently stretch, making the front of the knee appear too flat. This results in a hollow in the back of the knee, with a bulge above the knee. The hyperextended dancer carries the body weight on the heels. This condition affects speed and elevation.

With hyperextension the flexors of the knee contract to unlock the knee. Some dance teachers think hyperextension is aesthetically pleasing; precautions must be taken with this condition because of its potential for injury. Hyperextension often causes a chain reaction of postural misalignment that is especially dangerous when landing from jumps or leaps.

This kind of spinal misalignment result from hyperextension of the knees:

- Head is forward.
- Shoulders are back (cervical misalignment).
- Hips are back, and lower back sways forward to compensate (lordosis, or "swayback").

- Upper shoulders are round (kyphosis).
- Scapula bows outward.
- Pelvic inclination increases.

> ### *Simple Test:*
> View the dancer in parallel First position from both the side and the back. Notice if the knees touch and if the legs are swayback (hyperextended).

Retraining for Knee Variances

The process for retraining applies to dancers who are knock-kneed, bowlegged, and hyperextended. When dancers are either knock-kneed or bowlegged, they usually exhibit some degree of hyperextension.

To begin the process of retraining the student's musculature and alignment, place the dancer in First position parallel, facing the barre with both hands on the barre. The teacher assists the dancer to shift the weight from the heel, where it falls naturally, to the center of the foot triangle. Dancers who are bowlegged roll out (supinate) on the outsides of their feet. For the knock-kneed dancer, standing in parallel First position with feet touching is contra-indicated because the knees overlap. Pressing the knees together without overlapping, in turn causes the knees to hyperextend. Dancers with knock-knees should avoid rolling in (pronating) on their feet because this misalignment increases the tendency to injure the medial side (of the knee).

To determine how a knee variance relates to body alignment, view the dancer standing in First position parallel from both back and side views. Then appraise the dancer in the following ways:

1. Look at the hips and their relationship over the feet.

2. Look at the rib cage and its relationship to the hips and the legs; determine if the ribs are forward and the hips are back.

3. View the head and its relationship to the shoulders, hips, knees, and ankle bones.

4. Visualize the aplomb line (see chapter 3) dropping from the ear of the dancer to the floor. Notice the parts of the body out of alignment.

The teacher centers the student's pelvis forward over the foot triangle (see chapter 3, figure 3.5). With repositioning, the dancer's knees soften gently. The pelvis centers with the "bones" (iliac crests) perpendicular to the floor. Aid the student to visualize correct alignment by placing the hips over the arch (foot triangle) and avoid concentrating on the knees. In the hyperextended student, the ribs are forward of the vertical alignment. Move the ribs gently back into vertical alignment. Align the neck and head with the rest of the body. The teacher verifies the vertical alignment by visualizing a vertical line drawn down the side of the body from the ear to the front of the ankle bone.

The next stage of retraining alignment is executing a demi-plié and a relevé. Ask the student to stand in parallel First position and sense if the body weight is over the foot triangle. Remind the dancer to keep the back long so that the hips do not change position. Before the dancer executes a demi-plié, ask to place your hand just below her waist. Guide the dancer as she stretches and descends into the demi-plié, raising up to relevé and stretching down keeping the knees straight (abaissé) to the full-foot position with the body weight vertically centered over the foot triangle. After completing the relevé, the teacher again checks all points of the dancer's vertical alignment to make subtle adjustments. Then the student repeats the exercise with the teacher either guiding or observing the student's movements.

In this new aligned position, the knees feel bent until the retrained muscles are strong enough to hold the new position. The student practices relevés in parallel First position and then in classic turned-out positions facing the barre. Weight placement and alignment are crucial to the retraining process of the dancer.

To achieve a near to normal alignment, the student practices relevés repeatedly with one hand on the barre as the teacher monitors the student's performance. The student then practices this exercise in the center. When the dancer kinesthetically feels and sees correct performance, then he or she is able to take responsibility for retraining. In the beginning of retraining, the teacher guides and monitors all variables for the dancer to practice. After the dancer performs the retraining exercises, the teacher continues to monitor the student's work to ensure progress. The student masters the relevé before undertaking more difficult exercises and combinations that require transfers of weight, changes of level, and jumping techniques.

Evaluation Tools in the Ballet Class

In the ephemeral art of dance, teachers and students must keep a clear vision of what they are trying to accomplish daily and for the entire course. The

teacher establishes a set of performance criteria to make sound judgments about each student's level of performance in relationship to the expected standards for classical ballet.

Performance evaluation measures the psychomotor domain and is the major part of determining a grade for a technique class. Balance performance evaluation by testing the cognitive domain with written work and other factors. Written examinations cover the terminology, theory, and history of ballet. Another evaluation tool that enhances the student's overall experience is after attending a dance performance, the student writes a dance concert report. Another variable to consider as part of overall grade is attendance. These evaluation tools provide you with wide range of choices.

Short- and Long-Term Evaluation

The ballet teacher implements both a daily and long-term evaluation of each student and the class. Through careful observation of students the teacher creates a daily (or formative) evaluation. This evaluation covers what was learned in today's class and what needs to be practiced in the next class. After each class the teacher writes down notes regarding what the class has accomplished, what they need to practice, and any notes on individual student problems. Reviewing these notes aids the teacher in planning the next class.

A summative evaluation occurs at the end of a unit, term, or year. Like a final examination, this evaluation shows the progress of the student dancer in the course. The summative evaluation provides a profile of the student's technical development in relationship to the expected standards for beginning ballet. Both formative and summative evaluations are necessary in the ballet class. They combine with other evaluation tools to form the basis for the student's final grade for the course.

Criterion-Referenced Evaluation

In ballet class, objectivity is essential for evaluation. Criterion-referenced evaluation provides the method that allows each student to achieve personal best while learning the expectations of the art. This type of evaluation gives the student the responsibility for learning and achievement and the teacher the ability to direct the teaching/learning process. Too often ballet and other dance forms have been construed as not being difficult courses. Because of the nature of dance, the testing is subjective. Implementing a performance testing strategy based on set criteria that are demanding, yet fair, gives the course validity and the teacher more credence as a professional educator.

Criterion-referenced evaluation establishes a criterion, or set of standards, that the students must meet. Ballet, with its specific standards for executing exercises and steps, lends itself well to this method of evaluation. Evaluate each student in terms of how well their performance meets the criteria established. The teacher selects exercises, steps, and criteria appropriate for each beginning level of study.

Students and teachers are partners in this type of testing. Everyone knows the exercises and steps that will be tested and the criterion for performance that have been taught and practiced before the test. In addition, students have had the opportunity to ask questions about the performance test items, and the teacher has given each student feedback to improve performance. This creates a win-win situation in performance testing.

Objectives guide the teaching/learning process and what will be tested. Many subject areas such as dance history, pedagogy, and terminology use the paper and pencil test, others cannot. Evaluating dance technique means evaluating performance. Once the performance is over, it is over. Performance test items evaluate the abilities of the students as they perform. The advantages of performance evaluation are that you can test each part of the performance, make specific comments about technique, and give immediate feedback to students.

Developing the Criteria

The teacher selects the specific items that make up the criteria for performing a step and determines the expectations for an excellent, good, average, below average, or poor performance. These criteria provide a measure by which to test student learning. Students know the criteria for performance testing while they are learning the set class. Repeat the same criteria consistently during learning and during testing. Explain the rating scale and its application to the material being tested. Since students with diverse backgrounds of performance experience are in the beginning class, clearly state a student's performance is not compared to others in the class but to the established criteria.

By implementing the self-check and the reciprocal teaching styles before a performance testing situation, students become more responsible for meeting the performance criteria (see chapter 2). They also become more responsible and aware of their own performances.

The two teaching styles of self-check and reciprocal encompass set criteria for evaluation. Each style uses a criterion checklist. If you choose these teaching styles as an evaluations mode, here is a different approach to self-check and reciprocal: The teacher selects criteria for performing the exercise or step and creates the self-check or reciprocal checklist. The student does a self-check, or in pairs students rate each other using the self-check list. If a student receives a score of four points on a five-point scale and wants to obtain a perfect score of five, the student requests the teacher to observe his or her performance. The teacher rates the student using the same checklist. The teacher, as an expert, observes the student's performance of the exercise, step, or combination. If the teacher observes excellence in the performance, then the student receives a five or perfect score, depending upon the rating scale.

Administering Performance Examinations

Evaluating students in ballet class is done primarily through performance examinations. These examinations in the beginning class cover basic exercises and steps presented in short combinations. Since most beginning students are not familiar with performance examinations, the teacher prepares and rehearses them. By the end of the semester, the beginning student performs an entire ballet class as a technique examination, as a music student performs a jury.

To insure enough time for testing, schedule two class periods for a performance examination. This gives the teacher a safety factor; if a student is absent for the first day, then test that person the next test day. This provides a way for the student to be tested with a group, rather than alone. Explain to students the importance of attendance on a performance examination day. Include in the course syllabus procedures to handle absence on a performance examination day. If there is a large number of students in the class, the teacher may not be able to see them all perform the entire set class in one day. By allocating two days for testing, the teacher can control these variables in performance evaluation.

Preparing Students for the Test

When preparing students for a performance examination, the students should know the material with some level of comfort and responsibility for their performance. The students practice the examination several times in class with time allotted for questions and suggestions on how to improve their performance. Conduct practice sessions facing away from the mirrors. Keep the practice sessions as similar as possible to the actual testing situation.

Ask students to memorize the exercises and combinations so they concentrate on technique and applications of principles. Before the examination day, tell students several times the specific criteria for testing technique and principles as they apply to each exercise or step. This focuses students on the important aspects of each exercise or step. Question students as to what the criteria are for performing specific exercise or step (e.g., "What criteria will I be looking for in the battement dégagé?"). Explain to students that they should not worry if they forget a sequence, that you are assessing their technique, or how they perform an exercise or step.

Beyond testing the technique in executing a step, exercise, or combination, other components of the performance examination include knowledge, rhythm, quality, poise, and overall performance. Define each of these terms as part of the teaching process before the technical examination.

- *Technique* is the skill used to execute the step, exercise, and combination accurately, combined with the application of ballet principles.

- *Knowledge* refers to knowing or remembering the step, exercise, or combination.

- *Rhythm* includes performing the step to the music with the correct tempo, counts, and accents.

- *Quality* of movement relates to the dancer performing the step with dynamics, using breath phrasing, and giving the movement sequence proportion.

- *Poise* encompasses using the performance attitude with confidence and assurance.

- *Overall performance* is the summary of these attributes combined into the dancer's performance.

> *Rule:*
>
> You can only say the correction; students have to implement, retrain, and internalize it.

Preparing Yourself for Testing

The exercises and combinations you construct are short and repetitive so that students remember them easily, and you can test several students at one time. After you have set the exercises and combinations, try not to change them during the practice sessions. Changing the set exercises or combinations leads to confusion and frustration for the beginning dancer. The number of practice sessions necessary depends on the level of the class and how fast the class learns. Usually three practices of the set class is sufficient for the beginning level student. Students rehearse and perform facing a wall in the studio that does not have mirrors so that the teacher may observe if students are following dancers in the front line or if they genuinely know the material.

Prepare for the examination day through this process:

1. Memorize the criterion for evaluating each test item. It is imperative to have this checklist in mind while evaluating student performance.

2. Rehearse for the test and memorize it to ensure that the exercises, steps, and combinations are the same in rehearsal as in the testing situation.

3. Write out the exercises and combinations clearly with the corresponding record or compact disc name, side, and selection number. Include counts, preparation, combination, ending, and comments.

4. Revise these notes during practice, and bring them to the performance exam as a reference. The notes clarify any questions or discussions that students might have regarding the counts or sequence of an exercise or combination.

Evaluating Barre Exercises

Before testing the barre exercises, ask the students to line up in the order in which their names appear on your roll. This helps you in observing and recording the test information quickly. All of the students, half the class, or smaller groups execute the exercises at the barre. One of the problems in small groups is that the remainder of the class becomes cold while waiting to perform.

These are the steps for the barre portion of the performance test:

1. Begin by demonstrating and verbally presenting the exercise to the music.

2. Check the tempo of the music with the students before the actual performance.

3. Answer any questions students might have before they execute the exercise.

4. Train yourself to view several students at the same time to determine if their work meets the criterion established.

5. View both sides of the exercise; this provides a double check for evaluating the movement.

For the beginning student, accuracy is more important than speed in performance.

Evaluating the Center

To test students efficiently in the center, the teacher divides the class into small groups of three or four students to perform the center barre exercises and combinations. Number the groups one, two, three, and so on. Decide if group one is comprised of those students whose last names begin or end at the alphabet. With each center combination, rotate the groups so that different groups of students become the first group. For the first combination, the first group performs first. For the second combination, group two performs the combination first, followed by group three, and so on.

Groups comprise three or four students. Direct students to stand in a specified formation in their group: in a triangle or staggered square, and have the students change from back to front positions or lines between each combination. These formations help you to view all students at once as they dance. Before the group performs the second side, they invert the triangle or switch lines in the square formation from front to back so that everyone has an opportunity to perform in the front line. The round robin process ensures that each group performs a combination first.

These are the steps for the center portion of the test:

1. The teacher presents the combination with music.

2. The class practices the combination with music before they perform it in groups.

3. The teacher asks if there are any questions. If necessary, the teacher reviews the combina-

tion by performing it with the students before testing them in their groups.

4. The teacher starts with one group dancing at a time, while the others wait outside the studio. This provides a quiet atmosphere for the group performing to concentrate on their work without background noise or distractions.

5. The teacher observes the performance of the combination on both sides before evaluating it.

6. The teacher repeats the combination a total of four times for petit allégro, then begins the combination on the other side. Adagio combinations include both sides. The teacher executes grand allégro combinations, depending on their length, two to four times.

7. The teacher asks the students to repeat the combination if unsure of their scores.

For grand allégro combinations traveling across the studio, the first group completes the combination, before the next group begins. For jumping, or sauté, combinations (e.g., changement, échappé sauté) ask each group to stand facing front in different parts of the studio. One group at a time performs the jump combination for you to observe and rate. A short musical interlude between each group's performance gives you time to score and move on to the next group.

Rating and Grading the Performance Examination

The performance examination contains exercises and steps. These components have a criterion for performance and a rating scale for determining how well a performance meets the criterion.

Choosing the Rating Scale

Rating ballet performance can be done in several ways. The fastest and simplest way is to create the checklist. List the exercises, steps, or combinations in a column. In a second column, rate the student's performance with either a check or a minus. The advantage of using a checklist is that it is fast; the disadvantage is that the checklist does not provide details. This type of test does not discriminate how the step or exercise was performed.

The Likert scale is another type of performance test. The rating scale range is from five to zero, five being the highest score and zero, the lowest. Another variation of the Likert scale uses four as the highest rating and zero as the lowest. Using a rating scale provides levels of discrimination. These are grades with the five-point scale:

- Five represents an excellent execution of the step; all components and important parts are present at least 90 percent of the time.

- Four is a good execution of the step with most components and important parts present in performance at least 80 percent of the time.

- Three is average execution of the step, performed accurately at least 70 percent of the time, indicating that this step or exercise needs practice.

- Two designates that the step or exercise is below average, performed accurately less than 70 percent of the time, and needs a great deal more practice and refinement.

- One refers to a poor execution of the step, performed with less than 60 percent accuracy. This score indicates the student is not on the right track.

- Zero indicates that the student did not perform the step at all because of he or she is unable to dance or is absent from class.

Another method of evaluating characteristics of performance such as technique, sequencing, coordination of arms and head, transitions, musicality, and presence uses percentages. Allocate a specific percentage to each characteristic of performance depending on its importance, with the total categories equaling 100%.

Rating the Performance Examination

To prepare for recording ratings in the testing situation, do the following:

- Draw a grid that lists the students' names down the left side of the paper.

- Write the steps, exercises, and other components across the top of the paper.

- Organize students in alphabetical order at the barre and in groups in the center to facilitate evaluating a large group of students.

Before evaluating students in a beginning class,

- the teacher presents the step or combination with music and counts, and

- the students practice the step or exercise and ask questions before they begin the actual performance testing.

During the evaluation, the teacher

- observes one or two students' performance in each direction of the exercise or the alternation of a combination before making a judgment;

- looks at the entire body of the student or students performing, not just at the feet and legs;

- allows for "technical difficulties." Beginning students may be nervous when asked to perform even though they may know the steps; and

- permits students to perform the exercise or combination again.

You can defuse tension from student performance examinations by planning ahead. The teacher does the following:

- Prepares the students for the performance examination.

- Selects the exercises, steps and combinations that will be evaluated at the end of the unit. The performance examination contains content from the unit that the students have completed.

- Memorizes the list of criteria for each exercise and step before the performance examination.

- Remains objective and consistent while scoring without regards to the personality of the student and his or her behavior in class.

- Sets a level of discrimination in scoring that matches the course.

With practice, you will gain skill and speed, as well as discriminating powers in evaluating student performance.

At the final practice session and on the day of the performance exam, explain in detail how you score performance. You should do these things at the end of the performance examination:

- Show your scoring sheets to the students.

- Tell students if they do not understand why they got a certain score they should discuss it with you.

- Indicate that you need to see the student perform the exercise or combination again to explain the score. After performing an exercise or combination again students are usually able to tell you why they received that particular score.

- At the next class meeting, give students a slip of paper that translates their barre and center scores into numerical or letter grades.

Rules:

When scoring performance examinations, take into consideration that this may be the student's first experience in performing, but also the student's first experience in taking a performance examination. Remember, these are beginning students.

Grading the Performance Examination

Grading student performance in a beginning ballet class presents a dilemma for the teacher. When receiving a grade students who have had little or no ballet experience are intimidated by other class members who have had previous training. In an academic ballet class, explain to the students that they will not be compared to other class members when you are grading their performance. They will be evaluated in relation to the established criteria for performing basic ballet technique. In criterion-referenced evaluation, the teacher views each student's performance, regardless of previous training, in relation to the set standards for performance appropriate for beginning ballet. In part II of this book, each unit contains a guide for developing criteria for evaluation of performance, and an Assessment Checklist accompanies each exercise and step.

In a performance evaluation situation, the teacher rates each student by how well the student performs the given exercise or combination and meets its criterion. For this evaluation method to work successfully, explain how it works and what the expectations for individual performance are in the class. Reinforce how criterion-referenced evaluation works throughout the term and especially before any performance testing situation.

Performance evaluations make students nervous, since they may be unfamiliar with the methods used in dance performance testing. It is imperative that the teacher conduct the rehearsals and testing situation as identically as possible, without any unsettling or last-minute surprises. If problems arise during the test that are beyond your control, try to minimize them so that the students feel secure. There should be no surprises during the performance evaluation.

Written Reports and Examinations

Many beginning students have never seen a ballet or dance performance. During the term, the teacher can require students to attend a ballet or other type of dance performance and write a dance concert report. If a professional, university, or high school concert is unavailable, then a videotaped performance will suffice. After viewing the performance students write a report based on their observations and discuss the following aspects of the performance. Items students should discuss in their reports include

- choreography,
- performance qualities of the dancing, and
- production elements such as lighting and costuming.

The concert report assignment gives students an opportunity to see a live or videotaped dance performance and hopefully creates for them the desire to become an audience member at future concerts.

Written examinations reinforce learning ballet terminology, principles, rules, and protocols for the beginning student and further strengthen the movement-language connection. Written examinations include multiple choice, true-false, matching, and other types of questions. The first written examination tests students' ability to recognize ballet terminology and match definitions with terms. For the second written examination, expect students to memorize and write the ballet terminology. Presenting the ballet terminology in two stages, first recognizing and then writing the term, gives students a better chance to succeed. You may find that some students with previous ballet experiences consider it unnecessary to study for the written test. Often these students are surprised at their test results.

Summary

Assessment is a global term that encompasses evaluation and evaluation tools. Evaluation in the ballet class is formative, ongoing throughout the semester, and summative, conducted at the end of the semester. Evaluation tools measure the psychomotor, cognitive, and affective domains. In the ballet class, the major focus is on the psychomotor domain through the use of the performance evaluation. The performance exam is a criterion-referenced evaluation, where students are evaluated against a set of standards for performance of exercises and steps.

At the beginning of the term, pre-assessement of the class provides the teacher with a physical profile of each student's body type and knee variance. The teacher continually prepares the students for the performance test. Likewise, the teacher prepares for administering the performance test by selecting and memorizing the exercises and steps and the performance criteria for each, organizing the music, moving the students through the exam efficiently, and choosing a rating scale or checklist.

Written reports and examinations engage the cognitive domain and test ballet vocabulary, rules, and principles. Informally, the teacher monitors the affective domain through observing students during the class and how their self-esteem, confidence, and poise develops over the course. Grades are a compilation of performance, written reports and examinations, and class attendance.

Part I laid the foundation of the what, how, why, and when to teaching exercises and steps in the beginning ballet class. You are now ready to move on to part II, which presents four teaching units that guide you in constructing and teaching the beginning ballet class.

Teaching Progressions for Beginning Ballet Classes

Part II is a series of four units that present appropriate beginning ballet exercises and steps in a logical progression. Each unit represents three to four weeks of a high school or college term. Although each unit has been designed to be covered in a three- to four-week time period, it may take longer for students to acquire all the material. The number of class meetings, the amount of class time, and the rate at which the students in the class learn may all be influential factors. The materials in each unit are adaptable to studio and other teaching situations. The guiding principle in part II is "quality rather than quantity."

In each unit, there are several features. Opening each unit, a teacher's planner offers directions for implementing the teaching/learning process during the three- to four-week unit. Within each unit, the Teacher's Planner contains the following:

- Objectives in the cognitive, psychomotor, and affective domains
- Teaching strategies
- Assessment
- Teacher responsibilities
- Performance test content

Following the teacher's planner, the new barre exercises and new center steps are presented. Each exercise and step description includes the following information, as appropriate:

- Photographs showing the correct technique
- Definition with pronunciation cues for the French terms
- Principles that relate to the exercise
- Rules and protocols for performing the exercise or step
- Verbal depiction of the exercise describing in detail how the exercise or step is executed
- Arm positioning for barre exercises and center steps
- Purpose of the exercise
- Music and timing of the step
- Standard introductory movements or preparation describing the arm, foot, and head

movements used to get started (note: after unit I, the standard introductory movements are referred to as "preparation")

- Introductory and transitional steps with which the center step being described either introduces or links
- Proper breathing or breath phrasing to be used during execution of the exercises and steps
- Progressions include the sequence for learning the exercise or step
- Teaching cues presenting alternative ways to explain the movement
- Teaching images offering visual, anatomical, and kinesthetic aids for learning the movement
- Assessment Checklist providing the specific criteria for performing the exercise or step correctly
- Specific errors highlighting the problems associated with performance
- Standards and variations amplifying the extensions of the exercise or step appropriate for beginners

At the end of both the barre and the center's new steps are barre progressions and center progressions. These progressions indicate how to develop exercises and combinations for exercises and steps introduced in previous units (thus, they first appear in unit II).

In addition, each unit starts with an illustration of the Pyramid of Principles of Classical Ballet and highlights the principles covered in that unit. Notice that the principles build from the base of the pyramid and also extend vertically to include basic balance principles in each unit. As you introduce the principles, you'll notice that there are expected standards of performance. Be aware that there are common errors that may also be observed in your students' performance. The following chart (a) links the principles used throughout the units with their expected standards, and (b) identifies the most common errors encountered in applying the principles. Couple this information with the Assessment

Standards and Common Errors in Performance at the Barre and in the Center

Principle/Rule	Standard	Error
Alignment	• maintained	
Turn-out	• maintained	
Stance	• maintained	
Distribution of weight	• equal distribution/two feet • centered over one foot • foot triangle maintained	• unequal • incorrect or shifts
Transfer of Weight	• body weight shift from two legs to one leg • transfer at the base of the demi-plié	• incomplete shift
Counterpull	• demi- and grade plié	
Squareness	• shoulders squared • hips parallel to shoulders and floor	• twisted • hips tipped or twisted
Pull-up or Lift	• continuous in leg(s) or body	• no pull-up • settling/sitting
Aplomb	• vertical movements with relevé, demi-plié and fondu	
Counterbalance	• working leg extended over 20 degrees derrière	• not used
Balance	• body centered on two legs, full foot or relevé • body centered on supporting leg, full foot	• uncentered • uncentered

Checklist and Specific Errors with each exercise or step (in units I through IV) to get a complete picture of correct performance.

Part II presents a logical, sequential teaching plan for you to present the exercises and steps that should be included in the first term for the beginning bal-let student. Be aware that it may take students awhile before they are ready to be tested or to learn new material or to progress to the next unit. Thus, select from the materials provided in order to adapt it to your situation and to your students' skill levels.

Teacher's Planner for Unit I

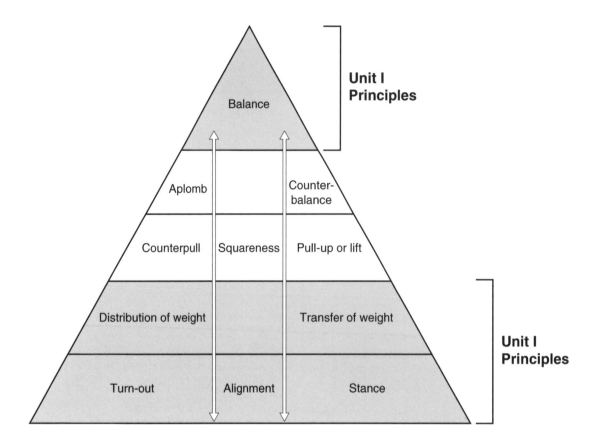

Unit I introduces students to the ballet class. In this unit, you'll find guidelines outlining teacher expectations for the first day in class. The first moving day acquaints students with basic positions, exercises, principles, and protocols practiced within the structure of the class. In this unit, the focus is on learning basic barre exercises that are repeated in the center, then simple steps are introduced. You may use the following information to plan your unit.

Objectives of the Unit

The objectives for the unit encompass the cognitive, psychomotor, and affective domains as follows.

Cognitive Domain

The students will be able to

- identify and say new ballet terms;
- translate action words to ballet terminology;
- follow directions given for performance of exercises and steps; and
- apply principles, rules, and protocols to class work.

Psychomotor Domain

The students will be able to

- execute classical foot and arm positions, First and Second port de bras;
- perform the following barre exercises: demi-plié; battement tendu; battement tendu with demi-plié; battement dégagé; rond de jambe à terre; foot exercises: point and flex, foot presses and pedals; and grand battement;
- execute the following center steps: coupé, pas de bourrée, walk, chassé, révérence;
- perform appropriate barre and center protocols; and
- transpose the same step to the other side.

Affective Domain

The students will be able to

- attend to directions given by the teacher,
- cooperate in class activities, and
- understand and demonstrate basic ballet protocols.

Teaching Strategies

The following teaching strategies apply within unit I:

- Teaching styles: command, practice, inclusive
- Teacher modeling: demonstration of new exercises and steps using English action words and French terms (i.e., "say" and "do"); verbal cues; and repetition to build a visual and motor memory of what is "correct"

Assessment

Consider the following methods of assessment:

- Pre-assess body types and knee variations.
- Assessment Checklist (the performance criteria) utilizes cues for the performance of each exercise and step.
- Periodic, informal evaluations monitor if knowledge and skills are attained.

Teacher Responsibilities

The following list is a self-check of your responsibilities when teaching unit I:

- Pre-assessment of each student identifies body type, knee variance, previous movement experience, and level of dance training
- Clear demonstration of exercises and steps
- Clear direction and cueing of exercises and steps
- Clear counting of music
- Clear explanation and application of principles, rules, and protocols
- Group feedback
- Individual attention
- Pace of the class
- Open and risk-free atmosphere

Performance Test Content

Student performance evaluations for unit I follow.

Principles and Rules

The student will demonstrate

- unit I principles: alignment, stance, turn-out, distribution of weight, transfer of weight, and balance; and
- unit I barre and center rules and protocols.

At the Barre

The student will demonstrate the following:

1. Classical foot positions
2. Demi-plié
3. Battement tendu
4. Battement dégagé (modified)
5. Point and flex the foot
6. Foot presses and pedals
7. Grand battement (modified)

In the Center

The student will demonstrate the following:

1. Stage directions
2. First and Second port de bras
3. Four battement tendu en croix
4. Coupé
5. Pas de bourrée
6. Ballet walks
7. Chassé
8. Révérence (not tested)

Written Examination

The student will

- define movements (in English), and
- associate a few basic French terms with the appropriate action.

First Day of Ballet Class

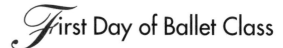

Generally, on the first day that the ballet class meets, the teacher reviews the course syllabus, expectations, attendance requirements, and dance attire for the class. Be specific about what type of dance attire and shoes should be worn for class, and suggest locations where students can purchase their attire. Ask students to have their dancewear and shoes by the next class meeting.

At this first class meeting, ascertain if any student has had an injury, surgery, or continued health problem. So as not to disclose personal information in front of the class, ask students who have these conditions to visit with you after the class is over. Talk with each student one at a time, away from the group, regarding their health problem. If a student had, for example, a broken foot or knee surgery, you need to know the extent of the injury, when the injury or surgery occurred, and if the student has a doctor's permission to dance. The student must be able to handle the intense work of the class. It is equally important to ascertain if a student has diabetes, epilepsy, asthma, or any chronic disease that requires immediate attention from a health professional. As the teacher you are responsible for the students in your class. Know their health history and prepare for any emergency. Be familiar before the class starts with school procedures for emergencies and accidents.

While you are talking about the course, pass a sheet of paper around to each student to indicate name and amount of previous movement or dance training. It is important to emphasize to the students that this is beginning ballet class and that dance experience is not necessary to enroll in the class.

Often in the beginning ballet class, the students' range of dance experience varies from none to many years of study. Beware, the number of years of training may not reflect the actual level of the individual. If the training lacked precise correction of the person's technique, the dancer exhibits bad habits. Retraining a dancer is not an easy process. The individual often resists instruction that differs from what they have known. Some students perform exercises and steps in a different manner, depending on the school or method under which the student studied. Ballet etiquette is for the student to follow the style of the teacher conducting the class.

If students indicate that they have had extensive dance training, ask them to stay after class is dismissed. Remind these students that the ballet class is for beginners, that the pace will be slow, and the content will cover only basic ballet technique. Their knowledge may be intimidating to beginning students who have no experience. These students should be encouraged to attend a class where you can observe and judge their technical level. Often programs hold placement classes for this purpose. Advise those students whose technique is beyond the beginning level to enroll in the appropriate class.

First Moving Class

The first moving class is the second class meeting. In this class, students take the first steps toward learning ballet. In these first few classes, the teacher presents only small amounts of material so that students are not overwhelmed and feel confident.

At the first moving class, spend time explaining the ballet class structure of the barre and the center. Then the teacher pre-assesses informally and quickly each student's body, and notes whether or not each has a knee variance before starting the classs.

Back and Front Views for Body Assessment

Ask the students to stand in parallel First position at the barre or standing in the center of the studio. Observe their body alignment by looking at their backs. Is the body symmetrical? Are the shoulders level? Are the hips level? How long is the back? How long are the legs? What are the body proportions? Does the individual have a long or short waist? How long is the neck? Does the student stand tall and straight or slouch?

While students are standing in parallel First position, it is important to note the hips, knees, and ankles. Especially check the knee structure. Are the knees hyperextended? Are the legs bowlegged? If bowlegged, does the leg bow out only in the lower leg or in both the upper and lower leg? Are the ankles perpendicular to the floor? Do the ankles roll inward or outward?

Side View for Body Assessment

Next, view the body from the side, and mentally draw a plumb line from the ear to the front of the ankle joint, passing through the shoulder, hip socket, and knee. This simple test indicates the student's body alignment and weight distribution in everyday life. Note, is the head forward or back? Is the rib-cage hyperextended? Is the student "sway-backed"?

There may be so many students in the class that conducting a body pre-assessment may seem overwhelming. With practice, you will be able to record all of these items in your mind for each student. In the beginning you may want to write notes about each student's body profile for you to refer to until you have it memorized. Review each person's body pre-assessment while planning your classes.

Teaching Classical Alignment

Alignment is a compilation of the body parts positioned together. The body is a dynamic structure that moves efficiently as a whole and is responsive to movement of its parts. The entire body is like a set of building blocks. If one block is out of alignment, it affects everything above or below.

Teaching Beginning Ballet Technique

Once the body is out of alignment, other body parts make compensations that cause misalignment and eventually injuries. All major joints (toes, ankle, knee, hip, and wrist, elbow, shoulder, and spine) are affected.

Practical Application Exercise for Standing Alignment

Students stand in parallel First position (knees and feet directed forward, with the insides of the feet parallel, slightly separated and directly under the hips), then in classical First position. Here is the practical application:

1. Head is posed and centered on top of the spine.
2. Eyes focus forward and slightly upward (as if looking just over the horizon or focusing into the balcony seats in a theater).
3. Neck stretches upward from the shoulder girdle.
4. Shoulders are down, level, and relaxed.
5. Ribs are relaxed (the rib cage is in a neutral position between expansion or contraction).
6. Abdominal muscles engage, lift, and press in toward the spinal column.
7. Hips are level and legs outwardly rotate deep within the hip socket.
8. Pelvis centers under the shoulders.
9. Tail drops downward.
10. Knees lift and stretch, but are not hyper extended.
11. Ankles and insteps lift.
12. All five toes remain on the floor.
13. The foot triangle is maintained (first and fifth metatarsals, and heel on the floor).
14. Weight is evenly distributed between both feet.
15. Standing in classical First position, the teacher visualizes the plumb or aplomb line drawn down the front of the body from the center of the head, through the sternum, through the center of the pubic bone, and down between the heels.
16. Viewing the body from the side, you mentally draw the plumb or aplomb line down the side of the body from the front of the ear; through the shoulder joint, hip joint, and knee; and falling in front of the ankle bone.

As the dancer stands in alignment, the arms hang slightly in front of the body with the elbows lifted outward and away from the body. The arms slightly round with the top of the arm facing upward and the palms facing the dancer.

Practical Application Exercise for Supine Alignment

You may teach alignment by having students lie down on the floor. The floor provides a stable surface on which the students are better able to sense this integrated position. When lying supine on the floor, the entire back rests on the floor in an aligned position with the curve at the waistline maintained. Imagine pulling the navel toward the spine. The hip bones lift slightly toward the bottom of the rib cage to create a minimal foreshortening that helps strengthen the abdominal muscles and lengthen the spine. The pelvis is not "tucked" to the extent that the third curve of the spine (at the waist) is touching the floor. To check this, the dancer should be able to slide a hand between the waist and the floor. The dancer strives to get the entire spine to rest on the floor, allowing for the natural curve in the lower back. This aligned position may not be possible in the beginning. An alternate option is to lie supine on the floor with the legs separated by the width of the pelvis, the knees bent, and the feet resting on the floor. To further relax the back into the floor, raise the head slightly. The teacher checks that the third curve remains. The dancer then lowers the head to the floor and slides the feet out along the floor until the legs are straight.

These supine positions on the floor support and reinforce a kinesthetic sense of good alignment that transfers to a standing position. The beginning student repeats these alignment exercises often to develop a kinesthetic sense and refine proper alignment.

Basic Principles

Carefully construct the first class in which the students move. In this class, introduce them to basic concepts of alignment, weight distribution, turnout, and stance (see chapter 3). Explain the use of the barre, how to stand facing the barre, and how the hands rest on the barre.

Weight Distribution

Use the following guidelines to establish correct weight distribution:

- Explain the importance of weight distribution as it relates to alignment and balance.
- Teach how to center the weight over the foot triangle.

- Place the body weight vertically centered over the foot triangle.
- Stress proper weight distribution that allows movement in any direction.

Practical Application Exercise for Weight Distribution

Stand in parallel First position, facing the barre. In an aligned position, bounce up and down gently, lifting the heels off the floor. Perform eight bounces and on the final bounce place the weight over the foot triangle. The entire foot rests on the floor. Ask students to place their weight over their heels, then return the weight to over their arches (center of the foot triangle). Repeat the bounce exercise again.

Turn-out

Use the following guidelines establish correct turn-out:

- Turn-out emanates from the hip joint and extends through the upper and lower legs and feet.
- Turn-out should be the dancer's natural rotation from the hip joints that is approximately 90 to 100 degrees and must be maintained equally by both legs.
- Knees align with the pelvis and the feet.
- The knee cap (patella) falls directly between the second and third toes.
- The ankles are perpendicular to the floor so that the feet do not roll either inward or outward.
- The vertical alignment from the hip through the legs, knees, ankles, and feet remains regardless if the joints are straight or flexed.

Practical Application Exercise for Turn-out

Stand in parallel First position facing the barre. In classical alignment, center the weight over the arches of the feet. Engage the abdominals and outwardly rotate the legs from the hip sockets. Again, center the weight over the arches, because it tends to settle back on to the heels in a turned-out position. Sense the outward rotation of the legs and feet; sense the weight centered over the arches.

Beginning students usually accomplish the turned-out position by first turning out their feet instead of rotating from the hips. To instill the fact that turn-out comes from the hip socket, direct students to lie on their backs. Ask them to place their legs in parallel position and then outwardly rotate the legs from the hips to the turned-out position. This exercise facilitates students' understanding of turn-out.

Stance

Next, students learn stance with weight shared equally by both feet. The classical foot positions are the blueprint for where movements pause. It is important to establish these positions in your students' movement and muscle memory.

Practical Application Exercise for Stance

Have students face the barre, and introduce First, Second, and Third positions of the feet. Explain to them that the dancer remains in these classical foot positions

- to kinesthetically learn the position,
- to rest, and
- to regain balance before shifting weight to one foot or in a different direction.

First Position: Heels are together with the legs rotating outward. This angle varies from 90 to 100 degree angle, depending on the structure and skill level of the dancer. Distribute the weight equally on both feet (see figure I.1a).

Second Position: Feet separate approximately shoulder-width apart, depending on the structure and skill level of the dancer. Both legs turn out the same amount, distributing weight equally on each foot. The great toes are on a straight line parallel to the dancer's front (see figure I.1b).

Third Position: Legs are turned out, with the front foot crossing to the instep or middle of the back foot. Distribute the weight equally on both feet (see figure I.1c).

Fourth Position: For the beginning dancer, Fourth position from First (figure I.1d) or Third position (figure I.1e) is the most appropriate. In all Fourth positions, one foot is in front of the other. The space between the feet is equal to the length of one foot. Each leg is equally turned out. Distribute the weight equally on both feet. Shoulders and hips remain square.

Fifth Position: Fifth position is executed in two ways. In the Cecchetti method, the feet cross with the heel of the front foot at the joint of the great toe of the back foot (figure I.1f). In the Russian School, the heel of the front foot crosses completely to the tip of the great toe of the back foot (figure I.1g). Distribute the weight equally on both feet. For the beginning dancer, the Cecchetti Fifth position is the most appropriate.

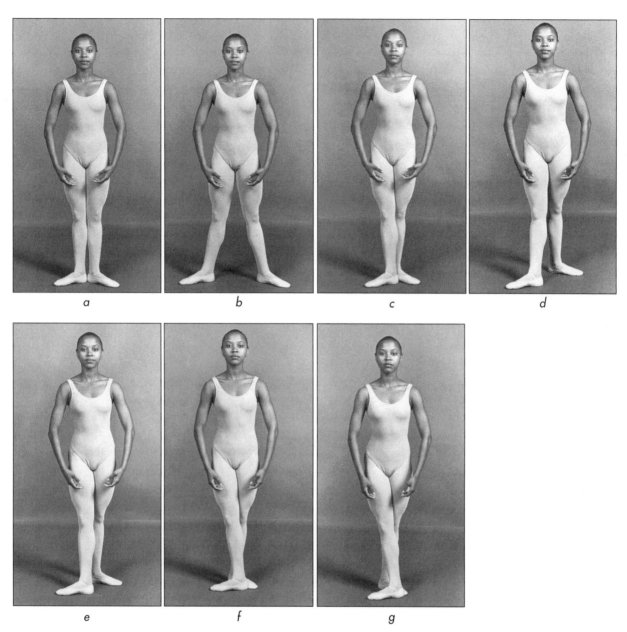

Figure I.1 Classical positions of the feet: a) First position. b) Second position. c) Third position. d) Fourth position from First. e) Fourth position from Third. f) Fifth position (Cecchetti Method). g) Fifth position (Russian School).

Unit I Barre

In unit I, the teacher introduces students to the ballet class environment. Before learning the basic barre exercises in this first unit, the teacher presents foundational principles, the classic foot positions, and explains the protocols practiced at the barre.

Demi-Plié
(duh-MEE plee-AY)

Definition: half-bend of the knees (see figure I.2)

Principles: alignment, stance, turn-out, weight distribution, transfer of weight

Rules and Protocols: standard introductory movement (preparation) and ending

Verbal Depiction: The demi-plié is usually part of the first exercise of the traditional barre. In all five classical foot positions, the knees bend as far as possible with the soles of the feet remaining on the floor.

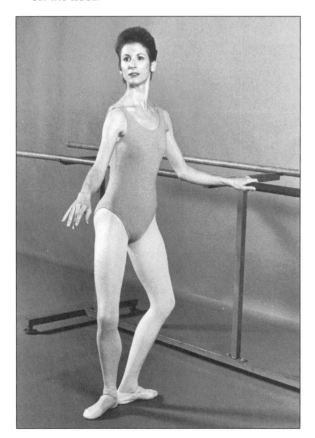

Figure I.2 Demi-plié, First position.

Arms: Beginning in the preparatory position (Fifth position en bas), the working arm opens to Demi-seconde during the descent of the demi-plié.

Purpose:
- Warms up the hip, knee, and ankle joints of the leg
- Increases strength and flexibility of the gastrocnemius, soleus, and other muscles of the lower leg

Music and Timing:
- Time signature: 4/4 or 3/4
- Tempo: moderate tempo with a legato quality
- Timing: Same number of measures for descent as ascent. In 4/4 time, two measures down and two measures up; in 3/4 time, one measure down and one up

Standard Introductory Movement or Preparation:
Start in Third or Fifth position, arms in the Preparatory position; execute a First port de bras. At the same time the arms open to Second position, the working foot extends to Second position. The working foot closes in the starting position while the arm away from the barre moves to its starting position. The arm nearest the barre extends for the hand to rest on the barre. The head movements for the preparation are standard: Tilt the head toward the barre as the arms lift; and then the head turns toward the center of the room as the arms extend to Second position.

If the demi-pliés begin with the feet in First position, the dancer executes a First port de bras that finishes in either Fifth position en bas, or the starting position for the exercise. At the beginning of the term, the teacher counts "1 - 2 - 3 - 4," then cues the movement as follows: on 5, "ready," count 6, "move the arms front" (First position), count 7, "side" (Second position), count 8, "place both hands on the barre." Once the dancers begin doing exercises with one hand on the barre, the teacher cues the dancers using the same movements for counts 5, 6, 7, and on count 8 of the music, place the hand on the barre.

During class, the term "side" often replaced "à la seconde or Second position." The teacher uses the term "side" as a cue for the direction or the position.

Breathing:
- On the preparation, the breath phrasing is standard.
- Inhale on the descent as the body counterpulls and the legs bend.
- Exhale on the ascent as the body continues to pull-up while the legs straighten.

Progressions: Introduce demi-pliés in First, Second, and then Third positions. Perform three demi-pliés in First, Second, and Third positions. Execute one side, stop, then do the other side.

Teaching Cues:

- "Engage your abdominals and lift in the torso while the legs bend."
- "Direct your knees between your second and third toes."
- "Inhale on the descent; exhale on the ascent."
- "Make the movement continuous."
- "Use all the music."
- "Dance the exercise."

Teaching Images:

- "Imagine a rubber band attached from the top of the head to the floor. As the body descends, the band stretches. As the body ascends the rubber band returns to its normal size."
- "Compare the demi-plié to an elevator, descending and ascending in the elevator shaft."

Assessment Checklist:

- ✓ Body weight centers over the legs through the descent and ascent.
- ✓ Turn-out from the hips through the legs and feet remains the same throughout the exercise.
- ✓ Alignment is stable throughout the exercise.
- ✓ The knees bend directly above the second and third toes of each foot.
- ✓ Distribution of weight over the foot triangle remains the same.
- ✓ Movement is continuous throughout the exercise.

Specific Errors:

- The foot triangle does not remain stable: instep drops and the feet roll in or out.
- Heel(s) lift at the bottom of the demi-plié.
- The movement stops at the bottom of the demi-plié.

Battement Tendu

(bat MAHN tahn-DEW)

Definition: stretched beating of the leg and foot (see figure I.3, a-d)

Principles: alignment, stance, turn-out, weight distribution, transfer of weight

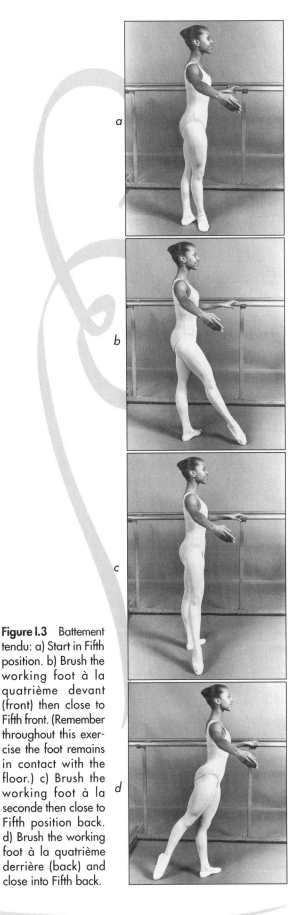

Figure I.3 Battement tendu: a) Start in Fifth position. b) Brush the working foot à la quatrième devant (front) then close to Fifth front. (Remember throughout this exercise the foot remains in contact with the floor.) c) Brush the working foot à la seconde then close to Fifth position back. d) Brush the working foot à la quatrième derrière (back) and close into Fifth back.

Rules and Protocols: use of the supporting and working leg, brushing and pointing the foot, use of directions

Verbal Depiction: From a full-foot position, the foot brushes along the floor as it extends through the instep/arch, the metatarsals, and the toes to a full point. In this position the tip of the first three toes rest on the floor in a fully extended position, supported by the arch, with the heel lifted high and forward. The toes never lift off the floor. On the return path, this sequence reverses. The foot flexes as it slides from the fully extended point through the toes, the metatarsals, and the heel into the closing position.

When executing a battement tendu, turn-out remains the same. The heel leads out to the pointed position and the toe leads back to the beginning full-foot position. In the battement tendu to à la seconde, the foot extends along the floor in a straight line to a point with the supporting great toe. On the return path, the heel leads back to the closing position.

Arms: The working arm may remain in Second position during the exercise.

Purpose:

- Increases flexibility of the ankles
- Develops full extension and proper alignment of the foot with the leg

Music and Timing:

- Time signature: 4/4 or 2/4.
- Tempo: moderate to fast tempo with a bright, sharp quality.
- Timing: In 4/4 time signature, use one measure for extension and one measure to close. Decrease to two counts out and two in; later, do one count in each direction.

Standard Introductory Movements or Preparation: Standing in First position (later in either Third or Fifth position), the dancer executes a First; all positions port de bras with standard head movements for either the two- or four-count preparation.

Breathing:

- On the preparation, use standard breath phrasing.
- Inhale on the extension phase.
- Exhale on the closing.
- Repeat this pattern over several repetitions or a complete set.

Progressions: Execute from First position, then from Third position; later, start in Fifth position; all positions facing the barre.

1. Before introducing battement tendu, teach the leg gesture directions separately: devant and à la seconde, and derrière.
2. Execute four battement tendu à la seconde, repeat on the other side, pause. Repeat exercise again beginning with the left leg.
3. Do four battement tendu devant, repeat on the other side, stop. Repeat exercise again beginning with the left leg.
4. Perform four battement tendu devant, repeat on the other side. Add four battement tendu à la seconde, repeat the other side. Delete the stops between the sequence.
5. Teach four battement tendu derrière, repeat on the other side, pause. Repeat the exercise beginning with the left foot.
6. Execute four battement derrière, repeat other side; add four battement tendu à la seconde, repeat other side. Delete the stops between the sequence.
7. Put the sequence together: four battement tendu en croix, stop; repeat other side.
8. Execute four battement tendu en croix on both sides, beginning with the right foot; then start the exercise again beginning with the left foot.
9. Decrease to two battement tendu en croix by the next unit.

Teaching Cues:

1. Battement tendu à la quatrième devant
   - "Heel leads out; toe leads in."
   - "Brush to a point directly in front of the shoulder, in line with the supporting heel."
2. Battement tendu à la quatrième derrière
   - "Toe leads out; heel leads in."
   - "Brush to a point directly behind the shoulder, in line with the supporting heel."
3. Battement tendu à la seconde
   - "On the extension, the working heel is slightly forward of the toes."
   - "Battement tendu extends to the Second position."

Teaching Images:

- "Imagine the foot brushing leaves away from you on the outward phase, and the leaves push the foot back on the inward phase."

- "Resist the floor as you articulate the foot from a full foot to a point and return the same way."

Assessment Checklist:

1. Battement tendu

   ✓ All five toes and the heel of the supporting leg maintain the foot triangle, lifting the instep.

   ✓ The working leg and foot stretches fully and is non-weight bearing.

   ✓ The foot keeps contact with the floor throughout the exercise.

   ✓ The working foot extends by brushing from the full-foot position and releasing in sequence the heel, the metatarsals, and the toes to a full-pointed position.

   ✓ On the return path, the working foot flexes and brushes in sequence the toes, metatarsals, and the heel to close in the full-foot position.

   ✓ The accent on the battement tendu is on the outward extension phase.

2. Battement tendu à la quatrième devant / derrière

   ✓ The foot slides in a straight line either directly in front or in back of the supporting heel.

   ✓ The fully pointed foot is directly in front or back of the heel of the supporting foot.

   ✓ On the extension phase, the supporting leg maintains turn-out; the heel leads forward (à la quatrième devant); the toe leads backward (à la quatrième derrière).

   ✓ On the closing phase, the toes lead in (à la quatrième devant); the heel leads forward (à la quatrième derrière).

3. Battement tendu à la seconde

   ✓ On the extension phase, the working heel is slightly forward of the great toe or the supporting foot.

   ✓ The working foot extends à la seconde with the great toes of both feet on the same line.

   ✓ On the return, the working heel remains forward of the great toe into the closing position.

Specific Errors:

1. Battement tendu

   - The heel drops toward the ground or sickles in or out.

2. Battement tendu à la quatrième devant / derrière

   - The working leg extends diagonally front or back.

3. Battement tendu à la seconde

   - The working leg extends to the side, behind or in front of Second position.

Standard Variation: Battement Tendu with Demi-Plié

Verbal Depiction: The battement tendu with demi-plié combines the two exercises of battement tendu and demi-plié. The battement tendu with demi-plié requires that both the supporting and working legs work in concert. The working leg performs the out and in actions of the battement tendu. At the same time, the supporting leg performs the down and up actions of the demi-plié. The body floats above these leg actions.

Progressions:

1. Perform battement tendu; demi-plié and straighten. Execute this modified exercise combination four times en croix.

2. Complete the battement tendu at the base of the demi-plié. From the demi-plié position, the working foot brushes out for the next battement tendu, while the supporting leg straightens simultaneously. Follow the battement tendu progression. Execute the battement tendu with demi-plié using the four, then later the two en croix patterns.

Battement Dégagé (Cecchetti) or Jeté (Russian)
(bat-MAHN day-ga-ZHAY or zhuh-TAY)

Definition: a beating of the entire leg and foot disengaged or thrown from the floor (see figure I.4, a-d)

Principles: alignment, turn-out, stance, weight distribution, transfer of weight

Rules and Protocols: use of the supporting and working leg, brushing and pointing the foot, and use of directions on and off the floor.

Verbal Depiction: The battement dégagé builds upon the action of the battement tendu, with the leg and foot continuing their extension barely off the floor. From either First or Fifth position, the

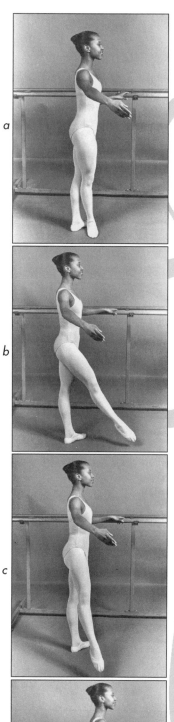

working foot brushes strongly along the floor through the extension phase of the battement tendu and continues to a full-pointed position off the floor. This extension is approximately two inches off the floor, or about a 20-degree angle. On the return phase, the pointed foot and leg stretch to the floor and through the battement tendu. The foot brushes out, releasing heel, metatarsals, and toes and returns to the floor in the reverse order to the closing position. The accent of the battement dégagé is on closing into the position.

Arms: The working arm remains in Second position during the exercise.

Purpose:

- Develops complete foot articulation and extension; consequently, increases suppleness of the ankle joint
- Facilitates sharp, quick, small movements of the entire working leg and foot in all directions

Music and Timing:

- Time signature: either 2/4 or 4/4.
- Tempo: moderate tempo, with a brisk, march-like quality.
- Timing: Brush out on "&"; close in on "the count" (e.g., "and, one").
- Modified timing: Brush out on count one, close in on count two.

Standard Introductory Movements or Preparation: Standing in Fifth position, the dancer executes a First port de bras with standard head movements for either the two- or four-count preparation.

Breathing:

- On the preparation, the breath phrasing is standard.
- Inhale on the extension phase.
- Exhale on the closing.
- Extend breath phrasing over several repetitions or a set.

Progressions:

- Begin in First position, brush to a point à la seconde on the floor, stretch off the floor, return to the point à la seconde on the floor, and close.
- Execute from First position devant and à la seconde; then teach derrière.
- Do one set of four in each direction creating the en croix pattern; go immediately to the

Figure 1.4 Battement dégagé: a) Start in Fifth position. b) Brush or dégagé the working foot 2 inches off the ground à la quatrième devant (front). c) Brush or dégagé the working foot 2 inches off the ground à la seconde (side). d) Brush or dégagé the working foot 2 inches off the floor à la quatrième derrière (back). Close in Fifth position.

other side without stopping, and repeat four times en croix.

- Execute from Third position four battement dégagé en croix in this modified form.

Teaching Cues:

- "&, in"; "out, in."
- "Keep the foot low, two inches off the floor."
- "Make your movement sharp."

Teaching Images:

- "Imagine your foot slicing or cutting through the air."
- "Cut through the air like a knife in exactly the same path (front, side, and back)."

Assessment Checklist:

1. Battement dégagé or jeté

   ✓ The working leg and foot stretch fully off the floor.

   ✓ The foot keeps contact with the floor through most of the foot extension phase of the exercise.

   ✓ The foot brushes and extends from the full-foot position, releasing in sequence the heel, the metatarsals, and the toes until reaching a full point off the floor.

   ✓ The foot and leg extend off the floor approximately two inches or 20 degrees.

   ✓ On returning to the floor, the foot flexes in sequential order (toes, metatarsals, heel) as it brushes to the full-foot closing position.

   ✓ The accent on the battement dégagé is on the closing.

2. Battement dégagé or jeté à la quatrième devant/derrière

   ✓ The foot slides in a straight line from the supporting heel.

   ✓ The fully extended foot is barely off the floor and directly in line with the supporting heel.

   ✓ On the extension phase, the heel leads forward (à la quatrième devant); the great toe leads backward (à la quatrième derrière).

   ✓ On the return phase, the toe leads back (à la quatrième devant); the heel leads forward (à la quatrième derrière).

3. Battement dégagé or jeté à la seconde

   ✓ The foot slides to a point off the floor in a straight line with the supporting toe.

   ✓ The heel of the working foot is slightly forward of the great toe.

   ✓ On the return path, the heel remains forward of the great toe to the closing position.

Specific Errors:

1. Battement dégagé or jeté

   - The foot and leg extend above 2 inches, or 20 degrees off the floor.

   - The heel drops toward the ground or sickles through the extension or return phase.

2. Battement dégagé or jeté à la quatrième devant/derrière

   - The working leg extends diagonally front or back.

3. Battement dégagé or jeté à la seconde

   - The working leg extends behind or in front of Second position.

Standards and Variations: Petit Battement Piqué (puh-TEE bat-MAHN pee-KAY): This exercise is also known as Battement Tendu Jeté Pointé (bat-MAHN tahn-DEW zhuh-TAY pwen-TAY). After the extension phase, the fully pointed foot taps the floor sharply one or several times. Each tap slightly rebounds to a dégagé. After the final battement dégagé (or jeté pointé), the working foot closes. Performing this exercise, students learn to use the working leg and pointed foot as an entity and acquire directional acuity. The progression for this exercise is en croix in decreasing repetitions of 4, 2, and 1.

Rond de Jambe à Terre en dehors or en dedans

(rawn duh zhahnb a tehr ahn duh-AWR) or (ahn duh-DAHN)

Definition: literally, the circular action of the leg on the floor. In reality, the working foot describes a half-circle on the floor performed in two directions. The working leg circles outward away from the supporting leg (or *en dehors*) and inward toward the supporting leg (or *en dedans*). (See figure I.5, a-d.)

Principles: alignment, turn-out, weight distribution

Rules and Protocols: supporting and working legs, brushing and pointing the foot, directions, and rotary movement

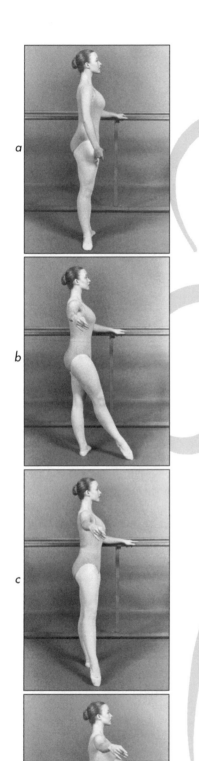

Verbal Depiction: The working leg, rotating from the hip joint, draws with the great toe a half-circle on the floor connecting the next half-circle by a battement tendu en cloche, which sweeps the working leg from either front to back or vice versa. The working leg circles outward away from the supporting leg (en dehors), and inward toward the supporting leg or (en dedans).

Regardless of whether the rond de jambe à terre en dehors begins in First position or à la quatrième derrière, the working leg brushes to battement tendu à la quatrième devant, with the heel of the working foot rotated up and forward. The working leg rotates through à la seconde with the heel slightly forward of the toe. When the working leg rotates to à la quatrième derrière, the heel of the working foot presses forward as the arch lifts slightly forward and upward extending the foot. To complete the rond de jambe à terre, the working foot brushes through the First position with all five toes and the heel on the floor. The foot should relax while moving through the First position before extending into the full-pointed position of the battement tendu.

The rond de jambe à terre en dedans reverses the directional pattern. Starting in First position or à la quatrième devant, the working leg executes a battement tendu en cloche and extends to battement tendu à la quatrième derrière. The leg rotates through à la seconde to a la quatrième devant, and ends with the brush of the full foot through the First position.

Throughout the execution of the rond de jambe à terre, center the body weight over the arch of the supporting leg, keeping the hips well turned out.

Arms: The working arm stretches in Second position.

Purpose: Develops the rotary movement of the entire working leg in a turned-out position, in both directions, while the pelvis remains stationary.

Music and Timing:

- Time signature: 3/4.

- Tempo: slow to moderate tempo with a light, flowing waltz quality.

- Timing: On the primary beat the foot brushes through First position to battement tendu; the two remaining counts of the measure complete the circular pattern. The accent is on the primary beat of the measure when the working foot passes through the First position.

Figure I.5 Rond de jambe à terre en dehors: a) Begin in First position. b) Working leg brushes à la quatrième devant (front). c) Rotate the working leg à la seconde. d) Continue to rotate the leg is à la quatrième derrière (back).

Standard Introductory Movement or Preparation: The beginning dancer performs a simplified version of the standard preparation. Standing in First position, the dancer executes a First port de bras. Standing in Fifth position, the dancer executes a battement tendu à la seconde, closing in Fifth position. A First port de bras and standard head movements for the preparation accompany the foot position changes. For the beginner, use a four-count preparation.

The standard preparation for rond de jambe à terre en dehors begins in Fifth position. The dancer executes a battement tendu devant en fondu, arms in First position. The working leg rotates to second position with the supporting leg straightening; the arms extend to Second position. The working leg rotates to à la quatrième derrière just before the first measure of the exercise. There are stylistic differences in the preparation depending on the school, the method, or the teacher.

Breathing:

- During preparation, inhale on the battement tendu devant en fondu; exhale on the rond de jambe portion.

- Inhale on the battement tendu phase.

- Exhale on the rotation phase.

- Extend breath phrasing up to four repetitions.

Progressions: In this unit, introduce the rond de jambe à terre in a modified form.

1. Define the pattern. En dehors (outward away from the supporting foot): Point the foot (pointé tendu) devant, hold for the measure; extend the working leg slightly off the floor and rotate and point the working leg à la seconde, hold for the measure; extend the working leg off the floor, rotate and point the working leg derrière, hold for the measure; close into First position, hold for the measure. Execute this exercise four times. Repeat the exercise en dedans (inward toward the supporting foot).

2. Another variation for teaching the step is point the foot (pointé tendu) devant, rond de jambe à terre en dehors to à la seconde, close in First position, hold. Pointé tendu à la seconde, rond de jambe à terre en dehors to derrière, close in First position, hold. Repeat the exercise four times. Reverse the one-quarter rond de jambes to perform en dedans.

Teaching Cues:

- "The working leg continually rotates in the hip socket throughout the circular path of the rond de jambe."

- "Front, side, back, First (position)."
- "Back, side, front, First (position)."
- "First (position), two, three."
- "Draw a half-circle with your big toe."
- "En dehors—out the door"; "en dedans—in the door."

Teaching Images:

- "Connect the dots—front, side, and back— with your big toe."

- "Imagine a piece of chalk attached to your big toe. This chalk outlines a perfect half-circle each time."

- "Imagine the working foot carving or scraping the inside of a wooden bowl."

Assessment Checklist

✓ The working foot keeps contact with the floor throughout the exercise.

✓ The foot brushes and extends from the full-foot position, releasing in sequence the heel, the metatarsals, and the toes until reaching a full-pointed position on the floor.

✓ The foot and leg rotate as a unit in a complete half-circular path from front to back (en dehors) or from back to front (en dedans).

✓ The hips remain quiet and do not move throughout the exercise.

✓ The foot flexes in sequential order (toes, metatarsals, heel) as it brushes to the full-foot position.

✓ The rond de jambe à terre exercise moves continuously without stops, except to change directions.

✓ The accent on the rond de jambe à terre is on the primary beat of the measure as the foot passes through the First position and extends into the battement tendu.

Specific Errors:

- The working foot does not draw a straight line from the supporting heel either in front or the back.

- The heel drops downward, resulting in a sickled foot throughout the exercise.

- The hip(s) move with the working leg during the execution of the exercise.

- The accent is either misplaced or not incorporated into the exercise.

- The toes come off the floor on the circular path.

Foot Exercises

To make the foot articulate as it releases or brushes to a point, the student learns and practices a series of foot exercises at the barre. The foot must be supple and responsive in all movements. There are two basic types of foot actions in ballet: 1. brushing from a full-foot position to a point and the return, and 2. releasing the foot from full foot through three-quarter relevé to a fully pointed foot on or off the floor and the return. In both of these foot actions, the sequence begins with a release through the heel, foot, metatarsals, and the tips of the toes, ending in touching the floor or pointing barely off the floor. On the return, first the tips of the toes touch the floor, if they have been off the floor, the toes flex continuing through the metatarsals and on through the foot until the heel returns to the floor. These two actions are the primary components of all exercises and steps that the student learns in ballet.

To fully articulate the foot, it becomes pliant, yet also resists releasing off the floor and returning to the floor. These qualities enable the dancer to gain control and dexterity in using the foot and are imperative for successful relevés and safe landing from steps performed in the air. Performing ballet depends a great deal on the foot actions that move the dancer through steps, poses, or movements. Aesthetically, a beautiful, expressive foot is a hallmark of classical ballet.

To prepare the student for the extensive footwork demanded by ballet, the beginning student executes foot exercises first at the barre and then in the center. These exercises include the following not only as preparation for learning steps in the center but also as a continued refinement of foot actions.

Principles: alignment, stance, turn-out, weight distribution, weight transfer, balance on two feet and one foot

Rules and Protocols: use of the supporting and working legs, articulation of the feet, pointing and flexing the foot

Verbal Depiction: In classical ballet, the pointed or plantar flexed foot is an important technical and aesthetic consideration. The foot points when it is in the air (en l'air). How the dancer points the foot is very important to the dancer's technique and development of line. The foot points from the ankle joint as an extension of the lower leg, forming a line from the knee downward through the toes. The front of the foot stretches long and away from the leg while lifting the arch and heel upward toward the leg. When the foot

points, the toes stretch, so that when the foot releases from the floor either by brushing, rising, or jumping, the entire bottom of the foot activates to execute the step or exercise. When the fully pointed foot rests on the floor in poses, positions or directions, this is called a pointe tendu.

Learning how to point the foot without tension gives it more flexibility and the ability to handle quick weight changes on and off the floor (see chapter 3).

Pointing and Flexing the Foot: The exercise begins in classical First position. The working foot brushes through battement tendu to à la seconde, later devant, and then derrière. In this exercise the entire foot points or flexes from the ankle. At the full extension of the working foot in its pointed position, the foot flexes: The heel presses forward; the foot sequentially flexes until the toes flex. At maximum flexion of the foot and toes, then the sequence reverses: First the heel, then the metatarsals, and finally the toes stretch back to the pointed position. The working leg remains at the same height, neither raising or lowering during the action. After executing the point and flex exercise, the working foot closes into First position.

Foot Presses: In First position, release the heel, and articulate through the foot until the toes and metatarsals remain resting on the floor. The objective is for the heel to lift to a height that it is perpendicular to the floor with all the toes and metatarsals firmly on the floor to the three-quarter relevé position. On the return, the heel remains high as the foot returns to the floor. During a foot press, imagine the foot resisting an outside force to complete a downward path, giving the action an image of power and strength.

Foot Pedals: Foot pedals are an extension of the foot press. In the foot pedal, the entire foot releases from a full foot to a pointed foot. The tips of the toes either rest on the floor or just above the floor. In performing the foot pedal, it is important that the foot initiates the action, not the leg. The foot resists the release, causing the knee to bend and the leg to raise slightly. On the return, the ankle flexes quickly or flicks to complete the final action of the foot stretching down toward the floor.

Arms: Facing the barre, the arms are near the sides of the body since both hands are on the barre.

Purpose: Develops articulation of the feet which is an important part of executing all exercises, steps, and jumps. In future units, execute the foot exercises before beginning the barre. The foot exercises become a pre-barre warm-up.

Music and Timing (foot points and flexes, foot presses and pedals):

- Time signature: 4/4 or 2/4.
- Tempo: Moderate with a sharp, bright quality.
- Timing: The foot points and flexes, with one measure for each action. The accent on foot pedals is "&, up."

Standard Introductory Movements or Preparation: Standing in First position facing the barre, the dancer executes a First port de bras ending with both hands placed on the barre.

Progressions: Perform foot points and flexes in a decreasing number from four, to three, to two, to one per side. Teach the exercise à la seconde, then devant and derrière. Execute the exercises on one side and then the other side. For example, brush to a point à la seconde, then flex and point three times, close in First position, and repeat the other side. Do the exercise in one direction on both sides; then add devant and derrière. Perform the exercise en croix, and later combine with battement tendu.

Execute foot presses in parallel First position, facing the barre. In this position, the path is directly up and down. Students monitor their performance by seeing and sensing when it is correct. Next, perform foot presses in classic First position.

For both foot presses and foot pedals the following progression is appropriate:

1. Eight in First position; repeat other side
2. Four per side twice
3. Two per side eight times
4. 16 foot presses/pedals with alternating feet

Teaching Cues:

- Point and flex: "Point and flex."
- Foot press: "Press the foot directly up, then down."
- Foot pedal: "Flick and press."

Teaching Images:

- Point and flex: "Draw a large arc up and down in space with your toes."
- Foot press: "Imagine a wad of bubble gum under your heel; your heel sticks to the gum as it lifts."
- Foot pedal: "Imagine your foot is on hot sand; you have to quickly lift it off the ground."

Assessment Checklist:

1. Foot points and flexes
   ✓ The entire foot points from the ankle.

   ✓ A straight line extends from the knee along the lower leg, the top of the foot, and the toes.

   ✓ In the pointed position the toes are straight.

   ✓ In the flexed position, the heel leads the articulation of the foot.

   ✓ The toes pull back in the flexed position.

2. Foot presses
   ✓ The heel lifts and the foot articulates to the three-quarter relevé position.

   ✓ All five toes and the metatarsals rest on the floor at the height of the press, with the weight centered over the foot triangle.

   ✓ The articulation is on a direct path upward and downward.

   ✓ The foot resists the upward and downward actions.

   ✓ The entire foot is relaxed in the full-foot position.

3. Foot pedals
   ✓ The entire foot articulates to a pointed position perpendicular to and just above the floor.

   ✓ The quality of the articulation is a flick, initiated with a sharp action at the ankle.

   ✓ The foot initiates the flick, not the knee.

Specific Errors:

1. Pointing the foot
   - The point comes from only the toes and metatarsals.
   - The ankle does not initiate the point.

2. Foot presses
   - The heel is not perpendicular to the floor.

3. Foot pedals
   - In the upward or downward path, the weight shifts inward or outward, causing the foot to roll in or out.

Grand Battement
(grahn bat-MAHN)

Definition: large beating or kicking action of the leg into the air (see figure I.6, a-e)

Principles: alignment, turn-out, weight distribution, transfer of weight

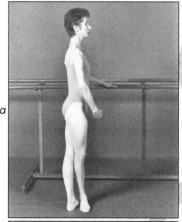

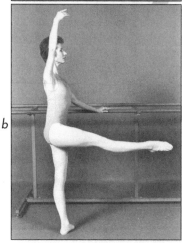

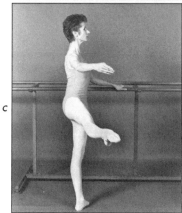

Figure I.6 Grand battement: a) Begin in Fifth position. b) Throw the leg à la quatrième devant (front) up to 90 degrees and close Fifth position front. c) Throw the leg à la seconde (side) up to 90 degrees and close Fifth position back. d) Throw the leg à la quatrième derrière (back) and close Fifth position back.

Rules and Protocols: use of supporting and working legs, brushing and pointing the foot, extending the stretched working leg 45 degrees off the floor, directions

Verbal Depiction: This exercise begins in First, later Third and then Fifth position. The working foot slides through a battement tendu and the leg is thrown upward 45, and later, 90 degrees. Think of the brush having a downward motion, pushing against the floor, which then creates an upward motion to the height of the extension. The action of the foot that pushes the leg into the air comes from the back of the pelvis. The leg then descends to the floor through the battement tendu to end in First, Third, or Fifth position.

The supporting leg remains perpendicular to the floor as the working leg extends in all directions. The pelvis remains centered and parallel to the shoulders except in the grand battement derrière, when the entire back and pelvis go into counterbalance (see chapter 3). The torso lengthens downward in the back and stretches upward in the front so that the body does not collapse and the leg kicks with ease.

Throw the working leg into the air quickly. The leg momentarily stops at the top of the extension and slowly descends into the closing position. Preserve turn-out throughout the exercise. Perform the grand battement with a straight supporting leg. The accent on the exercise is generally on the upward action. The "&" before the primary beat of the measure is the swift sweeping movement into the air.

Arms: Hold the port de bras for grand battement in Second position.

Purpose:

- Develops flexibility and strength of the working leg muscles
- Promotes flexibility of the hip socket

Music and Timing:

- Time signature: 2/4 or 4/4.
- Tempo: a slow to moderate march, gallop, or polka, with a quick, sharp quality.
- Timing: In 2/4 time brush up on "&" on count 1 stop at the top, brush down and close on "& 2." The close comes at the end of the measure.

Standard Introductory Movement or Preparation: Standing in First, Third, or Fifth position, the dancer executes First port de bras with standard head movements.

Teaching Beginning Ballet Technique

Breathing:

- Inhale as the leg extends in the air.
- Exhale on the return.
- Breath phrasing extends over several repetitions or a set.

Progressions: Teach the grand battement to students by instructing them to first lie supine on the floor. On their backs students should sense their alignment, keeping the three curves of the back. Stretch and outwardly rotate the legs directly underneath the body in classic First position. Initially, have students place their hands behind their waists to support the curve. Then without music, direct them to throw the leg devant as high as possible, and return to First position without the torso and hips responding. Execute four grand battements with the right leg devant and then with the left leg. Monitor the working leg so that it extends only to 45 degrees to control the hips and back.

When executing the grand battements à la seconde lying on their backs, ask students to place their hands on their hip crests, elbows out. Execute four grand battements à la seconde, and repeat the other side. Remind students that the working leg is off the floor and to press lightly on the opposite hip crest to keep the hips square and level.

The next phase combines the four grand battements devant, both sides, and the four grand battements à la seconde, both sides. After practicing this combination, have students try the exercise at the barre.

Facing the barre, execute four grand battement à la seconde; repeat the other side. With the back to the barre, perform four grand battement devant; repeat other side. Perform this exercise from First, Third, then Fifth position. Monitor alignment throughout the exercise.

Teaching Cues:

- "Quick up, s-l-o-w down."
- "Stop at the top."
- "Brush down into the floor, then throw the leg into the air."

Teaching Images:

- "Imagine kicking a beach ball."

Assessment Checklist:

- ✓ The foot slides along the floor, releasing heel, metatarsals, and toes through a battement tendu and then throws into the air.

- ✓ The foot action pushes downward into the floor, then lifts sharply upward followed by a slow descent.
- ✓ The accent is on the quick throwing movement into the air, followed by a momentary stop and a slow extension of the leg downward.
- ✓ The torso lengthens downward in the back and stretches upward in the front so that the body does not collapse or sink and the leg kicks with ease.
- ✓ The working leg slowly descends to the closing position with the body weight centered on both feet equally.
- ✓ Use counterbalance for grand battement derrière.
- ✓ The heel of the working leg is hidden in grand battement derrière.

Specific Errors:

- Both the supporting and working legs do not fully extend.
- The weight is back on the supporting heel.
- There is no control on the descent.

*𝒰*nit I Center

In unit I, the teacher introduces the students to the center portion of the class by acquainting them with performers, and dancers' stage directions and protocols. The students learn the classical arm positions and basic port de bras, and are introduced to center steps and later barre exercises. The teacher presents basic center steps that focus on transfer of weight and other principles introduced in the unit. The teacher concludes the class with the traditional révérence.

Performer Directions

In the proscenium stage space, directors and performers use standard terms to define the space. *Upstage* refers to that space farthest away from the audience and nearest the back wall of the theater. *Downstage* refers to that area of the stage nearest the audience. The space from the curtain line forward to the edge of the stage is the *apron*. These terms evolved from the raked stages of the eighteenth century. These stages slanted upward from the audience toward the back wall of the theater;

hence the term, raked stage. Directions for stage right and left are from the perspective of the performer, not the audience.

Stage Directions for Dancers: For dancers, stage directions specify corners and walls of the studio or performing space. There are two versions of stage directions: Russian and Cecchetti. Each uses numbers to denote corners and walls but starts counting from a different place. The stage directions are from the perspective of the dancer. The Cecchetti stage directions begin numbering the corners and then the walls of the studio or stage counterclockwise (see figure I.7):

> Direction 1: right front (or *down right*) corner
>
> Direction 2: left front (or *down left*) corner
>
> Direction 3: left back (or *up left*) corner
>
> Direction 4: right back (or *up right*) corner
>
> Direction 5: front wall (*en face*), or facing the audience
>
> Direction 6: left wall (or *stage left)*
>
> Direction 7: back wall (or *upstage)*
>
> Direction 8: right wall (or *stage right)*

Memorize the ballet stage directions because they are used continually in the center to indicate direction.

Progressions:

1. Point out the directions, corners, and walls with their corresponding numbers.

2. Test students by asking them to face the direction you have indicated.

3. Mix up the directions for them so they become familiar with them.

4. Repeat in the next class period as a review.

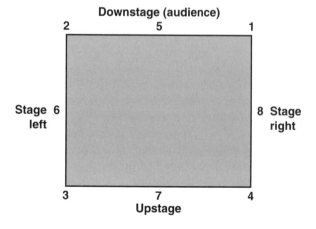

Figure I.7 Stage directions (Cecchetti).

Classical Arm Positions

Classical ballet arm positions originate from the anatomical position; the arms hang down from the shoulders, held near the body with the elbows and palms facing in toward the body. To achieve classical ballet arm positions, the elbows and wrists flex slightly to create a subtle curve throughout the arms and hands. For most classical arm positions, the arms curve and the palms face the dancer. Some positions have further requirements such as Second position. In Second position, the arms stretch away from the body to the side, just in front of Second position, the elbows flex slightly and rotate up facing the back of the room. Second position arms (Cecchetti Method) slope downward from the shoulder to the wrist in a gentle curve that finishes with the hand through the index finger.

Among the major ballet schools and methods, there are many arm positions; some positions are repetitive or variations of others. For the beginning student, it is best to keep the arm positions simple. The following classical arm positions meet these needs.

Preparatory Position (or *Fifth Position en bas*): Arms are rounded low in front of the body, with the fingertips in front of the thighs but not touching the body (see figure I.8a). Often in class this position is referred to as *en bas* (low).

First Position: Arms round in front of the middle of the torso at the bottom of the sternum, fingertips almost touching (see figure I.8b).

Second Position: Arms stretch from shoulder level, sloping downward, and are slightly rounded, immediately in front of the side of the body (see figure I.8c).

Demi-Seconde Position: Arms stretch at the side of the body, half the distance between First and Second position (see figure I.8d).

Third Position: Round one arm high over the head while the other arm stretches to Second position (see figure I.8e).

Fourth Position en haut (French): Round one arm high over the head; curve the other arm in front at the waistline (see figure I.8f).

Fourth Position en avant (Cecchetti): One arm curves in front at the waistline; the other arm stretches in Second position. Petit allégro and other combinations in the center use this variation (see figure I.8g).

Fifth Position en haut: Round both arms high, framing the head, diagonally upward from the hairline (see figure I.8h).

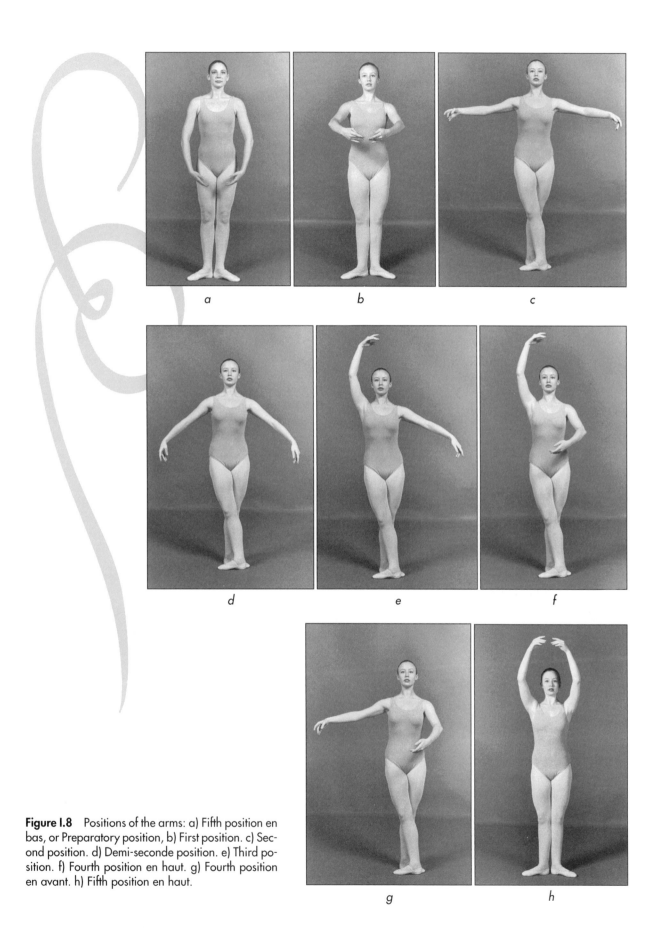

Figure I.8 Positions of the arms: a) Fifth position en bas, or Preparatory position, b) First position. c) Second position. d) Demi-seconde position. e) Third position. f) Fourth position en haut. g) Fourth position en avant. h) Fifth position en haut.

Progressions:

1. Ask students to stand with their arms in the anatomical position, and demonstrate the classical arm positions. Say and do the arm positions with the students. Ask students to demonstrate each of the positions.

2. Combine the arm positions with the classical foot positions. Hold each position three measures, and then change to the next position on the fourth measure.

3. Teach First port de bras: Begin in Fifth position en bas; move to First position (one measure); open to Second position (one measure); and rotate the elbows, the lower arms, and hands. Float back to the Preparatory position (two measures) (see figure I.9, a-c). Practice the port de bras four times with breath phrasing.

4. Teach Second port de bras: Begin in the Preparatory position. Move to Fifth position en haut by passing through First position (one measures); open and rotate the arms to Second position with a breath (one measure); rotate the elbows, the lower arms, and the hands. Float back to the Preparatory position (one measure) (see figure I.10, a-d).

Port de bras refers to moving through the classical arm positions. Port de bras is the first part of the traditional ballet center. Later, port de bras combines with other components of the center.

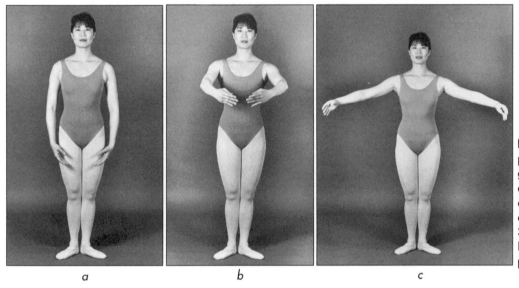

a   b   c

Figure I.9 First port de bras: a) Begin with arms Fifth en bas. b) Lift the arms First position. c) Move arms to Second position. d) End with arms Fifth position en bras.

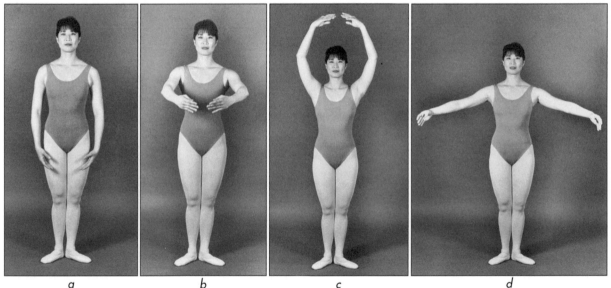

a   b   c   d

Figure I.10 Second port de bras: a) Place the arms Fifth position en bas. b) Lift the arms through First position. c) Move the arms Fifth position en haut. d) Open the arms to Second position. End with arms Fifth position en bas.

Center Barre

In center barre the students perform exercises from the barre in the center. This provides a reality check to see how well the individuals

- transfer weight from one foot to the other,
- maintain turn-out, and
- keep correct alignment while performing barre exercises.

The first barre exercise students perform in the center is battement tendu; other barre exercises include passé, battement dégagé, and grand battement.

Progressions: Perform battement tendu as a center barre exercise from First position, later Third, then Fifth position. This sequence of battement tendus is an extension of those at the barre presented earlier in this unit.

1. Four battement tendu en croix, stop, other side. Combine both sides.

2. Two battement tendu en croix, stop, other side; repeat combination.

3. Eight battement tendu en promenade en avant or en arrière; combine both directions of the exercise.

4. One battement tendu en croix, with the last battement tendu à la seconde closing in Third or Fifth position derrière, so that the combination can be reversed to the other side. Repeat the combination starting with the left foot.

The next progression is to teach battement tendu en promenade en avant or en arrière. The translation for this step is battement tendu walking (*en promenade*) forward (*en avant*) or backward (*en arrière*).

1. Perform battement tendu à la seconde, with the right foot, then left. Continue alternating feet until students have performed eight repetitions.

2. Practice this walking sequence in First position then Third or Fifth positions.

3. Start this sequence forward (en avant) from Third or Fifth position; the back foot executes a battement tendu à la seconde and closes front. Then the alternate foot closes front and so on. Performing this sequence backward (en arrière) from Third or Fifth positions, the front foot executes a battement tendu à la seconde and closes back. Then the alternate foot closes back, and so on, to complete the sequence.

Coupé

(koo-PAY)

Definition: to cut (see figure I.11, a-b)

Principles: weight transfer, pull-up (or lift)

Rules and Protocols: jumping and landing technique, position of the working foot on the supporting leg, articulating and pointing the feet

Verbal Depiction: Coupé is the position where the working foot rests either in front or back of the middle of the lower supporting leg. This position of the foot on the leg is the same as low retiré. Coupé is also a linking step in which the dancer leaps from one foot to the other underneath the body with the working foot changing from coupé derrière to devant or vice versa. During the transfer of weight the supporting leg and foot completely extend in the air, while the working foot remains in the coupé position.

This step is an extension of foot pedals, but performed from Third and, later, Fifth position devant and derrière. Perform this step in the center, by itself or as part of a combination.

Arms: Hold arms in Fourth position en avant with the same arm curved in front as the supporting leg regardless if the working foot is in front or back.

Music and Timing:

- Time signature: depends on the allégro combination
- Tempo: moderate
- Timing: "&" for the up movement, the count for the landing

Standard Introductory Movement or Preparation: Standing in Third or Fifth position, the dancer demi-pliés before the coupé.

Introductory and Transitional Steps: Coupé links with

- introductory steps such as glissade and pas de bourrée,
- jumps and other transitional steps in a series, and
- changes of weight and direction.

Breathing:

- Inhale on the ascent.
- Exhale on the landing.
- Extend the breath phrase over a movement phrase or combination.

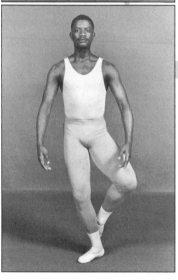

Figure I.11 Coupé devant, coupé derrière: a) Place the working leg in front on the middle of the lower supporting leg; coupé devant. b) Transfer the weight to the opposite foot ending with back foot on the middle of the lower supporting leg; coupé derrière.

Progressions:

1. Begin by marking the directions: the leg lifts back, close; front, close.

2. Connect the movements, performing the coupés slowly so the feet articulate properly.

3. Increase the tempo. At the barre, perform 16 counts alternating back and front in Third position.

4. Repeat in the center.

Teaching Cues:

- "And cut, and cut"
- "Up, cut"

Teaching Images:

- "Imagine the foot cutting the space like a knife."
- "Imagine the floor being hot, so the feet change in the air to escape the heat."

Assessment Checklist:

✓ The working leg goes to coupé at the top of the jump.

✓ The supporting leg and foot extend completely in the air.

✓ The working foot remains in contact with the supporting leg at the coupé position.

✓ The jump is high enough that the supporting leg and foot are completely off the floor.

Specific Errors:

- The working leg does not go to coupé immediately or too late.
- The working foot changes position on the back or front of the supporting leg.
- The jump is not high enough for the supporting leg and foot to extend completely in the air.

Pas de Bourrée

(pah duh boo-RAY)

Definition: step of the bourrée (see figure I.12, a-c)

Principles: transfer of weight, weight distribution, turn-out

Rules and Protocols: articulation and pointing feet, head movements accompany changes in arm positions, moving through foot positions and directions

Verbal Depiction: The pas de bourrée is composed of three steps. Pas de bourrée (dessous) begins in Third and, later, Fifth position. The front leg demi-pliés as the back leg coupés derrière. The back foot steps behind in Fifth position demi-pointe. Then the front foot steps to a small Second position three-quarter relevé. The back foot steps into Third or Fifth position devant, full foot. Both feet finish in Third or Fifth position demi-plié or the new back leg coupés behind to start

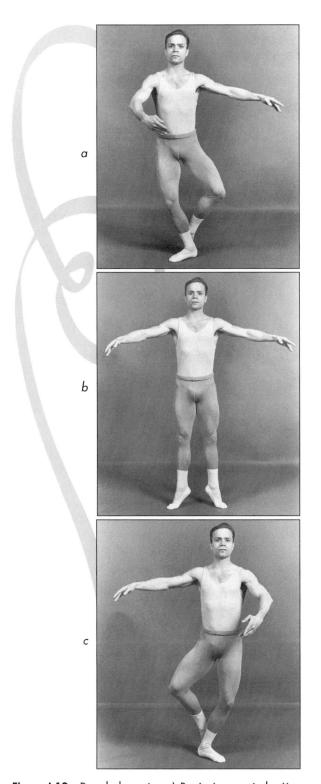

the pas de bourrée to the other side. Execute the coupé or dégagé sharply before the pas de bourrée. The position of the feet is very important in their relation to the quick transfer of weight during the step.

Arms (for pas de bourrée dessous, or under): With right foot in Third or Fifth position devant, right arm is front in Fourth position en avant. The arms move across the body to the other Fourth position en avant during the step. At the beginning of the step, the head tilts toward the right or front shoulder, looking over the arm curved in front of the body. During the step, the head changes to tilt toward the left shoulder as the feet change position and arms change so the left arm curves in Fourth position en avant. This will be illustrated in later units.

Music and Timing:

- Time signature: 3/4, 6/8, or 2/4

- Tempo: moderate to fast tempo, with a sharp, crisp quality but adaptable to a variety of qualities

- Timing: The rhythmic quality of the step is even like three beats on a drum. Execute the coupé on the "&" before the measure for the pas de bourrée. Each step takes one count—back, side, front. If the final step ends in coupé derrière, hold the "&" count before continuing to execute the pas de bourrée.

Standard Introductory Movements or Preparation: Standing in Fifth position, the dancer executes a First port de bras ending in Fourth position en avant with the curved arm in front of the supporting leg.

Introductory or Transitional Steps: A pas de bourrée is an introductory or transitional step in adagio and allégro combinations. It combines with other transitional steps to make more complicated transitions.

Breathing:

- Inhale at the beginning of the step.

- Exhale at the end.

- Extend the breath phrase over a series of pas de bourrées or a short movement phrase.

Progressions:

1. Teach the foot pattern of pas de bourrée from Third position on full foot: back, side (à la seconde), front, Third position, hold; repeat to other side.

Figure I.12 Pas de bourrée: a) Begin in coupé derrière (back). The back foot steps behind in Fifth position three-quarter relevé (not shown). b) Step to a small Second position three-quarter relevé. c) The back foot coupés derrière or both close in Fifth position (not shown).

2. Add the coupé derrière to the beginning of the step; end in Third position.

3. Connect both sides with a coupé: coupé, back, side, front, with the new back leg in coupé derrière, ready to start the second side.

Teaching Cues:

- "And, left, right, left"

- "And, up, up, down"

- "Ta, ta, ta"

- Pas de bourrée dessous (under): "back, side, front"

- Pas de bourrée dessus (over): "front, side, back"

Teaching Images:

- "Imagine yourself in a small space. You are trying to avoid stepping on beautiful flowers."

- "The steps of the pas de bourrée are very precise, like three taps on a drum."

Assessment Checklist:

✓ Perform sharp coupé derrière and demi-plié on the front leg simultaneously.

✓ Step in correct positions and directions.

✓ Feet are in three-quarter relevé.

Specific Errors:

- Incomplete coupé derrière is performed.

- Feet do not remain pointed.

- Weight is not centered on the relevé so that feet sickle in or out.

Standards and Variations: These are the basic standards and variations of the step appropriate for the beginning student:

Pas de Bourrée Dessous (Under): Begin in Fifth position, right foot front. The left foot coupés or dégagés in demi-plié à la seconde. The left foot steps on three-quarter relevé behind the right foot on three-quarter relevé. The right foot steps to a small Second position three-quarter relevé. The left foot closes in Third or Fifth position devant, demi-plié. The arms extend in Second position.

Pas de Bourrée Dessus (Over): Begin in Third or Fifth position, right foot front. The right foot coupés or dégagés in demi-plié à la seconde. The right foot steps on three-quarter relevé in front of the left foot on three-quarter relevé. The left foot steps to a small Second position three-quarter relevé. The right foot closes Third or Fifth position derrière, demi-plié. The arms extend in Second position.

Ballet Walks

Definition: stylized walk

Principles: alignment, turn-out, weight distribution, transfer of weight

Rules and Protocols: aristocratic attitude, articulating and pointing feet, utilizing poise, fluid movement, and grace while walking

Verbal Depiction: The ballet walk begins in the B+ position (chapter 3). The back leg and foot extend devant in a pointed position. The transfer of weight to that foot is through the toes, metatarsals (ball), and heel while the back foot releases the weight through the heel, ball, and toes. The body lifts and floats above this smooth transfer of weight as the dancer moves through the space.

Arms: Arms are held in either Fifth position en bas, Second, or Fourth position en avant.

Music and Timing:

- Time signature: 4/4, 3/4, or 2/4.

- Tempo: slow to moderate tempo, with a variety of qualities.

- Timing: Rhythmic quality of the step is very even.

Standard Introductory Movements or Preparation: Standing in the B+ position, the dancer executes a First port de bras ending in the Preparatory position, Second, or Fourth position en avant with the same arm curved in front as the leg pointed derrière.

Introductory or Transitional Steps: Use in adagio and grand allégro combinations.

Breathing: The dancer inhales at the beginning of the walks and breathes naturally over the movement phrase.

Progressions:

1. Ask students to walk across the studio as they walk outside of the dance studio (heel, ball, toes).

2. Demonstrate the ballet walk and ask students to execute the ballet walk across the studio (toes, ball, heel). Perform this exercise with the arms in demi-seconde or Fourth position en avant.

Teaching Cues:

- "Extend your leg and turned-out foot before you transfer the weight."

- "Walk with your sternum lifted."
- "Walk on a tight rope, one foot in front of the other."

Teaching Images:
- "Walk like a prince or princess."
- "Walk with a book on your head."
- "Walk as though you are gliding on silk."

Assessment Checklist:
- ✓ Turn out the extended leg and foot.
- ✓ Transfer the weight through toes, metatarsals, heel.
- ✓ Align the torso; lift it off the legs.
- ✓ Arms remain in position.

Specific Errors:
- The transfer of weight is reversed (heel, metatarsals, toes).
- Body weight settles with transfer to the foot.

Chassé
(sha-SAY)

Definition: chased; one foot chases the other (see figures I.13, a-e)

Principles: transfer of weight, weight distribution, turn-out, alignment

Rules and Protocols: jumping and landing technique, pointing feet, traveling in a direction

Verbal Depiction: The step begins in First, Third, or Fifth position demi-plié. The front foot slides on the floor to Second or Fourth position devant. The back leg pushes the body into the air (en l'air) where both legs close in either First or Fifth position en l'air. Land in First or Fifth position demi-plié. The weight then transfers to the back leg so that the front leg slides out easily for the next chassé.

Arms: Hold the arms in Second, Third, or Fourth position en avant or en haut.

Music and Timing:
- Time signature: 3/4 or 2/4.
- Tempo: moderate to brisk tempo.
- Timing: "One & a." Count one is the slide, "&" is the air movement, and "a" is the demi-plié at the end.

Standard Introductory Movements or Preparation: Standing in First or Fifth position, the dancer executes a First port de bras.

Introductory or Transitional Steps: an introduction to almost any step or use with other transition steps

Breathing:
- Inhale on the up movement.
- Exhale on the slide movement.
- Extend breath phrasing over several chassés or a short combination.

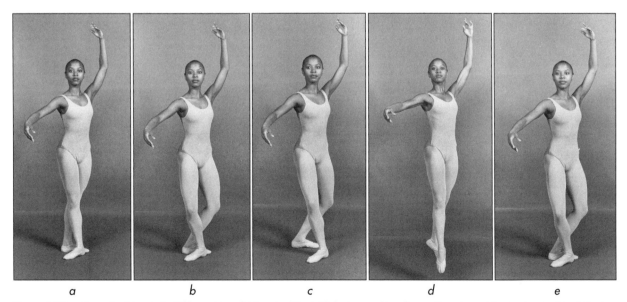

| a | b | c | d | e |

Figure I.13   Chassé: a) Begin in Fifth position. b) Demi-plié. c) Slide the working foot to Fourth position in demi-plié. d) Spring into the air, close the legs in Fifth position, traveling forward in the air. e) Land in Fifth position demi-plié.

Progressions:

1. Teach chassé to the side from First, then Third or Fifth position, with arms in Second or Fourth en avant. In chassé to the side, the working foot slides out to Second position.

2. Teach chassé devant from Third or Fifth position with the arms in Fourth position or Fourth en avant. In the chassé devant, the front foot slides out to Fourth position devant.

Teaching Cues:

- "Down, up" (voice in low then upper register).
- "Slide out in demi-plié."
- "Slide out, pull together."

Teaching Images:

- "The back leg chases the front leg across the floor."
- "Think of riding a wave with its up and down motion."

Assessment Checklist:

- ✓ Working foot slides out from the beginning position.
- ✓ Legs close in First or Fifth position in the air.
- ✓ Both legs and feet fully extend in the air.
- ✓ Foot positions are correct.

Specific Errors:

- The demi-plié foreshortens.
- The working foot flexes and steps out.
- Weight is unequal in Second or Fourth position demi-plié landing.
- The second leg does not close to meet the front leg in the air.

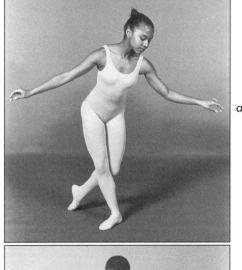

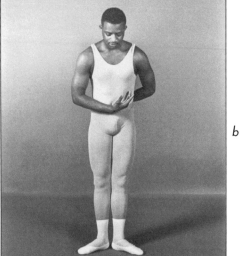

Figure I.14 Révérence: a) Female curtsy. b) Male bow.

Révérence

(ray-vay-RAHNSS)

Definition: curtsy or bow at the end of the class or in performance to acknowledge the teacher or the audience and their applause (see figure I.14, a-b)

Principles: transfer of weight, alignment, turn-out

Rules and Protocols: pointing feet, using port de bras

Verbal Depiction: The female curtsies and the male bows. There are many variations of révérence.

Female: Start in Third position. Right foot points to Second position (right arm does a First port de bras to Second position); transfer weight. Left foot points to Second position (left arm does a First port de bras to Second position); draw left foot back to B+ position and bow from the waist (arms return to Fifth position en bas). Upper body returns to vertical alignment. Repeat to other side.

Male: Begin in Third position. Right foot points to Second position (right arm does a First port de bras to Second position); transfer weight. Left foot points to Second position (left arm moves through a First port de bras to Second position). Draw left foot into Third position devant and bow from the waist (left hand curves in front at sternum level, right arm curves behind the back or extends along the side). Upper body returns to vertical alignment (left arm returns to Fifth position en bas). Repeat to other side.

Music and Timing:

- Time signature: 3/4 or 4/4
- Tempo: slow or moderate tempo with a flowing quality
- Timing: four measures of 3/4 or 4/4 music for each side

Teaching Cues:

- "Bow or curtsy."
- "Look at the audience from side to side in the orchestra and in the balconies."

Teaching Images:

- "Present yourself to the audience, and bow or curtsy."
- "Imagine you have just completed a performance and you are now taking your bow and curtsy. Acknowledge the audience's applause with style and grace."

Assessment Checklist: This combination is generally not assessed.

Teacher's Planner for Unit II

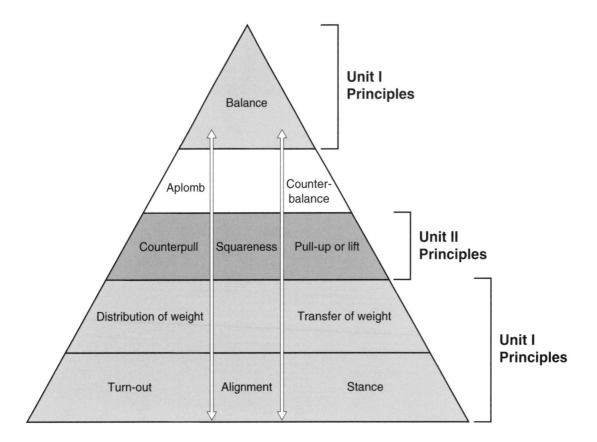

Unit II expands upon the basic barre exercises learned in unit I. In unit II, new types of exercises, directions, patterns, and sequencing are explored. In the center, the focus is on learning the Classical Positions of the Body and introducing basic petit allégro steps.

Objectives of the Unit

The objectives for the unit encompass the cognitive, psychomotor, and affective domains as follows.

Cognitive Domain

The students will be able to

- identify and say new ballet terms;
- translate the French ballet terms from unit I steps into correct movement; and
- apply units I and II principles, rules, and protocols to class work.

Psychomotor Domain

The students will be able to

- execute the following barre exercises: grand plié, battement tendu relevé, port de corps, retiré and passé, battement frappé, relevé, and sous-sus;

- perform the following center steps: battement tendu relevé, balancé, glissade, pas de chat, and jeté;
- learn the Classical Positions of the Body;
- perform appropriate barre and center protocols;
- refine execution of exercises and steps from unit I;
- execute a two-step combination and transpose it to the other side; and
- apply breath and breath phrasing to class work.

Affective Domain

The students will be able to

- accept and apply group corrections to personal work,
- receive and apply individual comments to personal work,
- respond to directions given by the teacher,
- demonstrate a professional attitude toward the work, and

- demonstrate initial self-reliance and movement confidence in classroom performance.

Teaching Strategies

The following teaching strategies apply within unit II:

- Teaching styles: command, practice, inclusive, self-check, guided discovery
- Teacher modeling: continued demonstration of new work using English action words and French terms, repetition, imagery, visual memory development and motor memory of what is correct

Assessment

Consider the following methods of assessment:

- Assessment Checklist utilizes cues for the performance of each exercise and step.
- Periodic informal evaluations monitor if knowledge and skills are attained.
- Written examination on ballet terminology, principles, and rules.

Teacher Responsibilities

The following list is a self-check of your responsibilities when teaching unit II:

- Clear demonstration of exercises and steps
- Clear direction and cueing of execution of exercises and steps
- Clear counting of music
- Clear explanation and application of principles, rules, and protocols
- Use of imagery in the teaching/learning process
- Group feedback
- Individual attention
- Pace of the class
- Open and risk-free atmosphere
- Development of barre and acquisition of new materials in the center

Performance Test Content

Student performance evaluations follow for unit II.

Principles and Rules

The student will demonstrate

- unit II principles: squareness, counterpull, pull-up or lift, balance; and

- unit II barre and center rules and protocols.

At the Barre

The student will execute the following:

1. Demi- and grand pliés, with relevé and balance
2. Battement tendus with and without demi-pliés
3. Battement dégagés in pattern
4. Rond de jambe à terre
5. Port de corps
6. Passés

In the Center

The students will perform the following:

1. Five, six, or eight positions of the body (this can be a test in itself—technique, sequence, body positions, directions)
2. Balancé combination
3. Pas de chats in a series
4. Pas de chat in two-step combination
5. Eight jetés en promenade en avant

Written Examination

The students will

- write answers in English, and
- identify French terms as well as write some French terms.

Unit II Barre

In unit II barre, the teacher builds upon the exercises introduced in unit I and expands the types of barre exercises performed. As in unit I, the teacher introduces some exercises in a modified form.

Grand Plié

(grahn plee-AY)

Definition: large bend of the knees (see figure II.1)

Principles: alignment, turn-out, weight distribution, squareness, counterpull

Rules and Protocols: movement is continuous during the exercises, equal time for descent and return to the full-foot position

Figure II.1 Grand plié in First position. Heels are off the floor.

Figure II.2 Grand plié in Second position. Heels remain on the floor.

Verbal Depiction: The grand plié is an extension of the demi-plié. While performing a grand plié, the legs flex at the hips, knees, ankles, and metatarsals. The dancer executes a complete demi-plié on both the decent and the ascent. Throughout the grand plié, the dancer maintains the turn-out established before the exercise. Later, perform demi-plié and grand pliés together.

In four of the five classical foot positions (the exception is Second position), the dancer descends to the base of the demi-plié and continues the descent by releasing the heels until the thighs are parallel to the floor. Distribute the weight equally over the foot triangle and, as the foot releases from the floor, to all five toes and the metatarsals. After reaching the depth of the grand plié, the thighs are parallel to the floor; the dancer begins the ascent to the base of the demi-plié and then to the straight-legged position. Throughout the execution of the exercise, the movement is continuous and without accent. The descent and the ascent of the exercise use an equal amount of measures.

In First, Third, Fourth, and Fifth positions, the heels release off the floor on the descent. In Second position, because the space between the feet is approximately shoulder-width apart, the heels do not release from the floor. At the bottom of the grand plié in Second position, the thighs are parallel to the floor (see figure II.2).

In the grand plié, center the body weight over both legs. The body counterpulls (stretches upward) as the dancer descends. On the ascent the body lifts upward, appearing to float over the legs.

Arms: First port de bras is appropriate for beginning dancers.

Purpose

- stretches the muscles of the inner thigh, in addition to those muscles stretched by the demi-plié (see unit I)
- applies the principles of turn-out, vertical alignment, distribution of weight, and counterpull.

Music and Timing:

- Time signature: 4/4 or 3/4.
- Tempo: moderate tempo, legato quality.
- Timing: In 4/4 time signature, use one measure down and one up; in 3/4 time signature, two measures for the descent and two for the ascent.

Preparation: Starting in Third or Fifth position, arms in Fifth en bas; execute a First port de bras. As the arms open to Second position the working foot extends to Second position. The working foot closes in the starting position, while the arm away from the barre moves to its starting position. The arm near the barre extends and the hand rests on the barre. Standard head movements are used for the preparation.

Breathing:

- Inhale on the descent.
- Exhale on the ascent.
- Breath phrasing extends over several repetitions.

Progressions:

1. Facing the barre, teach First and Second positions; then add Third position.
2. Combine demi-plié and grand plié in one exercise.
3. Change Third position to Fifth position.
4. Teach relevés and add them as an ending if the dancer is facing the barre.
5. Introduce Fourth position grand plié in unit IV, depending on student abilities.

Teaching Cues:

- "Inhale on the descent; exhale on the ascent."
- "Dance the exercise."
- "Use all the music."
- "Make the movement continuous."

Teaching Images:

- "Imagine the legs opening and closing like an umbrella."
- "In the grand plié as the legs bend, the body descends and ascends vertically as it goes down and up like an elevator."

Assessment Checklist:

- ✓ Center the body weight over the legs through the descent and ascent.
- ✓ Maintain turn-out from the hips through the legs and feet during the exercise.
- ✓ Direct the knees above the second and third toes of each foot.
- ✓ Release both heels and replace them simultaneously while maintaining the foot triangle during the demi-plié phase; distribute the weight over five toes and metatarsals during the grand plié.
- ✓ The body counterpulls (stretches upward) as the legs bend.
- ✓ The grand plié is a continuous movement.

Specific Errors:

- The knees fall in front of or behind second and third toes.

- The foot triangle is not maintained, causing the instep to drop and the feet to roll in or out.
- The heels release off the floor too soon or return to the floor at different times.
- The movement stops at the bottom of the demi-plié either on the descent or ascent and/or at the bottom of the grand plié.
- The heels lift into a high relevé at the bottom of the grand plié.
- One knee drops lower than the other at the base of the grand plié (unequal weight distribution).

Battement Tendu Relevé

(bat-MAHN than-DEW ruhl-VAY)

Definition: raised beatings (see figure 11.3, a-c)

Principles: weight distribution, transfer of weight, turn-out, pull-up, squareness, alignment, counterpull

Rules and Protocols: The working foot slides into a smaller Fourth position derrière to maintain alignment.

Verbal Depiction: Battement tendu relevé is a combination of the battement tendu joined with the working foot articulating from the pointed to the full-foot position and the reverse. The battement tendu and the battement tendu relevé have the same extension phase (see unit I). At maximum extension, the working foot releases from a full point to a full-foot position on the floor, with the body weight transferring from one supporting leg to both legs equally. In this position, both legs are either straight or in a demi-plié. On the return phase of the exercise, the body counterpulls. The body weight shifts from both legs back to the supporting leg just before the working foot releases to a full point and returns to the closing position. The accent is on the release of the working foot from its full-foot position to the full-pointed position.

During the execution of the battement tendu relevé, the dancer maintains turn-out and, especially, a squared body position (see figure II.3, a-c, battement tendu relevé à la seconde). The accent on the battement tendu relevé is on the release of the working foot from the full-foot position to the full-pointed position. There is a slight spring in the movement as the weight shifts back to the supporting leg. Accent the spring. Perform

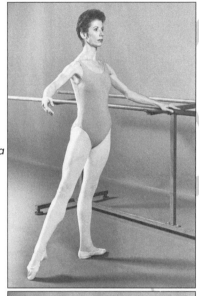

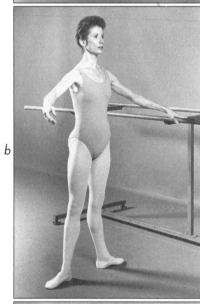

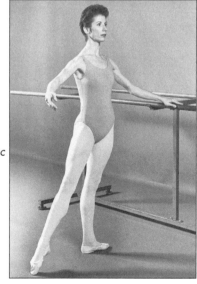

Figure II.3 Battement tendu relevé à la seconde: a) Brush the working foot to full point (pointé tendu) à la seconde. b) Lower in Second position to the full-foot position. c) Release the working foot to pointé tendu à la seconde. Close to Fifth back.

the battement tendu relevé with the weight transfer onto two straight legs or with a demi-plié.

Battement tendu relevé à la quatrième devant/derrière: These positions are in line with the supporting heel or from Third position depending on the dancer's ability to keep the body square. Performing the exercise derrière, the working foot slides into a smaller than standard Fourth position with the transfer of weight in order to maintain squareness. Then the working foot stretches back to the pointed position. (See figure II.4, a-f.)

Battement tendu relevé à la seconde: In performing this direction, the dancer uses his or her best Second position while maintaining turn-out and a squared position.

Arms: The working arm remains in Second position during the exercise.

Purpose: The battement tendu relevé develops the insteps and the transfer of weight from two legs to one and from one leg to two. This basic concept is paramount to beginning ballet technique. The goal for the dancer is to transfer weight efficiently and effortlessly during execution of the exercise. The control of the body and the weight transfer is key to performance of more complex exercises and steps.

Music and Timing:

- Time signature: 4/4.
- Tempo: slow to moderate tempo, with a strong to light quality.
- Timing: Count 1: battement tendu out; count 2: press working foot from a full point to full foot, on straight legs or in demi-plié, with the body weight shared equally on both feet; count 3: working leg extends to pointed position, while weight transfers to supporting leg; count 4: close in Fifth position.

Preparation: Standing in Fifth position, the dancer executes a First port de bras with standard head movements for either the two- or four-count preparation.

Breathing:

- Inhale on the extension phase.
- Exhale on the closing.
- Extend breath phrasing over several repetitions or a set.

Progressions:

1. Teach the battement tendu relevé facing the barre to Second position and then devant; then teach derrière.

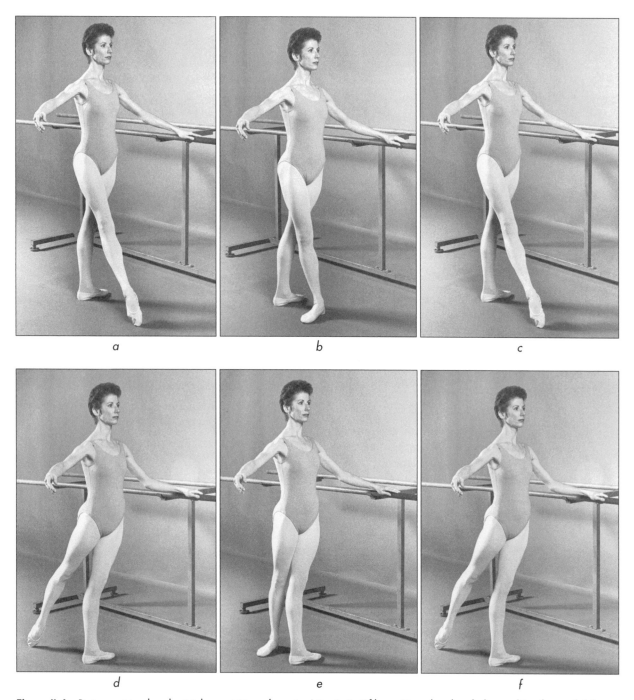

Figure II.4 Battement tendu relevé à la quatrième devant: a) Begin in Fifth position, then brush the working foot to full foot à la quatrième devant. b) Lower the working foot to Fourth position devant. c) Release the foot to pointé tendu to à la quatrième devant. Close to Fifth. Battement tendu relevé à la quatrième derrière. d) Brush the foot out to à la quatrième derrière. e) Lower the working foot to the smaller Fourth position. f) Lift the working foot pointé tendu to à la quatrième derrière. Close to Fifth position back.

2. Execute the exercise without demi-plié in the en croix pattern.

3. Add the demi-plié to the battement tendu relevé. Battement tendu relevé combines easily with battement tendus and battement tendus with demi-pliés.

Teaching Cues:

- "Point, lower, point, close."
- "Stretch and plié, stretch and close."
- "The working foot accepts the weight, releases the weight."
- "Spring to the top of the supporting leg."

Teaching Images:

- "The working foot moves like you are stretching a taut spring."
- "Press the spring into the floor through your foot; let it release your foot to a point."

Assessment Checklist:

1. Battement tendu relevé
   - ✓ The working leg and fully stretched foot are not weight-bearing.
   - ✓ The foot brushes from the full-foot position, releasing in sequence the heel, the metatarsals, and the toes to a full-pointed position, keeping contact with the floor.
   - ✓ The working foot flexes from a pointed position through the toes, metatarsals, and heel to a full-foot position on the floor to accept the weight transfer.
   - ✓ The body counterpulls before and during the transfer of weight to the new position and before the return phase.
   - ✓ The accent occurs when the weight shifts from two legs to one leg as the working foot extends to the full-pointed position and the supporting leg accepts the transfer of weight.
   - ✓ On the return path, the foot flexes and brushes in sequence of the toes, the metatarsals, and the heel to a full-foot closed position.

2. Battement Tendu Relevé à la Quatrième Devant/Derrière (this assessment includes the points listed in the Assessment Checklist for the battement tendu, see unit 1)
   - ✓ The foot slides in a straight line either in front or in back of the supporting heel.

   - ✓ The full-pointed foot position is directly behind the supporting foot.
   - ✓ In derrière, the pointed foot slides into a small Fourth position, maintaining alignment.
   - ✓ On the extension phase, the heel leads forward (à la quatrième devant); the great toe leads backward (à la quatrième derrière).
   - ✓ On the return phase, the toe leads back (à la quatrième devant); the heel leads forward (à la quatrième derrière).

3. Battement Tendu Relevé à la Seconde:
   - ✓ The heel is slightly forward of the great toe.
   - ✓ The foot extends to a point in line with the great toe of the supporting foot.
   - ✓ On the return the heel remains forward of the great toe into the closing position.

Specific Errors:

1. Battement Tendu Relevé
   - Weight shifts toward or away from the barre, and is not centered over the supporting leg.
   - Weight falls onto the working leg during the execution of the exercise.
   - Body weight is not equally shared by both legs in Second and Fourth positions.
   - The heel drops toward the floor or sickles.

2. Battement Tendu Relevé à la Quatrième Devant/Derrière
   - The working leg extends diagonally front or back.
   - The Fourth position derrière is not shortened.

3. Battement Tendu Relevé à la Seconde
   - The working leg extends to the side, behind or in front of the Second position.

Port de Corps
(pawr duh kawr)

Definition: Literally, port de corps means the carriage of the body; but as an exercise at the barre, port de corps refers to bending the body in any direction. *Cambre* refers to bending the torso sideways or backward (see figure II.5, a-g).

Principles: squareness, pull-up, alignment, turnout, balance on two feet.

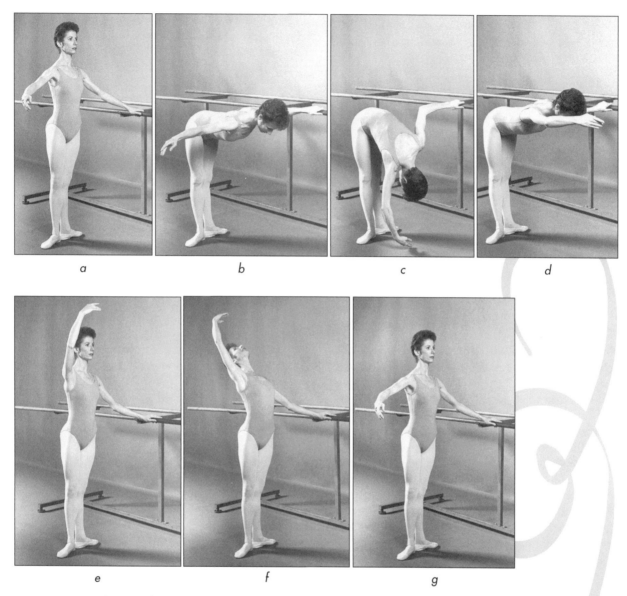

Figure II.5 Port de corps devant: a) Begin in First position with the arm in Second position. b) Bend forward to a flat back (or hinge position) parallel to the floor. c) Elongate the back toward the floor. d) Reverse the path to the hinge position. e) Return to a vertically aligned position, with the arms Fifth en haut. f) Bent or cambre derrière with the face lifted toward the ceiling, arm remains Fifth en haut. g) Return to vertical alignment with the arm rotating to Second position.

Rules and Protocols:

- Stretch in vertical alignment before beginning the port de corps.

- In the hinge position, the torso forms a right angle to the legs, which are perpendicular to the floor.

Verbal Depiction: Execute port de corps in all five positions on full foot later en relevé. The body bends in all directions: devant, à la seconde, and derrière. The movement is continuous and smooth. A secondary accent initiates a movement or change of direction. The secondary accent accompanies and begins the breath phrase for the port de corps. The dancer pauses momentarily in vertical alignment to end a port de corps before moving in the next direction.

In this unit, execute port de corps in First; Second; and, later, Third or Fifth positions and in the following directions:

Port de Corps Devant: There are two ways to perform port de corps devant. In the first type, the head stretches down and the back begins to curl, vertebrae by vertebrae, with the pelvis remaining centered until the body folds at the hips. At maximum extension, the crown of the head is directly in line with the floor. When the back is rounding, the abdominals continue to lift and the legs stretch upward while remaining perpendicular to the floor. On the return path, the unfolding action begins at the base of the spine. The back continues to unfold upward to the beginning vertically aligned position, with the head the last to return.

In the second type of port de corps devant, the head and back in an aligned position stretch upward and forward at an angle to the hips. This tilt continues until the back reaches a 90-degree angle to the legs, known as the hinge position. From this position, the back stretches down until the crown of the head is in line with the floor. On the reverse path, the head leads. With a straight back, the torso stretches outward and upward from the hip joint in an arc pathway through the hinge position and back to the vertically aligned position. During the port de corps, the body weight centers over the legs, which remain perpendicular to the floor. The head remains in a centered position and lifts slightly upward, but keeping the neck lengthened, during the return phase of the port de corps devant. Later the head turns and tilts toward the working arm and anticipates the arm changes that accompany the port de corps devant.

Port de Corps Derrière: Beginning in the centered, aligned position, the dancer stretches backward with the face lifted toward the ceiling while keeping the neck long. The bend continues through the upper back to the waist (Cecchetti Method). Some schools allow the bend to continue to the hips. On the return to the aligned position, the spine unfolds from its base until the body realigns and centers. The head is the last to return.

The head begins in a centered position and, for the beginning level dancer, can remain in this position throughout the port de corps derrière. In some schools, the dancer turns the head to the center of the room during the port de corps derrière. The head remains in front of the Fifth position en haut arm during the port de corps derrière.

Arms: The port de bras for the port de corps devant begins in either Second position or Fifth en haut. If the port de bras starts in Second position, the arm moves to the Fifth position en haut when the body folds over the legs. The arm stretches in that position outward and upward as the body unfolds. If the port de corps derrière follows, no transitional arm movement is necessary. If the port de bras begins in Fifth position en haut, the arm remains stretched overhead during the entire port de corps devant.

Purpose:

- Develops flexibility in the torso

- Coordinates the arms and head as the body fluidly bends or moves in all directions above a stable base of the hips and legs

Music and Timing:

- Time signature: 3/4, 4/4, or 6/8.

- Tempo: slow to moderate tempo, an adagio type exercise.

- Timing: Take four to eight measures to complete the port de corps in each direction.

Preparation: Stand in First, Second, or Fifth position to begin the port de corps. Often, port de corps combines with other barre exercises; therefore, a preparation is unnecessary.

Breathing:

- Inhale as the body stretches upward to align, center the body vertically, and pull up before executing the port de corps.

- On the port de corps devant: exhale on the forward and downward path, and inhale on the return to alignment.

- For the port de corps derrière: inhale on the backward movement, and exhale on the return to alignment.

- The breath phrasing contributes to building the dynamics of the port de corps.

Progressions:

1. Introduce port de corps in First and Second position. Later, execute it in Third, then Fifth position.

2. Teach port de corps devant, curling down and up, and then with the hinge movement.

3. Teach port de corps derrière facing the barre.

4. With one hand on the barre, combine the devant and derrière port de corps. This exercise combines with other barre exercises such as rond de jambe à terre or demi- and grand pliés.

Teaching Cues:

- "Keep the movement connected, flowing, and constant."

- "Never stop moving."

- Port de corps devant: "Fold at the hips."

Teaching Images:

- "Imagine the body sweeping the walls and the ceiling."

- "Create a large arc to the floor and an even larger arc back to alignment."

Assessment Checklist:

✓ The body extends upward with an inhalation before beginning the port de corps.

✓ The back remains stretched through the port de corps devant using the flat hinge position, or the back curls down and unfolds sequentially.

✓ Shoulders and hips are square at the beginning and end of the exercise.

✓ The torso bends back starting with the head and continuing to the waist.

✓ The legs remain perpendicular to the floor during the port de corps.

✓ Port de bras and head movements coordinate with the port de corps.

Specific Errors:

- Hips and/or shoulders are forward or back.

- The port de corps derrière does not start with the head or stop at the waist.

- The back does not unfold starting from the waist up.

Sur le Cou-de-Pied

(sewr luh koo-duh-PYAY)

Definition: Position of the working foot at the ankle of the supporting leg. Literal translation is "on the neck of the foot."

Verbal Depiction: Sur le cou-de-pied is the position the dancer passes through as the working foot releases from the floor to active foot positions on the supporting leg. In the standard sur le cou-de-pied devant, the side of the little toe touches the front of the ankle. In the sur le cou-de-pied derrière, the inside of the working heel touches the back of the ankle. Both positions require level hips and equally turned out legs. The dancer balances by centering weight over the foot

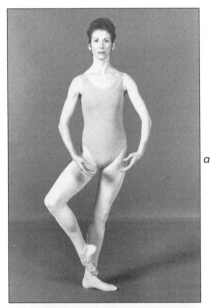

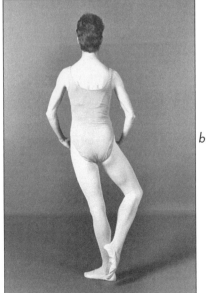

Figure II.5 Sur le cou-de-pied devant and derrière: a) Foot position in front of the ankle. b) Foot position in back of the ankle.

triangle of the supporting foot. The beginning dancer learns the following variations as part of exercises and steps.

In the sur le cou-de-pied position (Cecchetti Method) the toes and metatarsals rest on the floor. The metatarsals flex and the heel lifts to create a perpendicular line to the floor. In devant, the sur le cou-de-pied position is in front of the ankle of the supporting foot in the full-foot position (see figure II.6a). In the sur le cou-de-pied derrière, the heel is perpendicular to the floor and positioned at the back of the ankle on the supporting foot (see Figure II.6b).

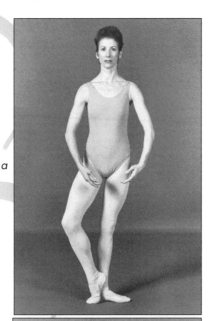

a

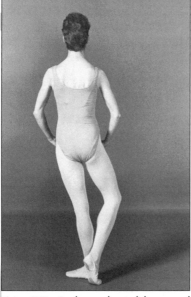

b

Figure II.7 Sur le cou-de-pied devant and derrière: a) Flex toes on the floor in the front of the ankle (Cecchetti). b) Flex toes on the floor in the back of the ankle (Cecchetti).

In the sur le cou-de-pied position (Russian School), the foot flexes from the ankle. In the devant position, the working heel rests in front and on top of the ankle and parallel to the floor. The position derrière rests at the back of the ankle or on the lower part of the leg (see figure II.7 a, b). Use this version of the sur le cou-de-pied positions to teach battement frappé.

Purpose: This position is important for developing foot articulation in the battement frappé and petit battement.

Battement Frappé
(bat-MAHN fra-PAY)

Definition: a beating of the foot that strikes the floor (see figure II.8, a-c)

Principles: balance, pull-up or lift, squareness, turnout, alignment

Rules and Protocols: The thigh is stable and not moving while the lower leg and foot extend from the knee. The strike of the working foot derrière is behind the heel of the supporting foot.

Verbal Depiction: The starting position for the foot is either the Cecchetti or Russian versions of the sur le cou-de-pied position. The toes and metatarsals strike the floor, followed by the foot brushing the floor quickly and extending off the floor in a pointed position. Only the lower leg extends and stretches, while the upper leg remains stable. The foot returns to sur le cou-de-pied. Throughout the execution of the battement frappé, the upper leg remains quiet and well turned-out. The accent is the lower leg and foot brush and quick extension.

Arms: The working arm stretches in Second position.

Purpose:

- Develops isolated movement in the lower leg and foot
- Builds flexibility in the ankle joint and develops foot articulation

Music and Timing:

- Time signature: 4/4 or 2/4.
- Tempo: brisk to moderate tempo, with a light quality.
- Timing: Strike the toes and metatarsals on the "&" beat, momentarily holding the beat at maximum leg and foot extension, before snapping the foot back to sur le cou-de-pied by the count (e.g., "&, 1").

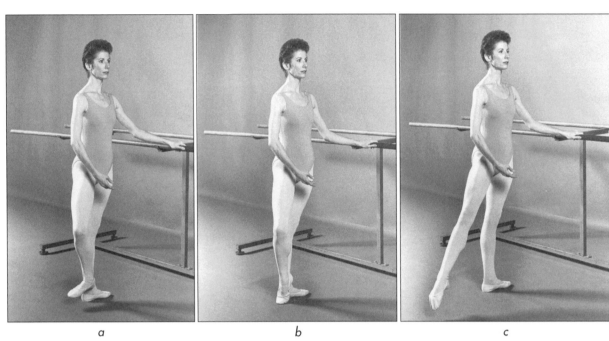

Figure II.8 Battement frappè: a) Begin with a flexed foot sur le cou-de-pied devant. b) Strike the toes and metatarsals on the floor. c) Continue to stretch the lower leg and working foot to a full point à la seconde off the floor.

• Modified timing: Strike and hold on "&, one," and return to sur le cou-de-pied on count two.

Preparation: Begin in Fifth position, arms in the Fifth position en bas. The arms rise to First position and extend to Second position as the working leg extends and foot the points à la seconde. The working foot then moves to the sur le cou-de-pied devant position. The preparation is done in two or four counts.

Breathing:

• Inhale as the arms and working leg extend on the preparation; exhale as the working foot returns to the sur le cou-de-pied position.

• Exhale on the extension of the frappé; inhale on the return phase.

• Breath phrasing extends over two or four repetitions, or an eight-count phrase.

Progressions: The battement frappé is taught in several steps:

1. First, the student locates sur le cou-de-pied devant and derrière. Facing the barre, the toes and metatarsals tap the floor eight times decreasing to four, then two times.

2. Repeat the process in both devant and derrière positions and repeat on the other side. This exercise develops the ankle action necessary for the strike in the battement frappé.

   Next, teach the battement frappé as a series of movements.

1. In the sur le cou-de-pied position, tap the floor with the toes and metatarsals and hold that position.

2. Brush the toes and metatarsals on the floor to extend the lower leg.

3. Hold and stretch in this position.

4. Snap the working foot back to the sur le cou-de-pied position; hold. In the initial stages, use one measure for each of the four actions. Then condense the time into two counts. By the end of the term, the battement frappé may be executed in one measure at a moderate tempo.

Teaching Cues:

• "Tap, brush, stretch, snap" (back to the sur le cou de pied)

• "Strike, hold"

• "Brush, extend"

• "Let me hear you strike the floor!"

Teaching Images:

• "Imagine your foot striking a door."

• "Imagine your lower leg and foot like a rubber band being stretched and then snapping back into place."

Assessment Checklist:

1. Battement Frappé

   ✓ Body weight shifts from two legs to one leg before pointing the foot à la seconde on the preparation.

✓ From the sur le cou-de-pied position, the toes and metatarsals strike the floor evenly.

✓ The toes and metatarsals keep contact with the floor throughout the striking phase of the exercise.

✓ The working leg and foot stretch to a pointed position two to four inches off the floor.

✓ The accent on the battement frappé is the quick, striking action before the outward extension phase.

✓ Hold the extended, pointed position.

✓ The foot quickly returns to the sur le cou-de-pied position.

2. Battement Frappé à la Quatrième Devant/Derrière

✓ The foot strikes in a straight line either in front or in back of the supporting heel.

✓ The fully extended position is directly in front of or behind the supporting heel.

✓ On the extension phase, the heel leads forward (à la quatrième devant); the toe leads backward (à la quatrième derrière).

3. Battement Frappé à la Seconde:

✓ The heel should be slightly forward of the toes as the foot extends in a straight line extending to a point off the floor and parallel with the supporting great toe.

✓ On the return, the heel remains forward of the toes of the working foot closing into sur le cou-de-pied.

Specific Errors:

1. Battement Frappé

• The toes and/or metatarsals do not contact the floor during the striking phase.

• The sole of the flexed working foot is not parallel to the floor.

• The working foot does not strike the floor near the supporting heel (derrière).

• The entire leg and foot do not extend as a unit.

• The battement frappé extends too high off the floor.

• The knee moves and/or the thigh does not remain stable throughout the exercise.

• The accent on the battement frappé is either not used or misplaced.

2. Battement Frappé à la Quatrième Devant/Derrière

• The working leg extends diagonally front or back.

3. Battement Frappé à la Seconde

• The working leg extends to the side, behind or in front of the à la seconde position.

• The heel does not lead to the pointed foot position or on closing sur le cou-de-pied position.

Retiré and Passé
(ruh-tee-RAY) and (pa-SAY)

Definition: Retiré means withdrawn; passé means passéd.

Principles: squareness, pull-up or lift, transfer of weight, balance, weight distribution, turn-out, stance, alignment

Rules and Protocols: Hip crests are level during retiré and passé.

Verbal Depiction: Retiré is the position of the working foot under the knee either in the front or back (see figure II.9, a-b). In this position it is important that the hips are level and that the body is square in order to support the position on one leg. The knee of the working leg is bent and open in Second position. In the retiré devant position, the side of the little toe of the working foot touches underneath the knee cap (patella), with the working heel slightly forward of the toe. In the retiré derrière position, the heel of the working foot touches at the back of the knee with the toes slightly away from the supporting leg. The accent is on the quick upward movements to retiré position. In passé, the accent is slight and quick on the articulation of the working foot from full foot through the sur le cou-de-pied position.

Passé begins from Fifth position. The working leg moves up the front or back of the supporting leg to under the knee, passes to the side of knee, and continues down the other side of the leg to close in Fifth position (see figure II.10, a-d).

Arms: The arm(s) stretch in Second position.

Purpose: Retiré is the position on the supporting leg that many center steps depend upon for execution. Passé is a transitional step by itself and part of many center steps. The working leg in the position of retiré requires transfer of weight and balance in a more demanding way. Moving through passé, the dancer transfers weight from

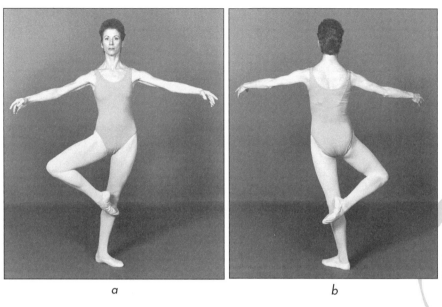

a   b

Figure II.9 Retiré: a) Retiré devant. b) Retiré derrière.

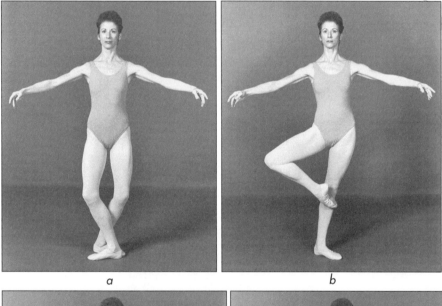

a   b

c   d

Figure II.10 Passé: a) Start in Fifth position demi-plié. b) Move up the front of the supporting leg to under the knee. c) Pass to side of the knee. d) Move to back of the knee down the back of the supporting leg. Close Fifth position.

front to back or vice versa. Acquiring balance on one leg is crucial for the beginning dancer.

Music and Timing:

- Time signature: 4/4
- Tempo: slow to moderate tempo, with a strong to light quality.
- Timing: The working foot moves up the supporting leg in one measure and down the supporting leg in one measure; later these two actions are completed using one measure.

Preparation: Standing in Fifth position facing the barre, the dancer executes a First port de bras with standard head movements for either the two- or four-count preparation.

Breathing:

- Inhale on the lift phase.
- Exhale on the closing.
- Extend breath phrasing over several repetitions or a set.

Progressions:

1. Facing the barre, review the positions of coupé devant and derrière.
2. Locate retiré devant, both sides; test balance on the supporting full foot (check that hips are level).
3. Locate retiré derrière, both sides; test balance on the supporting full foot (check that hips are level).
4. Practice the passé route front to back, close; back to front, close; both sides.
5. Practice passés; testing balance.
6. Practice four passés backward (en arrière); then four passés forward (en avant), moving away and toward the barre.

Teaching Cues:

- Retiré devant: "Hips level, knee out, side of little toe touching."
- Retiré derrière: "Hips level, knee out, heel touching behind the knee with toes away from the leg."
- Passé: "Up in the front, down in the back" (or reverse).
- "Toe in the front; heel in the back" (or reverse).

Teaching Image:

- Passé: "Draw a straight line up the leg and down the leg."

Assessment Checklist:

- ✓ The path of the working leg is directly up and down the front or back of the supporting leg.

- ✓ The position of retiré is under the patella or directly behind the knee.
- ✓ Hips remain square and level.
- ✓ Body weight centers and pulls up through the supporting leg.
- ✓ The side of the little toe touches the front of the supporting leg under the patella. Then the toes slide to behind the knee, changing so that the heel of the working leg touches the back of the supporting leg. The toes do not touch the supporting leg.

Specific Errors:

- The entire side of the foot touches the front of the supporting leg.
- The toes touch the back of the supporting leg.
- The working foot sickles.

Relevé and Sous-Sus
(ruhl-VAY) and (Soo-SEW)

Definition: Relevé means to rise. Specific relevés include press relevé (see figure II.11), elevé, spring relevé, and sous-sus (see figure II.12).

Principles: alignment, pull-up or lift, balance, turn-out, weight distribution

Rules and Protocols: The legs and feet retain their initial turned-out position and the body is stable throughout ascent and descent; in the sous-sus position, the legs cross one in front of the other tightly and without space between them. On the

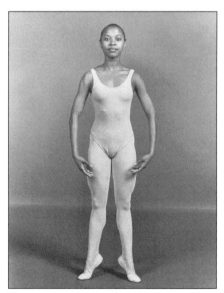

Figure II.11 Press relevé in First position.

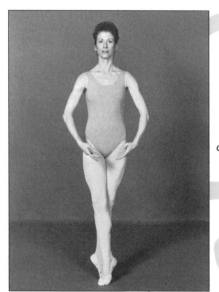

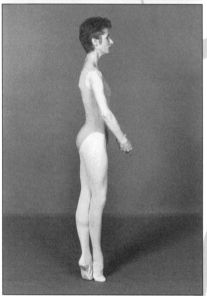

Figure II.12 Sous-sus: a) Front view. b) Side view.

descent, both legs descend simultaneously, both from relevé and sous-sus.

Verbal Depiction: Perform the relevé is in all foot positions. It begins in demi-plié. The feet quickly rise from the full-foot demi-plié to balance on the toes and metatarsals; hold this position. The body resists lowering as it returns to full foot. There are two distinct types of relevés (press and spring), and descents (with demi-plié and abaissé). The student should learn both of these types of relevés because they have different uses in ballet technique.

Press Relevé (French School): The press relevé is smooth and continuous on its rise and return to demi-plié. The toes and metatarsals remain in place on the ascent and descent. On the descent the heels

lower slowly from the three-quarter relevé position to full foot, ending in demi-plié.

Spring Relevé (Cecchetti Method): The spring relevé is a quick change from a full-foot position demi-plié to three-quarter relevé. Both feet hop lightly and alight simultaneously on top of the relevé. During the spring relevé, the body lifts vertically off the legs.

Elevé: The elevé is when the body rises from full foot to three-quarter relevé, without the demi-plié to initiate the movement.

Sous-Sus (Cecchetti Method): Sous-sus is a specialized relevé only performed in Fifth position. After a demi-plié, both feet pull together under the dancer, with a slight spring to three-quarter relevé. Both legs cross in Fifth position, equally turned-out with no space between them. On the descent from sous-sus, the dancer keeps the lift in the body as the feet slide out returning to demi-plié in Fifth position. The Cecchetti Method requires that both feet share the weight equally on the return to Fifth position demi-plié.

Demi-plié and abaissé are two methods of descending from the relevé position. On the demi-plié descent, the legs remain straight until reaching the full-foot position and then bend into the demi-plié. In abaissé, the legs remain straight as the feet slide out into a full-foot position. The body remains pulled up during both of these descents.

Arms: For relevés, hold the arms in Second or Fifth position en haut. For sous-sus, the arms often move from Fifth position en bas to Fifth position en haut on the ascent. If executing a series of sous-sus, the arms move and then remain in Fifth position en haut and return to Fifth en bas on the final demi-plié.

Purpose: Relevé develops the arches, weight distribution, and transfer of weight as the body moves from full foot to balancing on the toes and metatarsals in three-quarter relevé. Many poses and ballet steps are performed on relevé. The dancer's goal is learning to execute and control these various types of relevés efficiently and effortlessly.

Music and Timing:

- Time signature: 4/4, 3/4, or 2/4.
- Tempo: slow to moderate tempo, with a strong to light quality.
- Timing: The upward movement is on the "&"; descend on the count.

Preparation: Standing in First, Second, Third, or Fifth position, the dancer executes a First port de bras with standard head movements for either the two- or four-count preparation.

Breathing:

- Inhale on the rise.
- Exhale on the descent.
- Extend breath phrasing over several repetitions or a set.

Progression:

1. Review the point and flex and foot press exercises as the basis for learning relevé.

2. Face the barre, practice four relevés in First, Second, Third, or Fifth position. Perform these exercises slowly and alternate the Third or Fifth position with the right foot; then repeat, beginning with the left foot front.

3. Next, execute three relevés in each position and then test balancing on relevé in that position. At first simply lift the hands off the barre, then place the arms in Second position, next Fifth position en haut while executing the relevés.

4. Teach the sous-sus. Practice three sous-sus with hands on the barre and then balance; repeat to the other side.

5. Practice relevés and sous-sus with finger tips on top of the barre or without hands on the barre; then later practice in the center.

Teaching Cues:

- "And, up"
- "Inh-a-l-e, h-o-l-d, exhale"

Teaching Images:

- "Smooth and straight."
- "Go up and down like an elevator."

Assessment Checklist:

✓ Body weight centers over the full-foot triangle, then over the metatarsals and toes.

✓ The foot releases in sequence from the heel to the metatarsals and toes.

✓ All five toes and metatarsals remain on the floor.

✓ The body aligns and moves vertically up and down in the relevé.

Specific Errors:

- The heels release from the demi-plié before the knees straighten.
- The knees bend before the heels return to the floor.
- The foot falls toward the great toe or rolls out toward the little toe in relevé.

Barre Progressions

Demi-Plié:

1. Change Third position demi-plié to Fifth position demi-plié.

2. Teach grand pliés in First, Second, Third, and then Fifth position. Combine demi-pliés and grand pliés in one exercise. Arms begin in Fifth position en bas, open to demi-seconde, and return to Fifth en bas on the demi-plié; execute First port de bras on the grand plié.

Battement Tendu:

1. Perform en croix and other directional patterns.

2. Decrease the en croix patterns to two per direction with increased repetitions.

Battement Tendu With Demi-Plié:

1. Perform en croix, for example, four battement tendu en croix with demi-plié.

2. Decrease this pattern to two battement tendu en croix twice.

3. Combine with other steps, for example, two battement tendu en croix; two battement tendu with demi-plié en croix.

4. Or, execute two battement tendu (devant), two battement tendu with demi-plié (devant), en croix.

Battement Dégagé: Focus on practicing the exercise until it reaches its standard form but performed at a slower tempo.

1. Perform four battement dégagés en croix in their regular form.

2. Decrease to two en croix twice; execute from Third and perhaps Fifth position by the end of the unit.

3. Include three sequential patterns of three battement dégagés, hold in Third or Fifth position, en croix, twice; or three battement dégagés with the last one ending in demi-plié Third or Fifth position, en croix, twice.

Rond de Jambe à Terre: Concentrate on practicing the exercise in its standard form. Use the simplified preparation starting in Third or Fifth position (see unit I). Perform eight rond de jambe à terre en dehors, ending à la quatrième devant; eight rond de jambe à terre en dedans, ending à la quatrième derrière; finish in either Third or Fifth position. The exercise is still performed at slower than the standard tempo with two measures for each rond de jambe, in order to perfect the individual parts.

Teaching Beginning Ballet Technique

Grand Battements: Perform the grand battement in a modified form. Emphasize executing the exercise at the barre. Perform the grand battements from First, then Third or Fifth positions.

1. With the back to the barre: Execute four grand battements devant on both sides; this can be repeated.

2. Face the barre: Perform four grand battement à la seconde on both sides; this can be repeated.

3. Combine four devant right and then left, and four à la seconde right and left with the back to the barre. Then execute this combination with four grand battement devant, four grand battement à la seconde on the same leg; repeat other side.

4. Facing the barre, practice grand battements derrière; repeat both sides. Execute derrière and à la seconde combinations. These exercises prepare the student to perform grand battements with one hand on the barre.

Unit II Center

Classical Positions of the Body

The classical positions of the body comprise eight basic positions. In the beginning ballet class, the teacher presents some, or all, of the positions. Initially, execute the positions of the body with battement tendu in sequence on one side and then on the alternate side. There are several versions of these positions; some schools or methods have more positions or variations than others.

Principles: squareness, pull-up or lift, turn-out, weight distribution, transfer of weight, and alignment

Rules and Protocols: Open the legs and arms in the body position, Possess a send of the body position in relation to the stage direction. Close in the direction of the next body position.

Verbal Depiction: There are eight basic classical positions of the body. (Review stage directions presented in unit I).

Croisé Devant (kewah-ZAY duh-VAHN): The body faces direction 2. The right foot extends in battement

tendu devant. After the arms raise to First position, the left arm opens to Fifth position en haut while the right arm extends to Second position. The head is slightly tilted left and turned toward the audience (see figure II.13a).

A la Quatrième Devant (à lah ka-tree-EM duh-VAHN): The body faces direction 5. The right foot extends in battement tendu devant. Both arms raise to First position then open to Second position. The dancer looks straight ahead at the audience (see figure II.13b).

Ecarté (ay-kar-TAY) (devant): The body faces direction 2. The right foot extends in battement tendu to Second position, with the foot pointed toward direction 1. Both arms raise to First position; the right arm opens to Fifth en haut and the left arm to Second position. The head turns and lifts with the face focusing up into the palm of the right hand. The body may or may not tilt slightly toward the supporting leg (see figure II.13c).

Effacé (eh-fa-SAY) (devant): The body faces direction 1. The right foot extends in battement tendu devant. Both arms raise to First position, the left arm opens to Fifth en haut and the right arm to Second position. The head turns in front of the left arm and tilts upward as the dancer looks into the audience. The upper body, from under the shoulder blades, turns, lifts and tilts slightly backwards, opening toward the audience (see figure II.13d).

A la Seconde (ah la suh-GAWND): The body faces direction 5. The right foot extends in battement tendu à la seconde. Both arms raise to First position then open to Second position. The dancer looks straight ahead at the audience (see figure II.13e).

Epaulé (ay-poh-LAY): The body faces direction 2. The right foot extends in battement tendu derrière. The right arm extends forward in arabesque position (palm down). The left arm extends behind in arabesque position (palm down). Although the upper torso lifts and slightly twists to give the shouldered effect, the shoulders remain parallel to the floor. The head tilts down to the right shoulder as the dancer focuses on or beyond the fingertips of the right hand (see figure II.13f).

A la Quatrième Derrière (a-lah ka-tree-EM deh-RYEHR): The body faces direction 5. The right foot extends in battement tendu derrière. Both arms raise to First position then open to Second position. The dancer looks straight ahead at the audience (see figure II.13g).

Croisé Derrière (kawah-ZAY deh-RYEHR): The body faces direction 1. The left foot extends in battement tendu derrière to direction 3. Both arms raise to First position. The left arm opens to Fifth position en haut, and the right arm opens to Second position.

The body turns slightly toward the audience and the dancer looks out at the audience under the left arm (see figure II.13h).

Arms: After executing each body position, the arms return to Fifth position en bas using an outward route as the feet close in Fifth position. The head returns to a centered position.

Preparation: Standing in Fifth position, right foot in front, facing direction 2; execute First port de bras with standard head movements.

Music and Timing:

- Time signature: 4/4.

- Tempo: slow tempo with a smooth, legato quality.

- Timing: Performing each body position in 4/4 time, use one measure of four counts to slowly extend legs, arms, and head and complete subtle body changes. For measures two and three, stretch the lines of the body positions. At the end of the fourth measure, close in Fifth position facing the new direction for the next body position. This timing of the movement phrase gives the student adequate time to think about the parts of the body positions:

- The coordination of legs, arms, and head

- The next body position

- Directional changes

After learning the sequence of positions, the musical phrase for each body position condenses to two measures of 4/4 time.

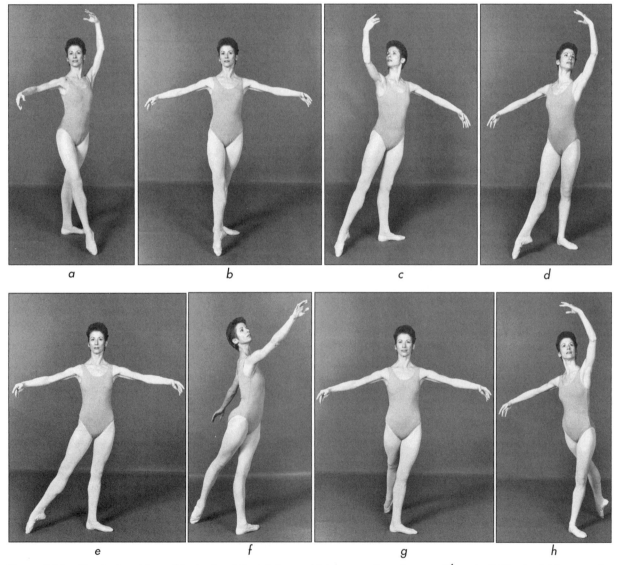

Figure II.13 Classical positions of the body: a) Croisé devant. b) A la quatrième devant. c) Écarté. d) Effacé. e) A la seconde. f) Epaulé. g) A la quatrième derrière. h) Croisé derrière.

Teaching Beginning Ballet Technique

In 3/4 time, the movement phrase shortens, with one measure to quickly open into the body position, measures two and three to stretch the line, and closing near the end of the fourth measure. The amount of time spent closing and preparing for the next body position lessens gradually as the dancer gains practice in finishing this transition.

Breathing: Breath and breath phrasing in conjunction with the opening into a body position give dynamics to the body positions in the sequence. Breath phrasing extends over one or more musical phrases but for no more than eight measures.

Progressions: The English translation of each of the eight positions provides clues for students to connect the pose to the name. Croisé devant or derrière means crossed in the front or back; à la quatrième devant or derrière refers to the Fourth position front or back; à la seconde refers to the Second position; effacé means shaded or shadowed; écarté, separated, thrown wide apart; épaulé means shouldered. Repeating the names of the body positions either out loud or to themselves helps students to remember the names and the sequence.

To teach the eight positions of the body to beginning dancers, break the positions down into a series of phases:

1. Begin with practicing battement tendu à la quatrième devant, à la seconde, and à la quatrième derrière from Fifth position. To make the combination complete or lasting for a phrase of 16 measures, repeat the à la seconde and close Fifth position derrière so that the combination repeats starting with the other side. These basic directions of front, à la seconde, back, and à la seconde are part of the center barre and enable the dancer to connect with the stage space and the audience. Teach this en croix sequence at the end of unit I or beginning as an extension of the battement tendu center barre exercises.

2. To teach the first section of the eight positions of the body sequence, face corner 2. Introduce croisé devant, à la quatrième devant, écarté, effacé, and à la seconde, then finish the sequence by closing Fifth position back. Complete the musical phrase with a First port de bras. Guide the students in transposing these body positions to the other side. This com-

pletes learning the first section of the combination. The working foot closes in Fifth position front for all the positions, except for the last position, à la seconde. To combine both sides, when closing Fifth position back, the body changes to corner 1 to execute the First port de bras and start the second side of the combination.

3. To teach the second section of the eight positions of the body sequence, face corner 2. Introduce the positions épaulé, à la quatrième derrière and croisé derrière. Execute a First port de bras at the end of this section for a musical phrase of four counts. Close the final position, croisé derrière, facing corner 1; execute the First port de bras and start the second side of the combination.

Combine the first and second sections of the combination; delete the port de bras. Depending upon the students, the teacher may select to teach six or all eight positions of the body. If the teacher chooses to introduce only six position, the sequence is croisé devant, à la quatrième devant, effacé, à la quatrième derrière, and croisé derrière, followed by a port de bras to complete the phrase before repeating the positions to the other side. In this version, do not perform the positions of écarté and épaulé. Introduce the six positions of the body in the same way as the eight positions of the body. In a combination of six positions of the body, the port de bras at the end of each section takes eight counts.

When the dancer changes directions between a body position, the dancer moves to the new direction while the working foot closes into Fifth position. This transition is smooth and complete to enable the dancer to open the working leg in the new position and direction at the start of the next measure.

Learning the body positions provides a challenge for beginning students a chance to memorize a sequence of movements. Remind students to use the photographs as references when learning the positions. After learning the positions of the body on one side, ask students to transpose this combination to the other side. This is an assignment that presents a challenge to beginning students. Learning to perform the positions of the body becomes a vehicle for teaching students the process for learning and performing extended movement sequences.

Balancé
(ba-lahn-SAY)

Definition: rocking step (see figure II.14, a-e)

Principles: transfer of weight, turn-out, pull-up or lift, alignment, balance

Rules and Protocols: feet point in the air, the working foot touches behind the supporting foot

Verbal Depiction: The balancé begins in either Third or Fifth position, right foot front, or the B+ position, with the right foot pointing derrière. On the first balancé, the right leg and foot extend and step to Second position. The weight transfers from the left by springing or stepping lightly to the right foot in demi-plié. The left foot steps onto three-quarter relevé behind or in front of the ankle, with the foot accepting the weight. The right foot lifts off the floor and then returns into demi-plié; then the left foot lifts off the floor at the ankle or sur le cou-de-pied.

Teach the balancé to Second position. Perform the balancé as either an adagio or an allégro step. The tempo and quality of the step is either with a smooth or a bouncy quality.

Arms: Begin in Fourth position en avant with the right arm curved in front. During the step the arms move to the opposite Fourth position en avant. The body and head incline to the right. The position of the head will be discussed in later units. Perform the next balancé to the left.

Preparation: Standing in the B+ position, the dancer executes a First port de bras ending in Fourth position en avant with accompanying head movements.

Introductory or transitional steps: Balancé is an introductory step in adagio, petit or grand allégro

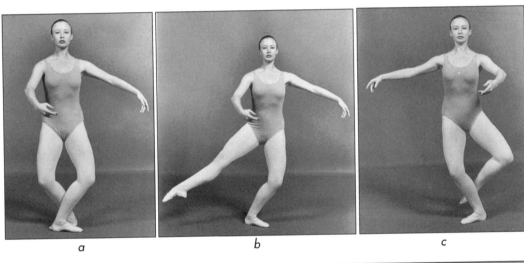

a   b   c

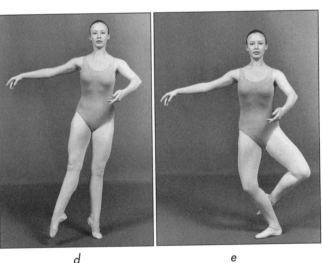

Figure II.14 Balancé: a) Begin in Fifth position demi-plié. b) Extend the leg to à la seconde. c) Step on the extended leg and bring the other leg to coupé derrière. d) Rise on the back foot while the front foot extends and leaves the floor slightly. e) End in coupé derrière.

d   e

combination, and links with steps performed in 3/4 or 6/8 time.

Music and Timing:

- Time signature: 3/4 or 6/8.
- Tempo: Slow to moderate with an adagio, lyrical, or bouncy quality. Teach the pattern at a very slow tempo before trying a slow-moderate tempo.
- Timing: On the "&" the working leg dégagés; and on count 1, the dancer transfers the weight to the new foot. On count 2, the other foot steps behind or in front of the ankle. Count 3, the first foot accepts the weight again. Modify the timing by using two measures for each movement.

Breathing:

- Inhale before the initial jump or step out.
- Exhale at the end of the step.
- Extend breath phrasing over a series of balancés or a short movement phrase.

Progressions:

1. Teach the step pattern: side, back, step in place; repeat on both sides.
2. Perform the step with the back foot in three-quarter relevé stepping behind the supporting foot.
3. Add the arms in coordination with the footwork.
4. Add head movements to the step: On the balancé to the right, the head turns to direction 1; on the balancé to the left, the head turns to direction 2.

Teaching Cues:

- "Side, back, step"
- "Side, front, step"
- "Right, left, right"

Teaching Images:

- "Imagine the movement of a rocking chair or see-saw as you dance."
- "Imagine performing the movement with a book balanced on your head—reach and glide smoothly across the floor."

Assessment Checklist:

- ✓ The working leg dégagés fully, extending with the foot pointed to Second position.
- ✓ The leg accepts the body weight in a deep demi-plié.

- ✓ The second leg steps immediately behind or in front of the supporting leg.
- ✓ The second leg is cou-de-pied derrière or devant.
- ✓ The quality of the step is either smooth or bouncy.

Specific Errors:

- There is no transfer of weight on the step behind or in front.
- The front leg extends above battement dégagé height.

Glissade

(glee-SAD)

Definition: to glide (see figure II.15, a-e).

Principles: transfer of weight, weight distribution, pull-up or lift, squareness, turn-out, alignment, balance

Rules and Protocols: Both legs fully stretch during the step. The feet close in quick succession.

Verbal Depiction: In Third or Fifth position, demi-plié and shift the weight to the supporting leg. While the supporting leg remains in demi-plié, brush the working leg in the direction in which the glissade moves. Push from the supporting leg, transfer the weight through fully extended legs to the working leg, and quickly brush the second leg into Third or Fifth position demi-plié. The accent is on the closing.

Some of the important points about performing the glissade are as follows:

- The working leg stretches further than its initial extension before accepting the transfer of weight.
- When the supporting leg extends, it completely stretches before quickly brushing into Third or Fifth position demi-plié.

To perform a glissade requires concentration on where the weight is and where the weight is going. This step includes a complete extension of the legs, with the body lifted off the legs so that they move smoothly for the quick transfer of weight from two feet to one, from one to one, and then from one to two.

The glissade is performed in two ways:

1. The legs fully extend with the toes touching the floor.
2. In the more common version, the working foot brushes barely off the floor and the legs and feet extend in the air just above the floor.

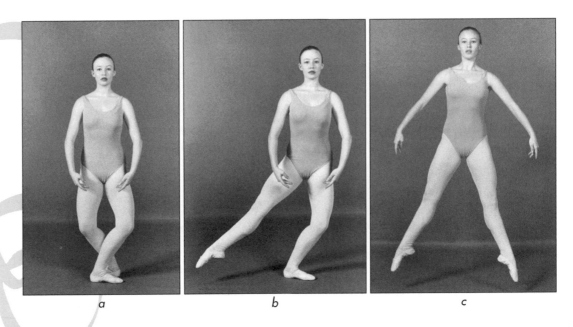

a   b   c

Figure II.15 Glissade: a) Begin in Fifth position demi-plié. b) Dégagé working leg à la seconde with the supporting leg in demi-plié. c) Legs extend in Second position in the air. d) Land on the first leg with the other leg extended à la seconde. e) Close in Fifth position demi-plié, with the same foot in front.

d   e

Arms: Standard arms for glissade begin in the Fifth position en bas or open on the glissade to the demi-seconde position.

Preparation: Begin in a strong, soft demi-plié, lifting the body weight up off the legs. At the bottom of the demi-plié, the weight transfers from two feet to the supporting leg so that the working foot and leg execute a strong brushing action. Meanwhile, execute a First port de bras.

Introductory or Transitional Steps: The glissade is generally an introductory or transitional step that combines a variety of adagio, and allégro.

Music and Timing:

- Time signature: 3/4, 4/4, 2/4, or 6/8.

- Tempo: a moderate to fast tempo, depending upon the combination.

- Timing: Brush out and glide in the air on "&." On the last count of the measure, close quickly into Fifth position with the second foot. The dancer learns to adjust the movement and speed of the glissade to the time signature for the combination. Perform the glissade in two measures or one, depending on the time signature; the style of the combination; and, especially, the dancer's level of experience.

Breathing:

- Exhale on the preliminary demi-plié.
- Inhale on the brush and air moment.
- Exhale on the closing.
- Extend breath phrasing to include a longer phrase of movement.

Progressions:

1. At the barre, first teach battement dégagé in demi-plié à la seconde; close with straight legs in Third or Fifth position. Alternate sides.

2. Teach glissade at the barre first in Third and/ or Fifth position; practice the step at the barre and then in the center.

3. In the center, perform four glissades devant to the right, stop; then perform the other side. The number of glissades decreases to two. Practice both sides of the combination: Three glissades devant and one derrière; repeat on the other side.

Teaching Cues:

- "And, close"
- "Glis-sade" (put the accent on the last part of the word like the closing of the step)

Teaching Images:

- "Imagine gliding over a highly polished floor."
- "Pretend you have a heavy book balanced on your head while you perform the glissade, so you stay down in the demi-plié."

Assessment Checklist:

- ✓ The entire working foot brushes on the floor and into the air.
- ✓ The supporting leg pushes the body into the direction of the extended working foot.
- ✓ Both legs completely stretch with the toes just above the floor.
- ✓ The working leg stretches further than its initial extension before accepting the transfer of weight.
- ✓ The second leg closes quickly into the Fifth position demi-plié.

Specific Errors:

- The timing of the push-off from the supporting leg is not in proper sequence; it is either too early or too late.
- The body "lopes" through the transfer of weight from one leg to the other.

- The working foot does not stretch to accept the weight of the body beyond where it initially extends.
- The second foot and leg close slowly into Fifth position demi-plié.

Standards and Variations: The glissade is a versatile step and can be performed in a variety of directions. The quality of the glissade can be both adagio and allégro.

Glissade Devant (glee-SAD duh-VAHN) (glissade front) travels to the side. In this variation, the right foot begins in front in Fifth position demi-plié. The left foot closes derrière in Fifth position. The step begins and ends with the right foot front.

Glissade Derrière (glee-SAD deh-RYEHR) (glissade back) travels to the side. In this variation, the working or right foot begins in back in Fifth position demi-plié. The left foot closes devant in Fifth position. The step begins and ends with the right foot back.

Glissade Changée (glee-SAD shahn-ZHAY) (glissade changing) changes feet. This refers to a glissade that closes with the opposite foot in front. If the step begins with the right foot front in Fifth position, then the step ends with the left foot front in Fifth position.

Pas de Chat
(pah duh shah)

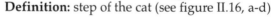

Definition: step of the cat (see figure II.16, a-d)

Principles: pull-up or lift, squareness, transfer of weight, weight distribution, turn-out, alignment, balance

Rules and Protocols: Apply the jumping technique; the two feet land in quick succession.

Verbal Depiction: The step begins from Third and, later, Fifth position left foot front. Demi-plié with the weight transferring at the base of the demi-plié from both legs to the left leg. The right leg draws up to the back of the knee (retiré derrière). Next, the left leg springs into the air while drawing up to the front of the right knee (retiré devant). The right foot lands first, followed immediately by the left foot into Third or Fifth position devant. The pas de chat is an up-and-over movement to the side. During the air moment, both legs bend in the air with the feet almost touching. The body lifts off the legs during the air moment through the landing. The accent for

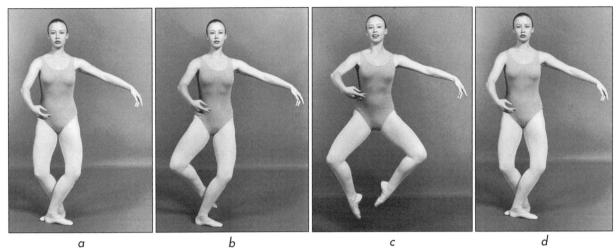

Figure II.16 Pas de chat: a) Begin in Fifth position demi-plié. b) Lift the back foot in coupé derrière (arms in Fourth position en avant). c) Spring into the air, with both legs bent. d) Land on one foot and immediately the other in Fifth position demi-plié, with the same foot in front.

the pas de chat is on the upward movement. The foot that begins the step from Third or Fifth position derrière remains behind at the finish of the step. Teach this step first with the legs lifting to coupé positions (see unit I).

Arms: If the pas de chat travels to the right (with right foot behind), the right arm curves in front of the body in Fourth position en avant, with the head turning slightly, looking out and down toward the direction traveling. The head movements will be illustrated in later units.

Preparation: Starting in Third or Fifth position, the dancer executes a First port de bras and demi-pliés.

Introductory and Transitional Steps: glissade, pas de basque, pas de bourrée, and assemblé

Music and Timing:

- Time signature: 2/4 or 4/4.
- Tempo: moderate to brisk tempo with a bright quality.
- Timing: "& a 1": On the "&," the first leg raises coupé derrière to the knee. On "a" the other leg raises to the knee while the first foot lands. On "count 1" the second foot closes in Fifth position devant in demi-plié.

Breathing:

- Inhale on the ascent.
- Exhale on the landing.
- Breath phrasing extends over a series of pas de chats or in the allégro combination.

Progressions:

1. Practice coupés then pas de chats first at the barre; then in the center.

2. Execute four pas de chats right, stop; four pas de chats left, stop.

3. Perform three pas de chats and battement tendu to change feet; repeat other side.

Teaching Cues:

- "Up, up, down, down"
- "Up and over"
- "& a 1"
- "Footfoot" (rhythmic cue for landing)

Teaching Images:

- "Imagine you are jumping and landing like a cat."
- "Jump over a fence."
- "Land like a kitten, not like a lion."

Assessment Checklist:

✓ The working leg draws up to the middle of the lower leg (coupé derrière) or to back of the knee of the supporting leg (retiré derrière).

✓ Before the working leg lands, the supporting leg springs off the floor.

✓ Both feet are in the air at the same time.

✓ The direction the step travels is up and over to the side.

✓ The first foot lands, then the second foot lands immediately after closing in Third or Fifth position.

✓ The feet remain in the same front/back position at the end of the step.

Specific Errors:

- The legs actions are disjointed or separate, causing a "loping" effect.

- Both legs do not share the air moment.
- Legs do not bend enough.

Jeté Devant

(zhuh-TAY duh-VAHN)

Definition: to throw or to toss (see figure II.17, a-d)

Principles: transfer of weight, pull-up or lift, squareness, turn-out, alignment, balance

Rules and Protocols: The entire foot brushes into the air, apply landing technique, place working heel on the middle of the back of the lower supporting leg.

Verbal Depiction: The jeté is a petit allégro step or, later, a grand allégro step. This step has many variations. In this unit, introduce the basic jeté or jeté devant (Cecchetti). As a basic petit allégro step, the jeté begins on one leg and ends on the other foot. The jeté starts in Fifth position demi-plié. The working foot brushes from behind and extends the leg en l'air à la seconde, while the supporting leg pushes into the air. The height of the jeté is determined by the height of the working leg off the floor. This height is between that of a dégagé—barely two inches off the floor—to under 45 degrees off the floor. In the air moment of the jump, both legs and feet are open and fully extended at an approximate 45-degree angle to the floor. On the descent the dancer lands on the working leg in fondu (demi-plié on one foot) with the other foot coupé derrière. The jeté does not move side to side; it is a vertical step.

Arms: Begin in Fourth position en avant; if the right foot brushes, the right arm begins in front.

Preparation: Execute a First port de bras opening to Second position and demi-plié with the body weight pulled up as the right arm moves from Second position to Fourth en avant. At the base of the demi-plié, the body weight transfers to the supporting leg so that the working leg is able to brush.

Introductory or Transitional Steps: A glissade, pas de bourrée, and other petit allégro steps introduce the jeté. The jeté combines with many other petit and grand allégro steps.

Music and Timing:

- Time signature: 2/4 or 4/4.
- Tempo: moderate to fast tempo, with a light and sprightly quality.
- Timing: On the "&" beat the dancer is in the air; the landing is on the count following "&." The dancer anticipates the jump part of the step.

Breathing:

- Inhale on the ascent.
- Exhale on the landing.
- Breath pattern extends over several repetitions of the step or a short sequence of allégro.

Progressions:

1. Facing the barre, execute the battement dégagé in demi-plié à la seconde; close in Fifth position front with the legs straight.
2. Teach the jeté at the barre.

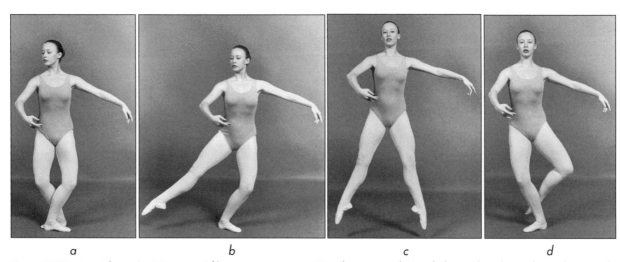

a   *b*   *c*   *d*

Figure II.17 Jeté (devant): a) Begin in Fifth position, arms are Fourth en avant. b) Brush the working leg en l'air à la seconde while the other leg remains in demi-plié. c) Spring off the supporting foot, both legs extend à la seconde in air. d) Land with the opposite leg with the working foot coupé derrière.

3. Practice the step at the barre and then in the center.

At the beginning level, execute the jeté step in a repetitive series that moves (forward) en avant. Usually this series is seven jetés en promenade en avant, closing with a jump onto both feet to complete the sequence.

Teaching Cues:

- "Brush, hop, cut."
- "Brush up; land on one."

Teaching Images:

- "Imagine there are rocks in your path and you have to leap over each one: right, left, and so on."
- "Imagine leaves are on the ground and you are kicking them away from your path."
- "Glue your heel in coupé derrière."

Assessment Checklist:

✓ Full working foot brushes into the air.

✓ Before completing the brush, the supporting leg pushes off quickly into the air.

✓ Both legs and feet fully extend in the air at a 45-degree angle to the floor.

✓ The body weight lifts and moves on a forward diagonal in the direction of the working leg.

✓ The working leg becomes the new supporting leg as it accepts the body weight when it lands in fondu.

✓ The new working leg bends at the knee with the foot touching in the coupé position.

Specific Errors:

- The step is disjointed or separates the actions of brushing and leaping.
- Both legs do not share the air moment.
- The working leg pulls underneath the body to land.

Center Progressions

Port de Bras: Continue to practice First and Second port de bras using breath phrasing. Focus on port de bras as part of studying the classical ballet positions, steps, and center combinations.

Center Barre:

Battement Tendu variations:

1. Perform two battement tendu en croix and alternate this pattern to the other side.

2. Decrease the en croix pattern to one in each direction, performed on both sides.

3. Repeat starting the combination with the left foot.

4. Increase the combination to two sets (right side, left side, repeat).

5. Continue practicing battement tendu en promenade en avant and en arrière, beginning with eight, decreasing to four, and repeating the set.

Pas de Bourrée:

1. Add stepping on three-quarter relevé (up, up, down—full foot).

2. Begin and end each pas de bourrée with a coupé. Close the last pas de bourée in Third or Fifth position.

3. Coordinate the arms in Fourth en avant with the step.

4. Combine the pas de bourrée with another step.

Ballet Walks: Continue to perform periodically.

Chassé:

1. Perform à la seconde and devant across the floor.

2. Coordinate with arms in Second position or Fourth position.

Teacher's Planner for Unit III

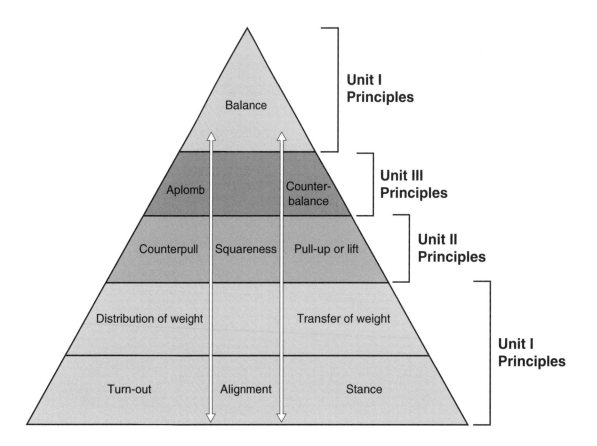

Balance

Unit I
Principles

Aplomb | Counter-balance

Unit III
Principles

Counterpull | Squareness | Pull-up or lift

Unit II
Principles

Distribution of weight | Transfer of weight

Turn-out | Alignment | Stance

Unit I
Principles

Teacher's Planner for Unit III

Unit III concentrates on adding the more complicated exercises to complete the barre. In the Center, adagio combinations expand, and petit and grand allégro steps combine, creating new challenges for the student. In this unit, the barre exercises and the center gain proportion and balance within the structure of the class.

Objectives of the Unit

The objectives for the unit encompass the cognitive, psychomotor, and affective domains as follows:

Cognitive Domain

The students will be able to

- identify and say new ballet terms;
- translate the French ballet terms from unit I and II steps into correct movement;
- apply units I, II, and III new principles, rules, and protocols to class work;
- assess execution of personal performance of exercises and steps; and
- foresee in performing exercises and steps the application of principles, rules, and protocols.

Psychomotor Domain

The students will be able to

- execute the following new barre exercises: battement dégagé en cloche, petit battement sur le cou-de-pied, battement développé, and grand battement derrière;
- perform appropriate barre and center protocols;
- learn the arabesque pose;
- perform the following new center steps: sautés, changements, temps levé, and assemblé;
- refine execution of exercises and steps from units I and II;
- execute a two- or three-step combination and transpose to the other side; and
- apply breath and breath phrasing to class work.

Affective Domain

The students will be able to

- accept and apply group corrections to personal work,
- receive and apply individual comments about work,

- respond to directions given by the teacher,
- demonstrate a professional attitude toward the work, and
- demonstrate self-reliance, movement confidence, and display a performance attitude in classroom performance.

Teaching Strategies

The following teaching strategies apply within unit III:

- Teaching styles: command, practice, inclusive, self-check, guided discovery, reciprocal
- Teacher modeling: continued demonstration of new work using English action words, French terms for unit I and II work, repetition, imagery, visual memory development, motor memory of what is correct, and more transfer of responsibility for learning to students

Assessment

Consider the following methods of assessment:

- Assessment Checklist utilizes cues for the performance of each exercise and step.
- Periodic informal evaluations monitor if knowledge and skills are attained.
- Written dance concert report.

Teacher Responsibilities

The following list is a self-check of your responsibilities when teaching unit III:

- Clear demonstration of exercises and steps
- Clear direction and cueing of execution of exercises and steps
- Clear counting of music
- Clear explanation and application of principles, rules, and conventions
- Use of imagery in the teaching/learning process
- Group feedback
- Individual attention
- Development of student responsibility for the movement
- Pace of the class
- Open and risk-free atmosphere
- Continued development of barre and acquisition of new materials in the center

Performance Test Content

Performance tests can include a self-check or peer evaluation. Student performance evaluations follow for unit III.

Principles and Rules

The students will perform

- unit III principles: counterbalance, aplomb, balance on one foot; and
- unit III barre and center rules and protocols.

Combining Exercises at the Barre

The students will execute the following:

1. Demi- and grand pliés with relevés and balances en relevé or sous-sus
2. Battement tendu, battement tendu with demi-plié, battement tendu relevé
3. Battement dégagé and battement dégagé en cloche
4. Rond de jambe à terre and port de corps

Single Exercises at the Barre

The students will demonstrate the following:

1. Battement frappé
2. Petit battement sur le cou-de-pied
3. Battement développé
4. Grand battement
5. Arabesque pose
6. Assemblé

In the Center

The students will demonstrate the following:

1. The three arabesques
2. Assemblé soutenu en promenade en avant
3. Three pas de chat, changement
4. Walk, walk, arabesque
5. Chassé, sauté, First arabesque
6. Sautés: 4 in First position and 4 in Second position

Written Assignment

The students will write a report after attending a dance performance.

Unit III Barre

In unit III, the teacher introduces the final group of exercises that comprise the beginning ballet barre. These exercises require strength and control to perform even at 45 degrees.

Battement Dégagé en Cloche

(bat-MAHN day-ga-ZHAY ahn klawsh)

Definition: swinging action similar to the action of a bell clapper (see figure III.1, a-d)

Principles: balance on one leg, alignment, pull-up, squareness, turn-out, weight distribution

Rules and Protocols: The body remains stable (aligned and squared) while the working leg swings from the hip devant and derrière off the floor.

Verbal Depiction: In a battement dégagé en cloche, the working leg swings front and back through First position. The body weight centers over the supporting leg, and remains perpendicular to the floor. Performing the battement dégagé en cloche, the working foot brushes through a battement tendu en cloche, swinging the working leg front and back to the height of a battement dégagé, about two inches from the floor (en l'air). The body remains stable and aligned. Later, the working leg swings up to a height of 20 to 45 degrees. The accent is on the extensions.

Arms: The working arm remains in Second position.

Purpose:

- Develops freedom of the working leg in the hip joint by swinging it front and back en l'air
- Requires control of the back, hips, and supporting leg to resist and balance the action of the working leg
- Builds a foundation for subsequent exercises performed en cloche

Music and Timing:

- Time signature: 2/4, 4/4, 3/4, and 6/8.
- Tempo: moderate to fast tempo with a light, bright quality.
- Timing: Accent is on the upward movement of the brush ("&, up").

Preparation: Standing in Fifth position, the working leg points derrière or devant, or the exercise begins in First or Fifth position. First port de bras and standard head movements accompany the foot movement.

Breathing:

- Inhale as the leg extends in the air.
- Exhale on the return to First position.
- Extend breath phrasing over several repetition or a set.

Teaching Cues:

- "And up, and up, and up."
- "Swing front and back through First position."

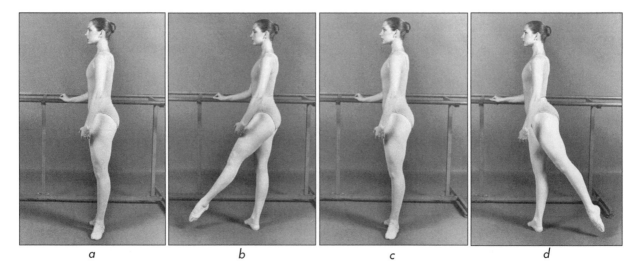

Figure III.1 Battement dégagé en cloche: a) Begin in First position. b) Dégagé or (brush the leg off the ground) à la quatriène devant. c) Brush working leg through First position. d) Dégagé the working leg à la quatrième derrière.

Teaching Images:

- "Sense your leg swinging like a bell clapper."
- "Imagine your foot brushing lightly front and back."

Assessment Checklist:

✓ The foot slides along the floor through a battement tendu en cloche on the extension and return.

✓ The foot brushes sharply into the air to dégagé height.

Specific Errors:

- Hips tip backward or forward or twist during the execution.
- The whole foot does not slide along the floor releasing heel, metatarsals, toes in sequence or the reverse on the return.
- Body alignment is not maintained during the exercise.
- The supporting leg does not remain perpendicular throughout the exercise.

Petit Battement sur le Cou-de-Pied

(puh-TEE bat MAHN sewr luh koo-duh-PYAY)

Definition: small beatings on the neck of the foot (see figure III.2, a-c)

Principles: turn-out, balance on one leg, pull-up or lift, squareness

Rules and Protocols: The working foot touches the sur le cou-de-pied positions devant and derrière. The toes and metatarsals of the working foot remain on the floor and trace an acute angle on the floor with the apex of the angle near Second position. The upper leg is stable; the movement initiates from the knee, and the lower leg and foot work as a single component.

Verbal Depiction: Beginning in Fifth position, the working leg prepares to execute the petit battement sur le cou-de-pied by extending à la seconde and then closing into the sur le cou-de-pied devant position. Turn out on both the supporting and the working legs. Center the body weight over the supporting leg. The hip, thigh, and knee of the working leg remain stable while the lower leg and foot work as a unit to execute the step.

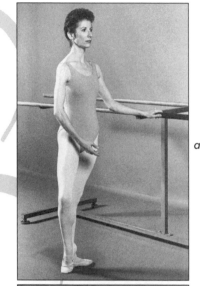
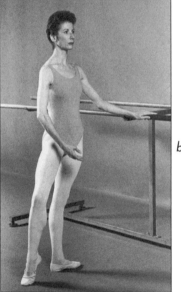
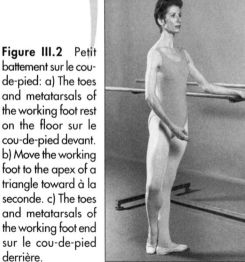

Figure III.2 Petit battement sur le cou-de-pied: a) The toes and metatarsals of the working foot rest on the floor sur le cou-de-pied devant. b) Move the working foot to the apex of a triangle toward à la seconde. c) The toes and metatarsals of the working foot end sur le cou-de-pied derrière.

The lower leg and foot describe a V-shaped pattern with the apex toward the Second position, as the lower leg and foot move from the front to the back of the supporting ankle. The portion of the working foot resting on the floor glides over the floor describing a V-shaped pattern. The working foot and leg remain well-turned out throughout the exercise.

For beginners to ensure turn-out and contact with the floor during the exercise, all five toes and the metatarsals of the working foot rest on the floor. In this position the foot remains in three-quarter relevé on the floor with the heel completely lifted during the exercises. Only perform the petit battement exercise on full foot. The accent on the foot brushing back in to sur le cou-de-pied position. Later, combine this exercise with battement frappé.

Arms: Arms are held in either Fifth position en bas or Second position throughout the exercise.

Purpose:

- Develops quick foot and lower leg gestures as foundation for allégro steps in the center
- Requires isolated movement of the lower working leg while the upper working leg remains stable and turned-out

Music and Timing:

- Time signature: 2/4 or 6/8.
- Tempo: moderate to brisk tempo with a sharp, light quality.
- Timing: The outward movement is on "&"; the accent is on the closing in the sur le cou-de-pied position on the count.

Preparation: Preparation for petit battement sur le cou-de-pied uses the same port de bras, foot preparation, and breathing sequence as the battement frappé (see unit II).

Breathing:

- Breath phrasing for preparation is the same as for the battement frappé.
- Inhale and exhale over several repetitions or a set.

Progressions:

1. Teach the exercise facing the barre. Find the sur le cou-de-pied positions, devant and derrière, and the position of the foot on the floor. Practice the in and out movement of the exercise, keeping the upper leg stable.
2. Practice 16 slow counts on each side, stopping in between. It is important that the student sense the squareness and turn-out of

both legs while balancing on one foot and centering the weight over the supporting leg.

3. Practice the exercise with one hand on the barre.

Teaching Cues:

- "Out, in"
- "And, one"

Teaching Images:

- "Imagine lightly dusting the floor with the toes and metatarsals of the foot."
- "With all five toes on the floor, draw a V-shape on the floor."

Assessment Checklist:

✓ All five toes and the metatarsals rest on the floor, with the heel slightly forward.

✓ Position the working heel at the front or back of the ankle.

✓ Shift the body weight from two legs to one leg before the preparation.

✓ Turn-out the working leg, flex the knee, and place the foot in the sur le cou-de-pied devant position.

✓ Keep the upper thigh of the working leg stable (not moving) in a turned-out position throughout the exercise.

✓ Perform the petit battement with the lower leg and foot working together.

✓ Describe a small V-shaped design with the apex toward the Second position on the floor.

✓ Start the V-shape design in the sur le cou-de-pied derrière position and end in the sur le cou-de-pied devant or vice versa.

✓ Execute the movement with a smooth, continuous quality.

Specific Errors:

- The working knee falls inward.
- The lower leg and foot do not work as a unit to execute the exercise.
- The working leg and foot move in an arc or forward and back pathway.
- The point of the V-shaped design is behind the Second position.
- The working foot does not touch sur le cou-de-pied devant/derrière positions.
- The sur le cou-de-pied positions are not at the same level; one is higher than the other.

Battement Développé
(bat-MAHN dayv-law-PAY)

Definition: unfolding of the leg (see figure III.3, a-g)

Principles: balance on one leg, pull-up or lift, counterbalance, squareness, turn-out, alignment, weight distribution

Rules and Protocols: The hips (iliac crests) remain level. The upper leg remains the same height while the lower leg extends. Counterbalance is used in executing the battement développé derrière.

Verbal Depiction: In a battement développé, the working foot moves from Fifth position through the sur le cou-de-pied position front or back of the supporting leg in a straight line to the retiré position. From this position, the working leg extends devant, à la seconde, or derrière. While the lower leg extends, the thigh of the working leg remains outwardly rotated and at the same height as in the retiré position. In executing the battement développé in front or Second position, the working heel leads the leg out, unfolding it continuously to its full extension at the same height as the retiré. In back, the toes direct the unfolding of the leg. At maximum extension, the working leg stops momentarily in the air before descending to a point on the floor and brushing into Fifth position. During the battement développé, the three curves of the spine stretch and lengthen keeping the body in correct alignment.

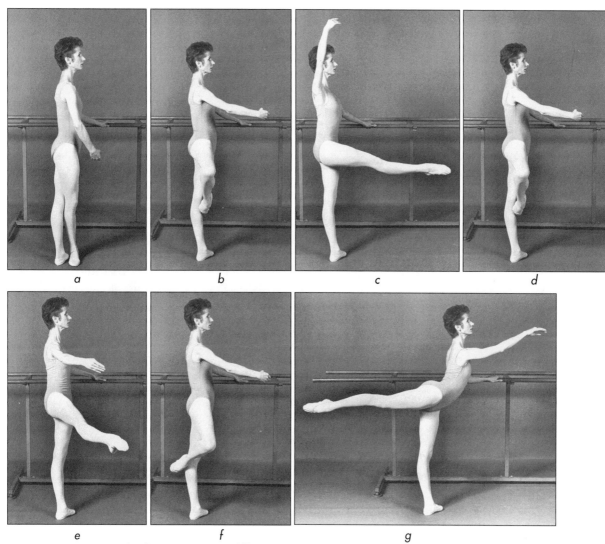

a   b   c   d

e   f   g

Figure III.3   Battement développé: a) Begin in fifth position. b) The working foot moves to retiré devant. c) The working leg unfolds à la quatrième devant to 90° and closes to Fifth position front. d) The working foot moves to retiré devant. e) The working leg unfolds à la seconde and closes to Fifth back. f) The working foot lifts to retiré derrière. g) The working leg unfolds to à la quatrième derrière and closes to Fifth position front.

In the battement développé derrière, the body counterbalances at the beginning of the extension phase from the retiré position. When the working leg returns to retiré or Fifth position from the back extension, the body returns to vertical alignment. Throughout the performance of the battement développé, from the initial position to the closing position, the working leg remains completely turned-out. The leg unfolds smoothly, with no accents in the movement.

To reach the position of retiré devant and retiré derrière, the working foot traces different paths. In the front, the little toe of the working foot traces the line up the front of the supporting leg from sur le cou-de-pied devant to retiré devant. In the back, the working foot releases through the sur le cou-de-pied position derrière and the heel draws a straight line up the back of the supporting leg to retiré derrière.

The battement développé exercise had been described as it generally is performed. Introduce the battement développé exercise using the coupé (or low retiré) position, instead of the retiré devant or derrière. Generally, beginning dancers are capable of keeping their hips (iliac crests) level in coupé devant and derrière positions, but not always in the retiré positions. From the coupé position, the working leg extends at 45 degrees, which is the correct height for the beginner's développé. Later, when the dancer gains the strength and ability to keep the hips level, then transfer to the retiré position, which opens the leg at 90 degrees.

Arms: The working arm may remain in Second position during the exercise.

Purpose

- Develops strength in the back and the supporting leg while the working leg extends in various directions
- Develops control of the working leg as it extends to positions up to 45 degrees
- Constitutes an important component of adagio movements both at the barre and, especially, in the center

Music and Timing:

- Time signature: 3/4 or 4/4.
- Tempo: slow, fluid adagio tempo and quality.
- Timing: Perform the retiré swiftly, allowing the maximum time to unfold the leg, accompanied by a slow descent and quick closing. In 3/4 time retiré on count 1, unfold the leg on count 2, and close on count 2. In 4/4 time, retiré on counts 1–2, unfold the leg on counts 3 and 4,

and close on count four. Later, the unfolding of the leg continues on through the final count to close at the very end of the measure.

Preparation: Standing in Fifth position, the dancer executes First port de bras with standard head movements.

Breathing:

- Inhale on the retiré and through the unfolding phase.
- Exhale on the return of the leg to Fifth position.
- Extend breath phrasing over several repetitions.

Progressions:

1. Introduce the battement développé with the same barre facings matching those of the grand battement (see unit II).
2. Perform one battement développé en croix with one hand on the barre, then repeat to build strength. The battement développé extends no higher than 45 degrees.

Teaching Cues:

- "Cou-de-pied, retiré, e-x-t-e-n-d, point, and close to Fifth position."
- "Up, extend, point, close."
- Counterbalance: "The torso tilts on a forward and upward diagonal when the leg unfolds derrière."

Teaching Images:

- "Imagine folding (retiré) and unfolding (développé) your leg like a bird's wing."
- "Draw the leg upward, graciously unfold it to a still point, then let it float back to the floor."

Assessment Checklist:

✓ Body weight shifts from two legs to one leg as the working foot passes through the sur le cou-de-pied position.

✓ The pointed working foot keeps in contact with the supporting leg to the retiré position.

✓ The working leg remains outwardly rotated throughout the exercise.

✓ The thigh remains stable at the same height throughout the exercise while the lower part of the leg extends front, to Second position, or back.

✓ The heel of the working leg unfolds the entire leg to its maximum extension of 45 degrees to the devant and to Second position.

- The toes lead the unfolding of the leg to the back.
- The movement is continuous and fluid.
- The torso counterbalances while the working leg extends derrière.

Specific Errors:

- The entire foot rests on the front of the leg or the great toe rests at the back of the leg.
- At the end of the développé either the supporting leg or the working leg and foot does not stretch to its maximum extension.
- Alignment is not maintained: Shoulders pull back, the back arches, and/or the ribs release or retreat.
- On the return of the leg from derrière, the torso or hips do not return to alignment from counterbalance.
- The working leg does not straighten on the développé.

Arabesque
(ah-ra-BESK)

Definition: The name *arabesque* derives from a Moorish architectural metal ornamentation.

Principles: balance (on one leg), pull-up, counterbalance, squareness, turn-out

Rules and Protocols: Hips and shoulders face the same direction. Counterbalance when the leg extends beyond 20 degrees derrière.

Verbal Depiction: Standing on one leg, the other leg extends à la quatrième derrière, the body counterbalances the leg. For the beginning dancer, the leg extends up to 45 degrees. The arms stretch in various positions. To continue the line of the arm in arabesque, the dancer holds the hands with palms facing down to the floor. Aesthetically, the arabesque in profile shows the dancer's longest lines.

For the three basic arabesque poses, the supporting leg is straight and presents the working leg in an open line. The arms are what distinguish each basic arabesque. The arms reverse when the dancer stands on the left foot.

First Arabesque: The right arm is in front of the shoulder at eye level. The eyes focus at and beyond the fingertips. The shoulders are squared. The left arm extends behind Second position (see figure III.4).

Figure III.4 First arabesque.

Second Arabesque: The left arm extends in front of the shoulder at eye level. The right arm extends behind the Second position. The shoulders are squared. The head tilts toward the downstage shoulder with the eyes focused on the hand. The arms form a diagonal line with the front arm higher than the back arm. The left arm extends behind Second position (see figure III.5).

Third Arabesque: Both the right and left arms extend in front of the body. The downstage arm is shoulder height, and the upstage arm is head height. The opening between the arms creates a window through which the dancer gazes. Third arabesque is also referred to as *arabesque a deux bras* (see figure III.6).

Purpose:

- Develops strength and extension up to 45 degrees for the beginning student
- Practices the arabesque as a foundation for adagio and allégro combinations
- Develops stability in executing the arabesque on full foot, in sauté (jumped), and en fondu (demi-plié) at the barre and in the center

Music and Timing:

- Time signature: 3/4 or 4/4.
- Tempo: slow, fluid adagio tempo and quality or moderate for grand allégro with an expansive quality.
- Timing: Performing the arabesque depends upon the variety of ways it can be executed and the context in which it is used as part of an exercise or combination.

Figure III.5 Second arabesque.

Figure III.6 Third arabesque.

Preparation: Often the arabesque is part of a combination, therefore there is no particular preparation for the pose. Instead, various arm positions designate the arabesques.

Breathing:

- Inhale as you perform the pose.
- Exhale as you leave the pose.
- Extend breath phrasing over several steps in the combination.

Progressions:

1. Facing the barre: Stand in Fifth position. Execute a battement dégagé derrière and continue extending the leg upward to under 45 degrees. Ask students to test their balance by taking their hands off the barre. Teach the arms for First arabesque. Practice the ara-

besque facing the barre and add the First arabesque arms. Repeat this process on both sides. Introduce Second and Third arabesque in the same manner at the barre. In the center, perform arabesque as a grand allégro step traveling across the floor or as part of an adagio.

2. Traveling across the floor: Walk, walk, step into First arabesque, stretch and hold; repeat on the other side. Perform the sequence in 3/4 time signature in a slow tempo.

3. Using arabesque in an adagio: Introduce First arabesque à terre on both sides. Students test balance by lifting the leg no higher than 45 degrees, then returning to a pointed foot on the floor and closing in Fifth position. Increase the length of the adagio by adding Second and then Third arabesque while changing arms. Create an adagio that includes the three arabesques.

Teaching Cues:

- "Walk, walk, stretch arabesque."

Teaching Images:

- "Float across the floor as you walk and stretch your arms and legs into the space."
- "Imagine performing the arabesque underwater."

Assessment Checklist:

✓ The body weight centers vertically over the supporting leg and the foot triangle.

✓ The working leg is directly behind the working shoulder.

✓ Use counterbalance when performing arabesques.

✓ Position the arms and head correctly for a specific arabesque.

Specific Errors:

- The working or supporting legs are not turned-out.
- The shoulders and hips are not square.

Arabesque Fondu
(a-ra-BESK fawn-DEW)

Arabesque fondu is a variation of the pose performed alone or as part of many steps. To teach the arabesque fondu, follow the steps for learning arabesque with a straight supporting leg at the barre.

In First arabesque, ask students to sense the counterbalance and the oppositional stretch of the body, the working leg and the arm position. With the hands on the barre, ask the dancer to execute a fondu (demi-plié) on the supporting leg. In this position, the dancer pulls up through the supporting leg as part of the oppositional stretching. Still facing the barre, practice stepping into First arabesque traveling across the floor combination of walk, walk, step into First arabesque and stretch the pose, then fondu, stretch and hold; repeat on the other side.

Barre Progressions

Perform all exercises at the barre from Fifth position.

Demi-Pliés and Grand Pliés:

1. Perform grand pliés in First, Second, and Fifth positions.

2. Combine demi-plié and grand pliés together.

3. End these combinations with a balancé in relevé in all positions.

Battement Tendu:

1. Execute two battement tendus en croix, repeat the sequence.

2. Practice transfer of weight execute four battement tendus devant, four battement tendus derrière, and eight battement tendus à la seconde.

3. Combine battement tendus and battement tendus with demi-plié combine with battement tendu relevés.

Battement Tendu Relevé:

1. Execute two, then one en croix.

2. Introduce sequential patterns such as one battement tendu relevé en croix; two battement tendu with demi-plié and repeat the sequence.

3. Combine with battement tendu with or without demi-plié.

Battement Dégagé (or Jeté):

1. Perform four battement dégagés en croix.

2. Decrease the sequence to two battement dégagés en croix twice.

3. Add directional patterns: with four battement dégagés devant, four battement dégagés derrière, and eight battement dégagés à la seconde.

4. Include battement dégagé ending in demi-plié.

5. Add battement dégagé en cloche ending in an arabesque balance on full foot, and later in fondu.

Rond de Jambe à Terre:

1. Perform eight rond de jambes à terre en dehors and en dedans (one measure at slow standard tempo).

2. Add the transition between en dehors and en dedans. A sequence of rond de jambes à terre en dehors ends à la quatrième devant; likewise, a sequence of rond de jambes à terre en dedans ends à la quatrième derrière.

3. The number of rond de jambes decrease to four en dehors, four en dedans, and repeat the sequence.

4. Add port de corps devant and derrière on full foot to the rond de jambe à terre exercise.

5. End with a balance in sous-sus.

6. Try variations: rond de jambe à terre with demi-plié during the battement tendu path, straightening the supporting leg on the circular path. Perform this variation in two measures and performed twice, and combine with four rond de jambe à terre en dehors; repeat en dedans.

Port de Corps:

1. Perform port de corps in Fifth position on full foot.

2. Combine with rond de jambe à terre or with demi- and grand plié combinations; add a balance in sous-sus at the end.

Battement Frappé:

1. Combine the four-step process of the battement frappé together and practice as an exercise.

2. Perform four battement frappé en croix at a slow tempo (two measures for each, then one slow measure for each); decrease to two battement frappé en croix twice.

Retiré and Passé:

1. Review retiré devant on full foot facing the barre. In this position test balance.

2. Practice retiré devant on full foot with one hand on the barre; later add as an ending to barre exercises.

3. Execute passés in the center en promenade derrière and devant on full foot.

Grand Battement: Introduce the principle of counterbalance.

1. Teach grand battement derrière facing the barre and introduce counterbalance. Follow the sequence for teaching grand battement in unit II.

2. Practice with one hand on the barre four grand battement en croix. Near the end of the unit, execute two grand battement en croix twice.

3. Introduce directional combinations: four grand battement devant, four derrière, eight à la seconde.

Relevé:

1. Practice relevés on two feet in different foot positions: First, Second, Fifth position, and sous-sus.

2. Combine with balances in each position and arms in Second or Fifth position.

3. Decrease the number of relevés from four to two.

4. Introduce facing the barre, on one foot: three times per foot then change; increase repetitions of the combination; test balance.

𝒰nit III Center

In unit III center, the teacher presents combinations of two and three steps. The new steps begin with sautés and changements and move on to the complex assemblé near the end of the unit.

Sauté

(soh-TAY)

Definition: jump in the air (see figure III.7, a-c)

Principles: aplomb, counterpull, squareness, pull-up, weight distribution, transfer of weight, stance, turn-out, alignment

Rules and Protocols: Apply jumping and landing technique. Both feet leave and return simultaneously. In the air, legs stretch and feet point to the floor.

Verbal Depiction: Begin in First or Second position. Demi-plié on both legs and jump simultaneously extending and pointing the feet while in the air. When first learning sautés, students should concentrate on extending the legs and articulating the feet to a complete point during the take-off from the floor . The feet remain pointed until the landing. Refer to jumping technique in chapter 3.

Arms: Arms extended in Fifth position en bas or other positions.

Music and Timing:

- Time signature: 2/4, 4/4, or 3/4.

- Timing: Take-off and jump are on the "&"; the landing is on the count.

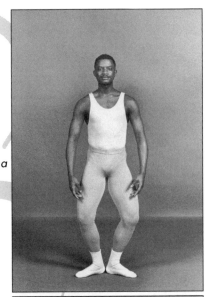

a

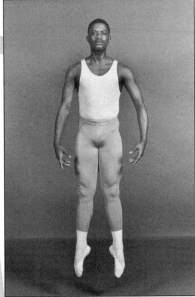

b

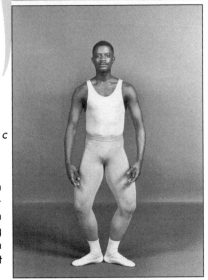

c

Figure III.7 Sauté in First position. a) Begin in First position demi-plié. b) Spring into First position in the air. c) Land in First position demi-plié.

Preparation: Standing in First or Second position, the dancer executes a First port de bras ending en bas with accompanying head movements and then demi-pliés.

Introductory or Transitional Steps: Perform the sauté as a series in one position or changing positions. The sauté is a preparatory step for other basic jumping steps.

Breathing:

- Inhale on the demi-plié and ascent of the jump.
- Exhale on the landing.
- Extend breath phrasing over a series of sautés.

Progressions:

1. Face the barre to introduce sautés in First, then Second, position.
2. Practice in the center performing eight sautés in First position and then stop. Repeat the sautés in Second position and stop.
3. Combine sautés in First and Second position; the number decreases to four per position; repeat the sequence.

Teaching Cue:

- "Stop at the top of the jump."

Teaching Image:

- "Imagine your legs are coiled springs."

Assessment Checklist:

- ✓ Knees are over toes in the demi-plié at the beginning and end of the step.
- ✓ Legs and feet extend completely in the air.
- ✓ Legs are in First or Second position during the jump.

Specific Errors:

- Knees are not over toes in the demi-plié at the beginning and end of the step.
- Legs and feet are not extended completely in the air.
- Legs are not held in First or Second position during the jump.

Changement
(shanz-MAHN)

Definition: to change. A changement is a jump with the feet changing from Fifth position front to back (or vice versa) while in the air (see figure III.8, a-c).

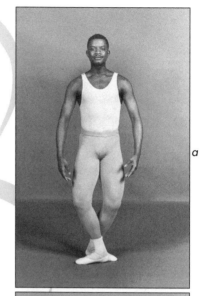

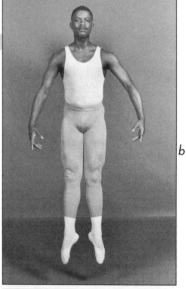

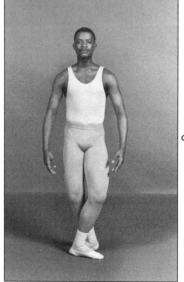

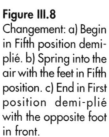

Figure III.8
Changement: a) Begin in Fifth position demi-plié. b) Spring into the air with the feet in Fifth position. c) End in First position demi-plié with the opposite foot in front.

Principles: aplomb, counterpull, squareness, pull-up, weight distribution, transfer of weight, stance, turn-out, alignment

Rules and Protocols: Apply jumping and landing technique. The change of position takes place at the top of the jump.

Verbal Depiction: Beginning in Fifth position, demi-plié, both legs jump at the same time extending and pointing the feet in the air. At the top of the jump, the legs exchange positions. Both feet land simultaneously in Fifth position demi-plié. The changement is a vertical jump that takes off and lands in the same place. The accent is on the ascent.

When first learning changement, concentrate on jumping high to extend the legs in First position pointing the feet completely, and changing the legs and feet at the top of the jump. The next progression is to keep the legs in Fifth position on the upward path of the jump, then change to Fifth position with the other foot front at the beginning of the descent.

Arms: Extend in Fifth position en bas or other positions.

Music and Timing:

- Time signature: 2/4, 4/4, or 3/4.
- Tempo: moderate tempo with light, bouncy quality.
- Timing: take-off and jump are on the "&"; the landing is on the count.

Preparation: Standing in Fifth position, execute a First port de bras ending en bas with accompanying head movements and then demi-plié.

Introductory or Transitional Steps: Perform the changement as a series or paired with many different steps: échappé sauté, temps levé, pas de chat, pas de bourrée, and other petit allégro steps.

Breathing:

- Inhale on the demi-plié and ascent of the jump.
- Exhale on the landing.
- Breath phrasing extends over a series of changements.

Progressions: Teach the changement after sautés in First or Second position. Practice changements at the barre and in the center. Perform eight changements as a single step.

Teaching Cues:

- "Stop at the top of the jump."
- "And, change, and, change."

- Look above the heads of the students at the top of the jump and say "I'm looking for you."

Teaching Images:

- "You are performing changements on the moon, where the gravity is 1/6 of the Earth's gravity."
- "Can you touch the ceiling with the top of your head?"

Assessment Checklist:

- ✓ Knees are over toes in the demi-plié at the beginning and end of the step.
- ✓ Legs and feet extend completely (in First position) on the air.
- ✓ Hold the legs in Fifth position on the ascent.
- ✓ Legs open to First position in the air before the change.

Specific Errors:

- Legs turn in during the changement.
- The jump moves forward or backward.
- One foot lands on the other because turn-out is lost during execution.

Temps Levé

Definition: Temps levé simply means time raised (see figure III.9 a, b, c)

Principles: aplomb, counterpull, squareness, pull-up, alignment, turn-out, weight distribution, transfer of weight, balance on one and two feet

Rules and Protocols: A hop takes off from one foot and lands on the same foot; a jump takes off from two feet and lands on one foot. The height of the hop or jump in the air allows the supporting leg to fully extend with the foot pointed.

Verbal Depiction: Temps levé is a jump or hop on one foot with the other leg in coupé, sur le cou-de-pied, or another position. The dancer hops high enough in the air that the entire supporting leg and foot are perpendicular to the floor. The other foot remains non-moving and in contact with the supporting leg during the air moment.

Arms: Fifth position en bas or varies depending upon the combination.

Preparation: Standing in Fifth position, demi-plié, execute a First port de bras with accompanying head movements.

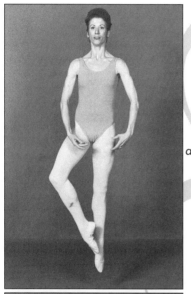

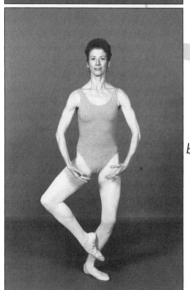

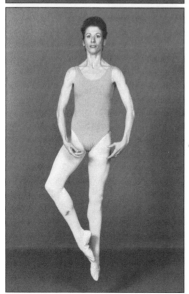

Figure III.9 Temps levé: a) Begin in demi-plié with the foot in coupé derrière. b) Spring off the supporting leg with the foot in coupé derrière. c) End in demi-plié, right foot front.

Introductory or transitional steps: Temps levé is one part of a variety of petit and grand allégro and linking steps.

Music and Timing:

- Time signature: any time signature, depending upon the allégro combination.
- Tempo: a light and buoyant quality.
- Timing: use "&" for the up movement; with the count for the landing.

Breathing:

- Inhale on the ascent.
- Exhale on the landing.
- Extend breath phrasing over a movement phrase or the combination.

Progressions:

1. Introduce temps levé after the relevés on one foot.
2. Practice temps levé facing the barre; three on the right foot, step change to the left foot and repeat combination.

Teaching Cues:

- "Lift, down."
- "Stop at the top of the air moment."

Teaching Images:

- "Imagine a spring-like action of the legs."
- "Pause in the air so that I can take a picture of you!"

Assessment Checklist:

If taking off two feet, both legs demi-plié and jump at the same time.

✓ The working leg goes to coupé at the top of the jump.

If taking off one foot, the supporting leg and foot extend completely in the air.

✓ The working foot remains in contact with the supporting leg at the coupé position.

✓ The jump is high enough so that the supporting leg and foot extend completely off the floor.

Specific Errors:

- If taking off one foot, the supporting leg and foot do not leave the floor sufficiently to extend fully.
- The working foot changes position on the back of the supporting leg.
- The jump is not high enough for the supporting foot and leg to completely extend in the air.

Assemblé
(a-sahn-BLAY)

Definition: literally, to assemble together. The assemblé begins on two feet and ends on two feet with the legs opening and coming together to land in Fifth position (see figure III.10, a-d).

Principles: pull-up, squareness, counterpull, turnout, weight distribution, transfer of weight, balance

Rules and Protocols: The height of the working leg is up to 45 degrees. The supporting leg executes a strong temps levé off the floor. Both legs meet and land together at the same time in Fifth position demi-plié.

Verbal Depiction: Beginning in Fifth position demi-plié, the working foot brushes to Second position up to 45 degrees off the ground. Following at nearly the same time, the supporting leg hops vertically into the air. Both legs and feet extend simultaneously in the air and land at the same time in Fifth position demi-plié. The basic assemblé is a vertical jumping step that remains in the same place. The dancer lifts the weight of the body off the legs to enable the important sequential timing of the leg actions and vertical jumping. For the beginning student, the action of the legs and feet coming together occurs when both feet land at the same time in Fifth position demi-plié. The accent is on the closing, with a secondary emphasis on the air moment.

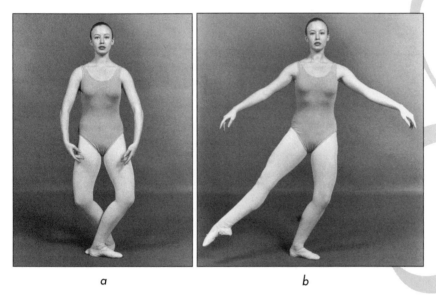

a

b

c

d

Figure III.10 Assemblé: a) Begin in Fifth position demi-plié. b) Brush the back leg à la seconde en l'air. c) Both feet and leg extend in the air with the supporting leg and foot vertical to the floor. d) Land in Fifth position demi-plié, working foot front.

Teaching Beginning Ballet Technique

Arms: When brushing the right foot, the right arm extends from Fourth position en avant and opens on an upward diagonal devant; the eyes focus on the hand. The left arm is in Second position. The arms remain in this position as the legs come together. The arms then float down to Fifth position en bas.

Purpose:

- Develops coordination of the legs
- Develops sequential timing of brushing, jumping, landing, and closure

Preparation: Execute a First port de bras. Begin the step with a strong demi-plié in Fifth position. At the base of the demi-plié, the weight transfers to the leg that propels the body into the air with the jump.

Introductory or Transitional Steps: A glissade, pas de bourrée, or other steps introduce the assemblé. The assemblé is a component of many petit allégro combinations.

Music and Timing:

- Time signature: 4/4, 2/4, or 3/4.
- Tempo: moderate to fast tempo with a brisk, lively quality.
- Timing: Use "&" for the preparation and air moment, the count for the closure on the floor. At the beginning level, the emphasis in executing the assemblé is reverse: primary for the landing together on both feet and secondary for the air moment.

Breathing:

- Exhale on the preliminary demi-plié.
- Inhale on the brush-jump sequence.
- Exhale and counterpull the body on the descent and demi-plié closure.
- Extend breath phrasing over several assemblés or the allégro combination.

Progressions:

Facing the Barre:

1. Practice battement dégagé to Second position; demi-plié on the supporting leg. Teach students to balance in the demi-plié (fondu) position with the working leg stretched to à la seconde, lifting the body off the legs. To test balance, ask the students to lift their hands off the barre for just a moment.

2. Alternate the battement dégagés from side to side in sequence up to eight times.

3. Practice the assemblé movement sequence, but without the hop.

4. Repeat with the supporting leg executing a relevé or adding the "hop, pull together."

In the Center:

1. Repeat the same battement dégagé exercises from the barre, with the arms in Second position. The student closes each time in Fifth position devant.

2. Add the "hop, pull together" to the combination. To teach the leg action sequence of the step, some teachers ask students to perform the assemblé movements with a relevé on the supporting leg instead of a jump.

3. After learning and practicing the leg actions at the barre and in the center, add the jump and practice the step informally. Then execute assemblé soutenu (see Standards and Variations).

4. Perform eight assemblé soutenus en promenade en avant (see Standards and Variations).

5. Combine the assemblé with another step, such as glissade, to create a petit allégro combination and perform on both sides.

Teaching Cues:

- "Brush, up, together"
- "Brush, hop, together, land"

Teaching Image:

- "Imagine gathering your legs in the air."

Assessment Checklist:

✓ The working foot completely brushes into the air.

✓ As the working foot leaves the floor, the supporting leg quickly extends into the air.

✓ Both legs are straight during the step with the supporting leg and foot perpendicular to the floor.

✓ The working leg is at a 45-degree angle to the floor.

✓ The height of the working leg relates to the height of the jump.

✓ The working and supporting legs close together in Fifth position demi-plié.

Specific Errors:

- The brush and jump are disjointed or separate actions.

- The battement dégagé is too high for the height of the jump.
- At the top of the jump, the supporting leg and foot are not fully extended.
- The dancer lands first on one foot and then the other.

Standards and Variations:

The assemblé is a versatile step with many variations. The following variations describe the step with the right foot. These steps are performed with the left foot as well.

Assemblé Soutenu: (a-sahn-BLAY soot-NEW) (assemblé sustained) combines an assemblé followed with a slow straightening action of the legs (soutenu).

In the center, assemblés are practiced in a repetitive series, such as a set of eight assemblés en promenade en avant or eight assemblés soutenu en promenade en avant. The assemblé soutenu gives the beginning dancer time to regain weight on both feet and rest before executing the assemblé again.

Assemblé Dessus: (a-sahn-BLAY duh-SEW) (assemble over) begins with the right foot front in Fifth position. The right foot brushes à la seconde en l'air and closes in Fifth position back.

Assemblé Coupé: (a-sahn-BLAY koo-PAY) (assemblé cut) begins with the working foot in the air, either in an open position or in coupé devant or derrière. The supporting foot pushes into the jump and both feet close together in the Fifth position demi-plié. This assemblé does not use a brushing action; use assemblé coupé to close a step that finishes in an open position such as a jeté or temps levé.

Center Progressions

Port de Bras: Review periodically and execute alone or combined with other center combinations.

Center Barre:
1. Execute a battement tendu and variations, battement tendu relevé and battement dégagé and variations in combined center combinations.
2. Explore directions and sequential patterns.

Classical Positions of the Body:
1. Review and refine performance.
2. Execute selected positions as part of other adagio combinations.

Balancé:
1. Practice with arms.
2. Combine with another step: balancé, First arabesque, sauté, repeat.

Glissade:
1. Practice as a step.
2. Combine with another step: glissade, assemblé, repeat other side.

Pas de Chat:
1. Perform in a two-step combination: three pas de chats, changement, other side.
2. Try to lift legs to retiré, devant and derrière positions during the air moment.

Jeté Devant:
1. Practice seven jetés en promenade en avant with arms; on the eighth measure, assemblé coupé ending Fifth position derrière.
2. Combine jetés in a two-step combination, such as three jetés, one assemblé or three jetés, pas de bourrée.

Pas de Bourrée:
1. Combine with another step into a two-step combination: two jetés devant, two pas de bourrée.
2. Try a three-step combination: glissade, two pas de chats, pas de bourrée.

Ballet Walks:
1. Practice periodically with port de bras.
2. Incorporate into combinations: two walks, step First arabesque and hold the pose, later fondu in arabesque.
3. Extend into running.

Chassé:
1. After learning arabesque as a pose, combine with chassé; alternate to other side.
2. Combine with two other steps.

Teacher's Planner for Unit IV

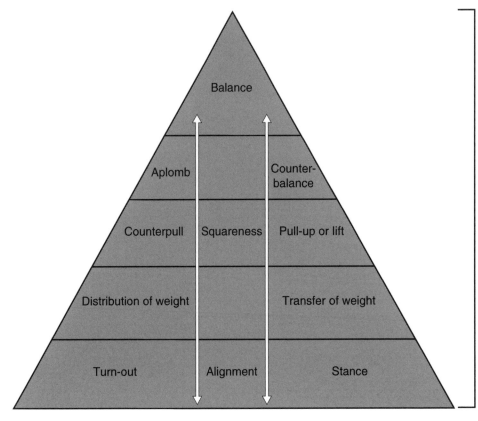

Unit IV
All principles
applied to
barre exercises
and center steps
and combinations

Unit IV is the capstone experience of the term. Since new barre exercises are not introduced, the attention is on enhancing the basic ballet barre through coordination of head and arms, breath phrasing, and quality. In the center, new steps are introduced that compliment and enlarge the center to gain its complete structure.

Objectives of the Unit

The objectives of the unit encompass the cognitive, psychomotor, and affective domains as follows:

Cognitive Domain

The student will be able to

- synthesize all principles into the beginning ballet barre and center at an adequate competency level;
- evaluate personal performance of all exercises and steps; and
- describe and define all exercises, steps, and body positions and poses.

Psychomotor Domain

The student will be able to

- perform the exercises that comprise a beginning ballet barre;

- continue to refine steps and exercises from units I, II, and III;
- execute two of the barre exercises together;
- perform some of the barre exercises with balancés on relevé or sous-sus;
- apply the rules and protocols to the barre exercises and center steps;
- perform the following new center steps: échappé sauté, pas de basque, développés, piqué en avant, three-step turn, grand jeté;
- execute the arabesque pose in center combinations;
- create center combinations of two, three, or even four different steps; and
- perform basic ballet technique with appropriate musicality, style, and performance attitude.

Affective Domain

The students will be able to

- demonstrate a professional attitude during the class,

- display performance confidence in executing exercises and steps from previous units,
- value the self-discipline and aesthetics gained from attaining competency in performing beginning ballet,
- value and transfer the benefits from the discipline of ballet into everyday life situations, and
- formulate the benefits received from participating in a beginning ballet class.

Teaching Strategies

The following teaching strategies apply within unit IV:

- Teaching styles: command, practice, inclusive, self-check, reciprocal, guided discovery
- Teacher modeling: demonstration of new work with English action words; use of French terms for unit I, II, and III content; little demonstration of previous content; predominantly verbal communication of exercises and steps; some repetition; imagery; continued development of visual memory; and continued transfer of responsibility for learning to the student

Assessment

Consider the following methods of assessment:

- Assessment Checklist utilizes cues for the performance of each exercise and step.
- Periodic informal evaluations monitor if knowledge and skills are attained.
- Performance examination.
- Written examination.

Teacher Responsibilities

The following list is a self-check of your responsibilities when teaching unit IV:

- Clear demonstration of new exercises and steps
- Clear direction and cueing of execution of exercises and steps
- Clear counting of music
- Clear explanation and application of principles, rules, and protocols
- Use of imagery in the teaching/learning process
- Group feedback

- Individual attention
- Development of student responsibility for the movement
- Pace of the class
- Open and risk-free atmosphere
- Continued development of barre and acquisition of new materials in the center
- Continued refinement of work at the barre and in the center

Performance Test Content

Performance testing may involve students doing a self-check, peer assessment, and teacher evaluation. Student performance criteria follow for unit IV:

Principles and Rules

The student will demonstrate

- unit I, II, and III principles; and
- unit I, II, and III rules and protocols.

At the Barre

The student will demonstrate

1. complete beginning ballet barre.
2. with combined exercises.

In the Center

The student will demonstrate the following:

1. Développé adagio or three arabesques in an adagio combination
2. Introduction and linking steps in combination or combined with adagio, petit allégro, or grand allégro combinations.
3. Jeté combinations
4. Assemblé combinations
5. Grand allégro combinations (single steps or combined)
6. Echappé sautés, changements.

Written Examination

The student will

- Translate French ballet terms to English, and vice versa, and
- write ballet terms in French.

Unit IV Barre

By unit IV, the beginning ballet barre is complete. Without new exercises being introduced in this unit, the teacher focuses upon students performing them in a variety of patterns and at standard tempos. In addition, the students apply appropriate principles, coordinate the arms and accompanying head movements, breath phrasing to all of the exercises.

Following are the exercises from units I, II, and III (in the order they are performed):

1. Demi-plié
2. Battement tendu
3. Battement tendu relevé
4. Battement dégagé
5. Battement dégagé en cloche
6. Rond de jambe à terre en dehors and en dedans
7. Port de corps
8. Retirés and Passés (or maybe incorporated into selected exercises)
9. Battement frappé
10. Petit battement sur le cou-de-pied
11. Battement développé
12. Grand battement
13. Relevés and sous-sus (or may be incorporated into selected exercises)

Barre Progressions

Barre:

1. Place one hand on the barre.
2. Steps and exercises use Fifth position, port de bras, breath phrasing, and coordinated head movements.
3. Some exercises may be executed with relevé or end with a balancé on relevé.
4. Standard musical tempo is used for exercises.

Demi- and Grand Pliés:

1. Perform demi- and grand plié combinations in First, Second, and Fifth positions. Introduce Fourth position demi- and grand pliés.
2. Include port de corps on full foot.
3. These combinations with relevés include extended balancés in sous-sus at the end of the exercise.

Battement Tendu:

1. Perform a variey of battement tendus in en croix and other patterns with and without demi-plié.
2. Combine battement tendu relevé with and without battement tendus, and with and without demi-plié.
3. Explore directional and sequential patterns of two, possibly three, varieties of battement tendus (e.g., two battement tendus, one battement tendu with demi-plié en croix twice).

Battement Tendu Relevé:

1. Perform a variety of en croix patterns with and without demi-plié.
2. Combine with battement tendu with and without demi-plié and into exercises.
3. Explore directional and sequential patterns with two varieties of battement tendu and/or battement tendu relevé.

Battement Dégagé:

1. Perform a variety of en croix patterns with and without demi-plié.
2. Combine battement dégagé en cloche into exercises.
3. Explore directional and sequential patterns of battement dégagé with and without demi-plié; combine with en cloche or with an ending balance.

Battement Dégagé en Cloche:

1. Combine with battement dégagé combinations as an ending.
2. End combination in arabesque balancing full foot or en fondu.

Rond de Jambe à Terre:

1. Perform rond de jambe à terre en dehors and en dedans at the standard tempo (one measure for each rond de jambe).
2. Practice rond de jambe with a demi-plié on the battement tendu en cloche and combine it with standard rond de jambes.
3. Perform port de corps devant and derrière together, full foot.
4. Extend balance at the end of the exercise in sous-sus.

Port de Corps:

1. Perform port de corps in devant and derrière in First, Second, and Fifth positions.

2. Execute the port de corps in full-foot position and as part of combinations with demi- and grand pliés and rond de jambes à terre, with accompanying balancés en relevé, especially in sous-sus.

Relevé:

1. Practice relevés on two feet and one foot (with the working foot coupé or retiré) facing the barre.

2. End the exercise en relevé.

3. Attempt some exercises with short relevé sequences.

Passé:

1. Insert passés into exercises at the barre and in the center.

2. Execute full foot.

Battement Frappé:

1. Practice directional combinations decreasing to two en croix or in other patterns (at standard tempo).

2. Attempt one battement frappé en croix.

3. Combine battement frappés with petit battement sur le cou de pied.

4. Execute some battement frappés en relevé, if appropriate.

Petit Battement sur le cou-de-pied:

1. Combine petit battement sur le cou-de-pied with battement frappé.

2. Attempt to perform petit battement on relevé if appropriate.

3. End the exercise with a balance on relevé.

Battement Développé:

1. Practice battement développé en croix and in other patterns.

2. Finish the battement développé in demi-plié or attempt it with a relevé.

Grand Battement:

1. Perform four, two, then once en croix.

2. Explore directional and sequential combinations with the grand battement with variations of grand battement closing in demi-plié.

3. Combine with other barre exercises.

Unit IV Center

In unit IV, the teacher introduces the new steps in the center, depending upon the class's competence in performing the steps from unit III. In this unit, concentrate on students executing two-, three-, or even four-step combinations and enjoying their performance accomplishments.

Échappé Sauté
(ay-sha-PAY soh-TAY)

Definition: Échappé means escape, and sauté means jump; so, échappé sauté is a jumping escape (see figure IV.1, a-e).

Principles: aplomb, counterpull, squareness, pull-up, alignment, turn-out, weight distribution, balance on two feet

Rules and Protocols: jumping and landing technique, vertical jump

Verbal Depiction: Begin in Fifth position demi-plié right foot front; jump and extend both legs immediately to à la Seconde and land in Second position. The Second part of the step reverses; jump extending the legs in Second position, change the feet during the air moment before landing in Fifth position, left foot front. This version is the petit version of échappé sauté, which is appropriate for the beginning dancer. The accent is on the upward and outward movement to Second position with a secondary accent on the return to Fifth position.

Arms: Open the arms to Second position with the jump out, and close to Fifth en bas on the return to Fifth position.

Music and Timing:

• Time signature: 2/4, 4/4, or 6/8.

• Tempo: moderate to fast tempo with a sharp, bright quality.

• Timing: On the "&" count, the legs spring upward and out from Fifth position. On count 1 the legs land in Second position demi-plié. On "&" the dancer jumps in Second position and on count 2 lands in Fifth position demi-plié.

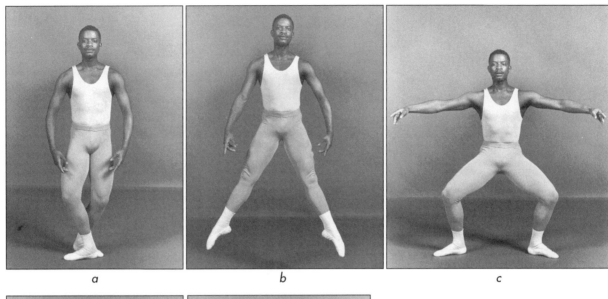

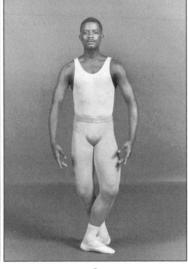

Figure IV.1 Echappé Sauté: a) Begin in Fifth position demi-plié. b) Spring into the air opening the legs to Second position. c) Land in Second position demi-plié. d) Spring into the air in Second position. e) End in Fifth position demi-plié, other foot front.

Preparation: Standing in Fifth position, the dancer executes a First port de bras with accompanying head movements.

Introductory or Transitional Steps: Perform échappé sauté in a series or with many different steps: changement, temps levé, and other petit allégro steps.

Breathing:

- Inhale on the extension phase.
- Exhale on the return to Fifth position.
- Extend breath phrasing over a series of échappé sautés or a short allégro combination.

Progressions:

1. Practice at the barre.
2. Perform in the center.
3. Combine échappé sautés with changements.

Teaching Cues:

- "Out, in"
- "Up and out, up and in"

Teaching Image:

- "Imagine your legs are like springs."
- "Imagine landing on down feathers."

Assessment Checklist:

✓ Both legs jump simultaneously.

✓ Both legs are extended and the feet pointed.

✓ The body counterpulls during the landing.

Specific Errors:

- The heels lift in demi-plié before the spring into the air.
- The legs and feet are not fully extended in the air.

- The feet roll inward in Fifth or in Second full-foot position.

Piqué en avant
(pee-KAY ahna-VAHN)

Definition: a pricked step (see figure IV.2, a-c)

Principles: counterpull, squareness, pull-up, alignment, turn-out, weight distribution, transfer of weight, balance

Rules and Protocols: The working leg remains straight during the step. The dancer springs onto the working leg that remains extended in front of the dancer. The weight completely transfers from one leg to the other. The back leg demi-pliés directly behind the supporting leg. The front leg releases to dégagé height off the floor to begin the next piqué.

Verbal Depiction: Piqué en avant or forward beings with extending the working leg pointing the front foot, to the length of a battement tendu from the supporting foot. With a quick, deep demi-plié on the supporting leg, the body weight quickly transfers through a springing action on to the three-quarter piqué relevé on the front leg. During this transfer of weight, the well turned-out front leg stays stretched and pointed, ready to accept the weight. The torso, with shoulders and hips square, lifts upward to alight on the top of the three-quarter piqué relevé. The back foot attaches in retiré derrière. After a momentary pause in this position, the back leg demi-pliés directly under the supporting leg. This sharp cutting action of the supporting leg allows the working leg to dégagé and begin the step again. The accent for the piqué occurs on the upward movement. The body lifts above the supporting leg when arriving on the piqué and counterpulls during the demi-plié.

Arms: For piqué en avant, the arms are in Fourth position en avant, with the arm curved in front of the working leg.

Music and Timing:

- Time signature: 2/4 or 4/4.
- Tempo: moderate to fast tempo with a light, sharp quality.
- Timing: The "&" is for the demi-plié transition; piqué on the count.

Preparation: Standing in Fifth position, the working leg extends and foot points (pointé tendu)

Figure IV.2 Piqué en avant: a) Begin with pointing the foot à la quatrième devant and the supporting leg in demi-plié. b) Step on three-quarter relevé on the front foot. c) The back foot raises to retiré derrière, then steps into demi-plié behind the front leg.

effacé devant. The arms open through First port de bras to low Fourth.

Introductory or Transitional Steps: A versatile introductory step, piqué combines with poses, many adagio steps, and is an integral part of turns.

Breathing:

- Inhale before the piqué.
- Exhale on the fondu.
- Breath phrasing extends over a series of several turns.

Progressions:

1. Teach the piqué action devant, facing the barre.
2. Practice piqués in the center in a series of four, later eight. Stop, and repeat on other side.
3. Add piqué into a combination.

Teaching Cues:

- "And, up, and, up."
- "Piqué, plié."
- "Up, down."
- "The front leg is always straight and the back leg is bent."

Teaching Image:

- "Imagine hopping to perch on a low wall on one leg."

Assessment Checklist:

- ✓ Transfer the body weight quickly from one leg to another.
- ✓ Spring onto the piqué relevé.
- ✓ Center the body weight on top of the new supporting leg.
- ✓ Perform the accent on the piqué part of the step.

Specific Errors:

- Legs and/or feet lose turn-out when stepping onto piqué.
- Body weight does not transfer quickly from one leg to the other.
- Body weight does not completely transfer from one leg to the other leg.
- Body weight is not centered on top of the leg in piqué relevé.
- Three-quarter relevé is absent during the step.

Pas de Basque

(pah duh bask)

Definition: step of the basque. This step originally derived from national dances performed by the Basque people. The step may be performed in either the Russian or Cecchetti version. The beginning student learns the Russian version of the step (see figure IV.3, a-e).

Principles: squareness, pull-up, alignment, turn-out, stance, weight distribution, transfer of weight, balance

Rules and Protocols: The body changes from one downstage corner to the other on the transfer of weight à la seconde. The pas de basque glides over or just above the floor. The weight completely transfers through First position to croisé derrière, and then closes before the next step.

Verbal Depiction: In the Russian version, the dancer begins facing direction 2, right foot front, Fifth position. Stretch the leg and foot pointing to direction 1 in Second position. The right foot accepts the weight in Second position and the left foot points. The body faces direction 1. The left foot brushes into First position and then slides to Fourth position croisé devant, accepting the body weight while the right foot points croisé derrière and then closes to Fifth position derrière. In the adagio version of the pas de basque, the toes stay in contact with the floor or as near as possible to the floor.

Arms: The arms open to Second position when the legs reach Second position. On the transition through Fourth position to the pause while pointing croisé derrière, the arms go through Fifth position en bas, to First position, to Third position with the upstage arm high. As the feet close in Fifth position, the arms open out and around down to Fifth position en bas.

Purpose:

- Develops coordination of the legs
- Introduces directional changes during a step
- Develops sequential timing of transfer of weight and change of direction

Music and Timing:

- Time signature: 3/4 or 4/4.
- Tempo: moderate tempo with a lyrical quality.
- Timing: On count 1, move the first foot to Second position pointing to other corner; on count 2, slide the Second foot into First position. On

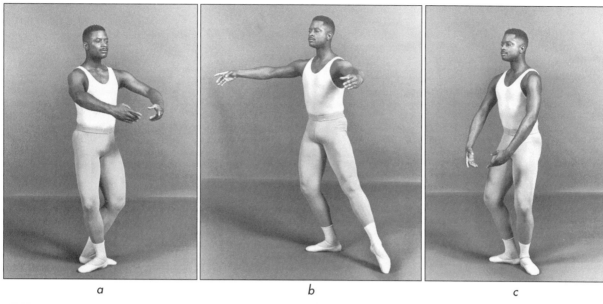

Figure IV.3 Pas de basque: Begin in Fifth position demi-plié. b) Brush the working foot à la seconde. c) Transfer the weight of the legs to First position demi-plié. d) In demi-plié, slide the foot to Fourth position croisé (crossed). e) Stretch the back leg, croisé derrière. Close Fifth position back.

count 3, slide into Fourth position pointing croisé derrière. On count 4, close in Fifth position derrière, just in time to start the step to the other side.

- Modified timing: When introducing this step, choose slow music and allocate two counts for each movement. Gradually increase the tempo of the music.

Preparation: Facing croisé devant, standing in Fifth position, the dancer executes a First port de bras.

Introductory and Transitional Steps: The pas de basque is often an introductory or transitional step in petit allégro, pirouettes, and grand allégro.

Breathing:

- Inhale as the foot extends to Second position.
- Exhale on the Fourth position croisé derrière.
- Breath phrasing extends over a series of steps or a short combination.

Progressions:

1. Introduce the step.
2. Perform the step on both sides four times.

Teaching Cue:

- "Second, First, Fourth (position), close"

Teaching Image:

- "Think of your body sweeping across the floor."

Assessment Checklist:

✓ Direction changes completely from one corner to the other.

✓ Weight shifts completely from one foot to the other.

✓ There are four shifts during the step.

✓ Step pauses pointing (pointe tendu) croisé derrière.

✓ Close in Fifth position derrière before starting the next step.

Specific Errors:

- Change of direction is incomplete.
- Weight shifts are incomplete.

Three-Step Turn

Definition: The three-step turn serves as an introduction to chaînés (see figure IV.4, a-e).

Principles: aplomb, counterpull, squareness, pull-up, alignment, turn-out, transfer of weight, balance on one leg

Rules and Protocols: piqué technique, turning technique, spotting technique

Verbal Depiction: To prepare for the turn to the right, begin in Fifth position right foot front, and point to the foot à la quatrième devant. The back leg demi-pliés and the right foot piqués onto three-quarter relevé in First position facing direction 5, or en face. With the body weight on the right leg, turn one-half turn to the right to face upstage, facing direction 7, closing the left

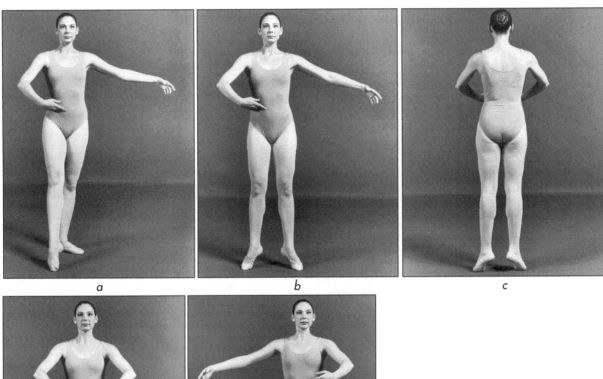

a   b   c

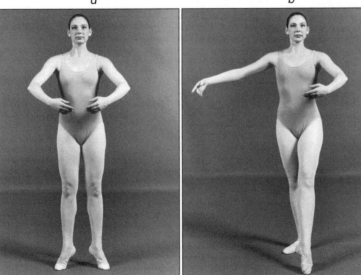

d   e

Figure IV.4 Three-step turn: a) Start by pointing the foot à la quatrième devant. b) Step into First position three-quarter relevé facing front. c) Execute a half-turn upstage, to direction 7, closing on three-quarter relevé in First position. d) Complete the turn and step on three-quarter relevé, in First position facing downstage, direction 5. e) Step full foot à la seconde and pointé tendu à la quatrième devant with the opposite foot.

Teaching Beginning Ballet Technique

foot in three-quarter relevé First position. Shift the body weight to the left leg and complete the turn to the right to face direction 5. With the right foot step full foot to à la seconde, and point the left foot à la quatrième devant. On the piqué the head turns to the right with the eyes looking at a place that is eye level; before the body completes the turn, the head snaps around to the same spot on the right side. As the left foot points à la quatrième devant, the head turns to the left with the eyes looking at a place that us eye level and returns to this place before the turn ends.

Arms: The arms begin with the right arm in Fourth position en avant. As the right leg steps the right arm moves to Second position. As the left foot steps both arms close to First position. As the right foot steps full foot, the left arm is in First position front with the right arm in Second position.

Music and Timing:

- Time signature: 2/4 or 4/4, later in 3/4.
- Tempo: moderate tempo with a steady beat.
- Timing: In 4/4 time signature, on "&", demi-plié on the supporting leg and on count 1, piqué relevé in First position. On count 2, execute the one half-turn and step on three-quarter relevé. On count 3, turn one half-turn to direction 5, and step full foot. On count 4, point à la quatrième devant. This sequence repeats to the other side. In 3/4 time signature, the full-foot step and pointe tendu à la quatrième devant occur during the final count of the measure.

Preparation: The right foot extends à la quatrième devant. The right arm is in First position and the left arm is in Second position.

Spotting Technique: When performing a turn, the dancer uses spotting technique. The basic technique begins with the eyes focusing on a spot or object at eye level. The body begins turning; the eyes and head look at the spot for as long as possible. The head quickly turns on a horizontal path, and the eyes refocus on the same spot or object. The body then completes the turn. Using the spotting technique in turns, the dancer avoids becoming dizzy.

Breathing:

- Inhale on the piqué relevé.
- Exhale at the end of the turn.
- Breath phrasing extends up to eight counts.

Progressions:

1. Practice step on full foot.
2. Learn spotting technique.

3. Practice spotting technique with turn.
4. Rehearse turn on three-quarter relevé.

Teaching Cues:

- "Look where you are going, where you have been, and where you will go."
- "Always come back to your spot."

Teaching Image:

- "Connect your feet in a small chain of steps."

Assessment Checklist:

- ✓ Working foot steps onto three-quarter relevé when closing into First position.
- ✓ Eyes focus on a spot and return to the same spot before stepping full foot.
- ✓ Head spots (focuses) in opposite direction at the end of the three-step turn.

Specific Errors:

- Feet are not on three-quarter relevé when stepping to First position.
- Eyes do not focus on a spot or return to the spot.
- Head does not focus in the opposite direction at the end of the three-step turn (to prepare for turning in the opposite direction).

Grand Jeté
(grahn zhuh-TAY)

Definition: The grand jeté is a leap, the transfer of weight from one leg to the other with an extended air moment (see figure IV.5, a-f).

Principles: transfer of weight, counterbalance, pull-up, turn-out, balance on one leg in fondu

Rules and Protocols: The extension of the front leg determines the height of the grand jeté. The back leg's push and extension propel the body. The classical grand jeté is a leap that curves over through space. The body counterbalances and the back leg extends upward during the landing in fondu.

Verbal Depiction: The grand jeté begins with the supporting leg stepping forward in demi-plié while the working leg brushes into a strong grand battement devant of at least 90 degrees to establish the height of the leap. The push into the air comes from the back leg as it straightens from demi-plié and extends to above 45 degrees in the air. In the air, both legs open to a 90- to

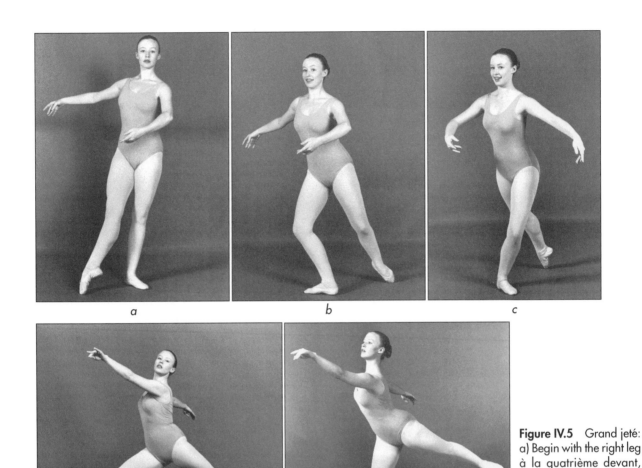

Figure IV.5 Grand jeté: a) Begin with the right leg à la quatrième devant, arms are Fourth position en avant. b) Run. c) Run. d) Both legs open 90 degrees in the air. e) Land in Second arabesque en fondu.

120-degree angle before descending. The body lifts and is vertical, with the shoulders slightly forward over the front leg during the leap.

Dancers strive for the illusion of being suspended in the air. Before the landing the body counterbalances. The leap lands on the front foot in a soft, deep fondu (demi-plié). The body remains in counterbalance, with the back leg fully extended behind at approximately 90 degrees for the beginning dancer. This pose stretches and holds for a visual effect before moving into the next step. During the grand jeté, the head focuses above the hand of the arm extending directly in front of the shoulder. The gaze is slightly above the third finger adding to the illusion of the height during the air moment and the landing.

Arms: The arms stretch in Second arabesque position (opposite arm to the opposite front leg) to compliment the extended legs. This natural opposition gives balance to the step by demanding attention to squareness in the body during the air moment. The timing of the arms is successive to the leg extension in the air. In the fondu, the arms continue to stretch.

Music and Timing:

- Time signature: 4/4 or 3/4.

- Tempo: moderate to slow tempo appropriate for grand allégro with a sweeping, often majestic, quality.

- Timing: Since count 1 of the measure is on the way to the top of the leap, the dancer starts the step and grand battement on the "&" before the first measure. Many grand allégro steps use this timing, which requires a quick, strong approach to the step. Students practice this to discover timing and how much energy they need to propel themselves into the air.

Likewise, the landing is equally strong, and not just an afterthought. When teaching beginning students grand jeté, two measures provides time to prepare, soar into the air, and hold the landing before the next step of the combination.

Preparation: Standing in Fifth position, execute a First port de bras while stretching the front leg pointing devant. Or stand in B+ with the working leg pointed behind, and execute the port de bras.

Introductory and Transitional Steps: Two runs before the grand jeté is a standard preparation for the leap and should be taught first.

Breathing:

- Inhale on the ascent and hold the breath.

- Exhale on the landing.

- Extend breath pattern over several repetitions of the step or a short sequence of grand allégro.

Progressions:

1. Introduce the actions of the legs in the grand jeté without and with the leap.

2. Execute two walks and a grand jeté, holding the landing pose before performing the combination to the other side.

3. Substitute runs for walks in the grand jeté combination.

Teaching Cue:

- "Step, step, grand jeté" (said in rhythm with the music)

Teaching Image:

- "Imagine leaping over a puddle."

- "Imagine leaping over a fence."

Assessment Checklist:

✓ The step forward is in a demi-plié.

✓ The grand battement devant is strong and at least 90 degrees.

✓ The back leg pushes the body into the air as it straightens and extends to above 45 degrees.

✓ The body is vertical with the shoulders slightly forward over the front leg during the air moment.

Specific Errors:

- The back leg does not straighten or extend to above 45 degrees.

- The body is not lifted during the air moment.

- The back leg drops on the landing.

Center Progressions

Port de Bras: Incorporated into center preparations, steps, and combinations.

Center Barre: Practice battement tendu, battement relevé, and battement dégagé exercises in the center in directional and sequential patterns.

Classical Positions of the Body: Integrate selected positions into adagio combinations.

Développé:

1. Perform en croix in the center. Then combine both sides.

2. Integrate several into adagio combinations.

3. Perform in some of the classical positions of the body such as croisé devant and derrière.

Arabesques:

1. Construct adagio combinations that use first, second, and third arabesques.

2. Integrate arabesque into adagio combinations.

3. Perform with sauté in grand allégro combinations.

Sautés and Changements:

1. Practice as single- or two-step combinations.

2. Refine performance of changement.

3. Combine changement with échappé sautés and into petit allégro combinations.

Temps Levé:

1. Combine with other steps such as arabesque.

2. Create two- or three-step combinations: two temps levés, two jetés; repeat.

Assemblé:

1. Create two-, three-, or four-step combinations: glissade, jeté, jeté, assemblé; glissade, pas de chat, jeté, assemblé.

2. Explore variations of assemblé.

Balancé: Combine with two or three steps in adagio or allégro.

Glissade: Combine with two or three petit allégro steps.

Pas de Chat: Combine with two or three petit allégro steps: two pas de chats, jeté, assemblé.

Jeté Devant: Combine with two or three petit allégro steps: glissade, jeté, assemblé, changement.

Pas de Bourrée: Combine with two or three petit allégro steps or integrate into other combinations.

Ballet Walks: Incorporate into adagio and grand allégro combinations.

Chassé: Incorporate into grand allégro combinations.

Adagio [a-DAHZH- yoh]—a slow, sustained movement

Air, en l' [ahn lehr]—in the air

Allégro [ah-lay-GROH]—brisk and lively movement

Arabesque [a-ra-BESK]—Performed with the working leg straight, extending behind the body and arms stretched in various positions.

Arqué [ar-KAY]—bowlegged

Arrière, en [ah na-RYEHR]—backward

Assemblé [a-sahn-BLAY]—assembled or joined together

Avant, en [ah na-VAHN]—forward

Balancé [ba lahn-SAY]—rocking step

Barre [bar]—a horizontal wooden pole used for support; also the beginning exercises for a ballet class

Bas, en [ahn bah]—low arms, refers to Fifth position en bas or Preparatory position

Battement dégagé [bat-MAHN day-ga-ZHAY]—disengaged battement; a brush barely off the floor

Battement, grand [grahn bat-MAHN]—large beating; a big leg kick thrown into the air

Battement développé [bat-MAHN dayv-law-PAY]—battement developed; an unfolding movement

Battement frappé [bat-MAHN fra-PAY]—struck beating; the toes and metatarsals strike the floor

Battement sur le cou-de-pied, petit [puh-TEE bat-MAHN sewr luh koo-duh-PYAY]—small battement, or beating on the ankle

Battement tendu [bat-MAHN tahn-DEW]—stretched beating

Battement tendu jeté pointé [bat-MAHN tahn-DEW zhuh-TAY pwen-TAY]—light touches of the foot on and off the floor in pointé tendu; also known as petit battement piqué [puh-TEE bat-MAHN pee-KAY]

Battement tendu relevé [bat-MAHN tahn-DEW ruhl-VAY]— battement stretched and raised; brush the working foot to full point, lower to full foot, return to full point, and close in Fifth position

B+ position—a preparatory position; standing on one leg, the other leg flexes at the knee, the foot points behind with only the great toe touching the floor

Center—the part of the ballet class comprised of steps and combinations executed in the middle of the studio or travelling across the floor

Center barre—exercises learned at the barre practiced during first part of the center portion of the class

Changement [shahnzh-MAHN]—change; jumping from Fifth, feet switch positions in the air and land in Fifth with the other foot in front

Changer, sans [shahn-ZHAY]—without a change

Chassé [sha-SAY]—one foot chases the other foot

Classical positions of the body—the eight positions are croisé devant (crossed in front), à la quatrième devant (to the Fourth front), écarté (separated), efaccé (shaded), à la seconde (to the Second), épaulé (shouldered), à la quatrième derrière (to the Fourth back), croisé derrière (crossed behind)

Cloche, en [ahn KLAWSH]—like the clapper of a bell; the working foot brushes through First position devant and derrière or vice versa; the foot may remain on the floor or swing into the air

Corps [kawr]—body

Cou-de-pied, sur le [sewr luh koo-duh-PYAY]—on the neck of the foot; position of the working foot at the ankle of the supporting foot

Coupé [koo-PAY]—to cut; position with the working foot on the middle of the lower leg, either in front or behind; a leap from one foot to the other in coupé position front or back

Croisé derrière [krwah-ZAY deh-RYEHR]—crossed behind; one of the Classical Positions of the Body

Croisé devant [krwah-ZAY duh-VAHN]—crossed front; one of the Classical Positions of the Body

Croix, en [ahn krwah]—in the shape of a cross; usually describes performing an exercise in a pattern of front, side, back, and side

Dedans, en [ahn duh-DAHN]—inward, toward the supporting leg

Dehors, en [ahn duh-AWR]—outward, away from the supporting leg

Demi [duh-MEE]—half

Demi-plié [duh-MEE-plee-AY]—half-bend of the knees

Demi-seconde [duh-MEE-suh-GAWND]—arm position halfway between Fifth en bas and Second position

Dessous [duh-SOO]—under

Dessus [duh-SEW]—over

Devant [duh-VAHN]—in front

Ecarté [ay-kar-TAY]—separated; one of the Classical Positions of the Body

Echappé [ay-sha-PAY]—escape

Echappé sauté [ay-sha-PAY soh-TAY]—jump from Fifth out to Second and back to Fifth

Effacé, effacée [eh-fa-SAY]—shaded; one of the Classical Positions of the Body

Élancer [ay-lahn-SAY]—to dart; one of the seven movements of dancing

En [ahn]—in, on

Epaulé, épaulée [ay-poh-LAY]—shouldered; one of the Classical Positions of the Body

Etendre [ay-TAHN-druh]—to stretch, one of the seven movements of dancing

Face, en [ahn fahss]—facing the audience; direction 5

Glissade [glee-SAD]—gliding step traveling from one foot to the other

Glisser [glee-SAY]—to glide; one of the seven movements of dancing

Grand, grande [grahn, grahnd]—big or large

Grand plié [grahn plee-AY]—big bend of the knees

Haut, en [ahn oh]—high

Jarreté [zhar-TAY]—knock-kneed

Jeté, grand [grahn zhuh-TAY]—large leap

Jeté devant [zhuh-TAY duh VAHN]—leap forward

Movements in dancing—there are seven movement in dancing: élancer (to dart), étendre (to stretch), glisser (to glide), plier (to bend), relever (to raise), sauter (to jump), tourner (to turn)

Pas de basque [pah duh bask]—basque step; an introductory or transitional step used in adagio and allégro

Pas de bourrée dessous [pah du boo-RAY duh-SOO]—bourrée step under: step behind, side, front

Pas de chat [pah duh shah]—step of the cat

Passé [pa-SAY]—passed

Piqué en avant [pee-KAY ah na-VAHN]—pricking forward; step onto straight leg with back leg retiré derrière, landing with the back foot cutting under, in demi-plié

Plié [plee-AY]—bent, bending

Plier [plee-AY]—to bend; one of the seven movements of dancing

Pointé tendu [pwent tahn-DEW]—pointed foot

Port de bras [pawr duh brah]—carriage of the arms

Port de corps[pawr de kawr]—carriage of the body

Positions of the arms—First, Second, Third, Fourth, Fifth en bas or Preparatory position, Fifth en haut, Demi-seconde, Fourth en avant

Positions of the feet—First, Second, Third, Fourth, and Fifth

Quatrième derrière, à la [ah la ka-tree-EM deh-RYEHR]—to the Fourth back; one of the Classical Positions of the Body

Quatrième devant, à la [ah la ka-tree-EM duh-VAHN]—to the Fourth front; one of the Classical Positions of the Body

Relevé [ruhl-VAY]—raised to the toes and metatarsals (three-quarter relevé)

Relever [ruhl-VAY]—to raise or lift; one of the seven movements of dancing

Retiré devant [ruh-tee-RAY duh-VAHN]—withdrawn in front; the working leg is bent and the side of the little toe is under the supporting knee

Retiré derrière [ruh tee-RAY deh RYEHR]—withdrawn in back; the working leg is bent and the heel is in back of the supporting knee

Révérence [ray-vay-RAHNSS]—curtsey or bow; performed at the end of class

Sauté, sautée [soh-TAY]—jump(s) or jumping in positions of the feet

Sauter [soh-TAY]—to jump; one of the seven movements in dancing

Seconde, à la [ah la suh-GAWD]—to the Second position

Sous-sus [soo-SEW]—under/over; spring onto both feet on three-quarter relevé with legs and feet tightly together

Sur [sewr]—on

Temps levé [tahn luh-VAY]—raised time; a jump from two feet to one or a hop on one foot

Terre, à [ah tehr]—on the ground

Tourner [toor-NAY]—to turn; one of the seven movements of dancing

Turn-out—the ability to turn out or rotate legs from the hip joints to a 90-degree position

additional readings

Beaumont, C.W. and S. Idzikowski (1975). *A Manual of the Theory and Practice of Classical Theatrical Dancing (Method Cecchetti)*. New York: Dover Books.

Feltz, D.L. and D.M. Landers (1983). "The effects of mental practice on motor skills, learning, and performance: A meta-analysis," *Journal of Sport Psychology*, 5, 1-8.

Fitt, S.S. (1983). *Dance Kinesiology*. New York: Schirmer.

Franklin, E. (1996). *Dance Imagery for Technique and Performance*. Champaign, IL: Human Kinetics.

Franklin, E. (1996). *Dynamic Alignment Through Imagery*. Champaign, IL: Human Kinetics.

Grant, G. (1982). *Technical Manual and Dictionary of Classical Ballet* (third ed.). New York: Dover Books.

Grieg, V. (1994). *Inside Ballet Techniques: Separating Anatomical Fact from Fiction in Ballet Class*. Pennington, NJ: Princeton Books

Jewett, A.E. (1985). *The Curriculum Process in Physical Education*. Dubuque, IA: W.C. Brown.

Karsavina, T. (1962). *Classical Ballet: The flow of movement*. London: Adam & Charles Black.

Kirstein, L., M. Stuart, and C. Dyer. (1952). *The Classical Ballet*. New York: Alfred Knopf.

Lawson, J. (1980). *The Principles of Classical Dance*. New York: Alfred Knopf.

Lawson, J. (1975). *The Teaching of Classical Ballet*. New York: Theatre Arts Books.

Lawson, J. (1975). *Teaching Young Dancers: Muscular Coordination in Classical Ballet*. New York: Theatre Arts Books.

Minton, S.C. (1989). *Body and Self: Partners in Movement*. Champaign, IL: Human Kinetics.

Mosston, M. and S. Ashworth. (1986). *Teaching Physical Education* (third ed.). Columbus, OH: C.E. Merrill.

Noverre, J.G. translated by C.W. Beaumont. (1966). *Letters on Dancing and Ballets*. New York: Dance Horizons.

Paskevska, A. (1992). *Both Sides of the Mirror: The Science and Art of Ballet* (second edition). Pennington, NJ: Dance Horizons.

Sheldon, W.M. (1954). *Atlas of Man*. New York: Harper & Row.

Sparger, C. (1982). *Anatomy and Ballet*. London: Adams & Charles Black.

Sweigard, L. (1974). *Human Movement Potential*. New York: Dodd & Mead.

Todd, M.E. (1976). *The Hidden You*. New York: Dance Horizons.

Vaganova, A. (1969). *Basic Principles of Classical Ballet*. New York: Dover Books.

Vickers, J.N. (1990). *Instructional Design for Teaching Physical Activities: A Knowledge Structures Approach*. Champaign, IL: Human Kinetics.

ectomorph 70, 71
effacé 133, 134
élancer (to dart) 40
elevé 131
en arrière (backward) 51
en avant (forward) 51
en croix patterns 48-49
ending, of class 44
endings
   of barre exercises 39-40, 50
   of combinations 42
endomorph 70, 71
energy, maximizing 56
English vs. French terms 6
en l'air, defined 52
épaulé 133, 134
errors, list of 83
étendre (to stretch) 40
evaluation 73-74. *See also* assessment, of students
examinations, performance 74-78
   specific units 87, 117, 145, 163
examinations, written 78
   specific units 87, 117, 145, 163

F
feedback, for students 17-19, 65-67
feet. *See* foot positions, classical; transfer of weight; weight
   distribution
Feltz, D.L. 15
Fifth position 90, 91
   arm position 104-106
   as beginning and ending position 42, 49, 50
   en bas (Preparatory position) 104, 105, 106
   en haut 104, 105, 106
   grand plié in 118
   stance 26
   weight distribution 26
first arabesque 30, 55, 151
First position 90, 91
   aplomb in 29, 31
   arm position 104-106
   demi-plié in 15, 92
   grand plié in 118
   moving to Second from 26
   sauté in 16
   turn-out in 24
floor, safety inspection 62
foot exercises 100-101
foot positions, classical 32-33, 91. *See also specific positions*
Fourth position 90, 91
   arm position 104, 105
   en avant (Cecchetti) 104, 105
   en haut (French) 104, 105
   grand plié in 118
   squareness in 28
Franklin, F. 9
French vs. English terms 6
full-foot position 25, 32, 50

G
gliding. *See* glisser (to glide)
glissade 137-139
   in combinations and progressions 52, 139, 160, 173
glisser (to glide) 40
grading 61, 78. *See also* rating, of examinations
grand allégro combinations 55, 63, 76
grand battement 101-103
   in progressions 103, 133, 153-154, 165
grand jeté 55, 171-173
grand plié 117-119, 153, 164
groups, dividing class into 62-63, 76
guided discovery style 14, 17
guided manipulation 66-67

H
hair style 60-61
hand positions, at the barre 36-37
hand positions, classical 33-34
head positions, classical 34-35, 38, 42
hyperextension, of knee 72-73

I
ideokinesis 9
imagery 8-9
inclusive style 14, 16-17
individualized instruction 16-17
introductory movements (preparation) 38, 41-42

J
jarreté (knock-knees) 71, 72-73
jeté 95-97, 153
jeté, grand 55, 171-173
jeté devant 141-142, 160, 173
jumping. *See* sauté; sauter (to jump)

K
kinesthetic imagery 9
knee variances 71-73
knock-knees (jarret,) 71, 72-73
knowledge, defined 75

L
Landers, D.M. 15
language (terminology) 6
learning 5-12
   class format and 5
   creating setting for 10-11
   cues and 7-8, 11, 46
   demonstration and 6, 14
   image of correct performance for 11
   imagery and 8-9
   levels of 11-12
   motor learning stages 6-7
   movement-language connections and 6
   teaching methods and 7
   visual memory and 9, 10, 11, 14
leg, positions of foot on 32-33

technique, defined 75
temperature, of studio 62
temps levé 156-157, 173
term, planning for 58
terminology 6
testing. *See* assessment, of students; examinations, performance; examinations, written
third arabesque 151, 152
Third position 90, 91
    arm position 104, 105
    grand plié in 118
three-step turn 170-171
tibial torsion 72-73
time management 64, 74
timing, of music 56
tourner (to turn), defined 40. *See also* turning
transfer of weight 25, 26, 50, 83
transposing movement 53-54
turning
    at barre 39
    in center combinations 43
    defined 40
    three-step turn 170-171
turn-out 22, 24, 83, 90

U
upstage, defined 103

V
verbal feedback 66
visual images 9. *See also* imagery
visualization (mental practice) 15
visual memory 9, 10, 11, 14

W
walks, ballet 110-111
    in combinations and progressions 52, 110, 142, 160, 173
weight distribution 24-25, 26, 32
    practical application exercise 90
    standards and common errors 83
    teaching in first moving class 89-90
weight transfer 25, 26, 50, 83
whole-part-whole method 7
working leg, at barre 38, 47, 50
written examinations 78
    specific units 87, 117, 145, 163
written reports 78

Gayle Kassing teaches dance at Jacksonville University in Jacksonville, FL. She has taught ballet technique for more than 25 years in various settings, including higher education, a university-based community dance program, and professional and civic dance schools. She has also owned and operated her own dance studios.

No stranger to publishing, Kassing has been writing ballet education articles that focus on teaching and assessment for more than 15 years. She also served as the publications director for the National Dance Association.

A member of the National Dance Assocation and the Florida Dance Association, Kassing earned her PhD in dance and related arts from Texas Woman's University.

Danielle M. Jay is an associate professor of dance education at Northern Illinois University. She has studied ballet since the age of three and has taught ballet at the college level for more than 25 years.

Jay has studied with Margaret Craske and Celene Keller at Jacob's Pillow and with David McLain, David Blackburn, and Oleg Sabline at the University of Cincinnati. She holds a PhD in dance and related arts from Texas Woman's University.

Jay is a member of the National Dance Association, which is a part of the American Alliance of Health, Physical Education, Recreation and Dance.